Japan's Arduous Rejuvenation as a Global Power

Victor Teo

Japan's Arduous Rejuvenation as a Global Power

Democratic Resilience and the US-China Challenge

Victor Teo
The University of Hong Kong
Pokfulam, Hong Kong SAR, People's Republic of China

ISBN 978-981-13-6189-0   ISBN 978-981-13-6190-6 (eBook)
https://doi.org/10.1007/978-981-13-6190-6

Library of Congress Control Number: 2019931024

© The Editor(s) (if applicable) and The Author(s) 2019. This book is an open access publication.
Open Access This book is licensed under the terms of the Creative Commons Attribution 4.0 International License (http://creativecommons.org/licenses/by/4.0/), which permits use, sharing, adaptation, distribution and reproduction in any medium or format, as long as you give appropriate credit to the original author(s) and the source, provide a link to the Creative Commons licence and indicate if changes were made.
The images or other third party material in this book are included in the book's Creative Commons licence, unless indicated otherwise in a credit line to the material. If material is not included in the book's Creative Commons licence and your intended use is not permitted by statutory regulation or exceeds the permitted use, you will need to obtain permission directly from the copyright holder.
The use of general descriptive names, registered names, trademarks, service marks, etc. in this publication does not imply, even in the absence of a specific statement, that such names are exempt from the relevant protective laws and regulations and therefore free for general use.
The publisher, the authors and the editors are safe to assume that the advice and information in this book are believed to be true and accurate at the date of publication. Neither the publisher nor the authors or the editors give a warranty, express or implied, with respect to the material contained herein or for any errors or omissions that may have been made. The publisher remains neutral with regard to jurisdictional claims in published maps and institutional affiliations.

Cover illustration: © PJF Military Collection / Alamy Stock Photo

This Palgrave Macmillan imprint is published by the registered company Springer Nature Singapore Pte Ltd.
The registered company address is: 152 Beach Road, #21-01/04 Gateway East, Singapore 189721, Singapore

For Mum, Sungwon and Jason

Preface

Japan's Arduous Rejuvenation as a Global Power assesses the profound impact that Japan's aspirations to become a great power have had for Japanese security and democracy. Rather than viewing the process of normalization and rejuvenation as two decades of remilitarization in the face of a rapidly changing strategic environment and domestic political circumstances, this volume contextualizes Japan's contemporary international relations against the longer grain of Japanese historical interactions. It demonstrates that policies and statecraft in Prime Minister Shinzo Abe's era are a continuation of a long, unbroken and arduous effort by successive generations of leaders to preserve Japanese autonomy, enhance security and advance Japanese national interests. Arguing against the notion that Japan cannot work with China as long as the US-Japan alliance is in place, the book suggests that Tokyo could forge constructive relations with Beijing by engaging China in joint projects inside and outside of the Asia-Pacific, in issue areas such as infrastructure development or the provision of international public goods. An improvement in Japan-China relations would enhance rather than detract from Japan-US relations, as Washington is likely to become more sensitive to Japanese needs and interests. Tokyo will find that its new-found independence in the US-Japan alliance would not only accord it more political respect and strategic latitude, but also allow it to ameliorate the excesses of US foreign policy adventurism, paving the way for Japan to become a truly great "normal" power in time to come.

Pokfulam, Hong Kong   Victor Teo

Acknowledgments

This book was inspired by the numerous student seminars the author has led at the University of Hong Kong's Department of Japanese Studies on the International Relations of the Asia-Pacific over the last decade. The lively discussions and interactions with the students stimulated much of the author's thinking and ideas on the subject matter. A great debt is owed to the School of Modern Languages and Cultures and the Faculty of Arts at the University of Hong Kong for support given to the author for this project. The author is also tremendously grateful to the following organizations for their kind support in the provision of fellowships and/or research grants that enabled the author to undertake extended leave to research for the various chapters in this publication: Hong Kong Research Council General Research Fund (Project HKU 753310H) for funding multiple research visits to Japan and a research fellowship at the University of Oxford; The Japan Foundation Short Term Fellowship Scheme for supporting a research stint at the University of Kyoto; the Harvard-Yenching Institute for fellowship as HYI Visiting Scholar at the Faculty of Arts and Sciences and Harvard Law School; the Academy of Korean Studies (AKS-2016-LAB-2250005) for funding a research associateship at the Harvard Program on US-Japan Relations at the Weatherhead Center for International Affairs and at Harvard Law School. A special note of acknowledgment must also go to the Doris Zimmern HKU-Cambridge Hughes Hall Fellowship for funding a stint at the University of Cambridge's Department of Politics and International Studies (POLIS). The author is also tremendously grateful to the University of Hong Kong Small Project Fund for funding the OA component of this project.

The author is also particularly grateful to the referees, scholars and colleagues who have read and commented on various chapters of the book. Special thanks must be conveyed to all the esteemed learned scholars in the US, the UK, Japan, China and Singapore for all the intellectual exchange, camaraderie, advice and encouragement. The author owes a great intellectual and professional debt to Professors Ezra Vogel, Susan Pharr, Michael Yahuda, Arne Westad, Heonik Kwon, Ian Nish, Khong Yuen-Foong, Antony Best and Lam Peng-Er for all the advice and mentorship over the years. Special thanks must also be given to learned colleagues and friends who have taken the time to speak to or engage the author on one occasion or more on Japanese foreign policy: Professors Thomas Berger, Sheila Smith, Andrew Oros, Yoshihide Soeya, Rosemary Foot, Caroline Rose, Akihiko Tanaka, Akio Takahara, Hitomi Koyama, Haruko Satoh, Yoneyuki Sugita, General Koichi Isobe and Shinju Fujihira among others. The author is grateful to Miss Man-Wai Lam, Miss Natalie Dabkowski, Miss Bea T.S. Leung, Ms Sudha Soundarrajan, Mr Tikoji Rao Mega Rao, Ms Linda Haylock, Ms Connie Li and Mr Brian Halm for their editorial assistance. The book was written over the course of many months while the author was at Cambridge (Massachusetts), Singapore and Hong Kong. Special thanks must be given to the following colleagues and friends for making the author's life in Cambridge so much more interesting and enjoyable: Susan Scott, Lindsay Strogatz, Francesca Coppola, James Flaherty, Li Ruohong, Edward Baker, Kendal Kelly, Jenni Ting, Nina Coomes, Melissa Smith and Mike Zaisser. The author is extremely grateful to the editors and staff at Palgrave Macmillan, particularly Miss Sara Crowley-Vigneau for her confidence in the author and for making this book possible. Last but not least, the author is grateful to his loving family for their support, without which his academic career would not have gone so far. Needless to say, the author is solely responsible for all errors in this book.

Contents

1 **The Rejuvenation of Japan**   1
   The Problem of Understanding Japan's Rejuvenation   1
   Understanding Japan's Foreign Policy: A Conceptual Survey   7
   Contradictory Tendencies, Democratic Resilience and Japan's Difficult Rejuvenation   12
   The Idea of Normalization and Rejuvenation   16
   Beyond Zero-Sum Games and Binary Choices: Transcending the US-China Divide   23
   Chapter Overview and Synopsis   27
   References   33

2 **Japan's Rejuvenation: Origins, Debates and Concepts**   41
   Japan's Political and Philosophical Traditions: Equality, Hierarchy and Exceptionalism   42
      The China Dilemma   42
      Japan's Exceptionalism   46
   The San Francisco System and the Making of an "Abnormal" Japan   50
   Mainstream Conservatism in Japanese Politics During the Cold War   53
   The Rise of Neo-Conservatism: From Normalization to the Rejuvenation of Japan   59
   The Contours of the Debate on Japan's Rejuvenation   63

    The Central Pillars of Rejuvenation   66
        Theme One: Constitutional Revisionism   66
        Theme Two: The Nature and Tone of the US-Japan Alliance   69
        Theme Three: Pacifism, the Use of Force and Global
        Engagement   76
    The Erosion of Pacifism: Can Democracy and Historical
    Revisionism Co-Exist?   85
    Neo-Conservatism and the Paradoxes of Japanese Democracy   90
    References   98

3 Japan's Rejuvenation and the US-China Divide   107
    Japan's Asia Strategy and the US-China Challenge   108
    Cautioning America's Unilateralism   115
    Is the "Anti-China" Position Necessarily Conducive to Japanese
    Interests?   122
    The Contestation in Southeast Asia: Winning Hearts and Minds   124
    References   130

4 Peacekeepers But Not Quite Peacebuilders: Japan's Evolving Role in the Middle East Peace Process   133
    Japan's Foray into the Middle East   134
    A Brief Synopsis of the Arab-Israeli Conflict   136
    Japan's Involvement in the Arab-Israeli Conflict   140
    The Need to Revamp Japan's Peacebuilding Strategy   144
    Fostering Better Socio-Economic Conditions   145
    Japan's Undisputable Credentials as a Peacemaker   149
    Losing Sight of the Forest for the Trees   153
    The Neo-Conservatives' Peacebuilding Efforts in the Trump Era   157
    References   161

5 The Provision of International Public Goods: Japan's Anti-Piracy Operations in the Gulf of Aden   167
    Piracy as a Security Challenge   167
    Genesis of Japan's Anti-Piracy Efforts   171
    Piracy in the Gulf of Aden: An Overview   175
    International Law and the Piracy Problem   177
    Japan's Response to the Piracy Problems in the Gulf   180

	Working with the Chinese PLAN and the Multilateral Provision of International Public Goods	184
	Conclusion	188
	References	189
6	**Recalibrating Japan's Foreign Policy**	195
	Japan's Rejuvenation from the Perspective of the US and China	203
	The US: The Preservation of Pre-Eminent Status	203
	Between Revisionism and Realpolitik: China's Japan Problem	206
	Resistance from Below: Democratic Resilience and Rejuvenation Challenges for the Future	209
		211
	Putting Japan's Self-Interest First: Asia and Beyond	211
	Pre-Requisites for Global Leadership: Gaining Respect of Asian Neighbors	215
	Working with US in the Asia-Pacific and with China Beyond	219
	References	222

Index 225

CHAPTER 1

The Rejuvenation of Japan

> My core vision for a future Japan is a "beautiful country" that is open to the world, and ready to face the challenges that come our way. Under my guidance, Japan will continue to advance a program of reforms and initiatives to achieve this vision.
>
> I believe it is important that we Japanese write a constitution for ourselves that would reflect the shape of the country we consider desirable in the 21st century.
>
> Do not fall into a brain-dead state of not daring to even lay a finger on the constitution or even avoid debating it. We will create with our own hands a constitution appropriate for the times.
>
> Shinzo Abe

THE PROBLEM OF UNDERSTANDING JAPAN'S REJUVENATION

In the aftermath of the 2018 June 12 summit between the US and North Korea, held in Singapore, there was vehement disagreement among experts and commentators over the question as to whether anything substantive had been established by President Trump and Chairman Kim Jong-un, or whether it was China, North Korea or the US that had emerged as a winner. The only consensus between various experts is that for the most part, Japan was the country that stood to lose most from this summit. However, this was not due to a lack of trying on Japan's part. On June 5, 2018, just five days before the Singapore summit, Prime Minister Abe flew to Washington D.C. to meet President Trump. The purpose was to lobby his purported new friend and buddy, whom the prime minister had meticulously courted—even before Mr. Trump was sworn in as president—on the importance of the North Korean issue to Japan's national interests.

The reaction of President Trump, in response to the overtures from the North Koreans to meet, is reminiscent of the Nixon shocks Japan suffered in 1972. This episode also raises questions for Prime Minister Abe's strategy and political instincts, as like his Liberal Democratic Party (LDP) predecessors (think Nakasone–Reagan or Koizumi–Bush), he strove to build good personal relations with his US counterpart. As the first prime minister of the G7 to personally call President-Elect Trump in New York, the prime minister ignored public and peer opinion in both Japan and the US, probably because he felt this gesture would ingratiate him as a true friend to the new US president and advance Japanese national interests. This strategy seemed to work out well, as President Trump has on various occasions called the prime minister his "good friend," and reaffirmed the US-Japan alliance in a way that provided much support for the prime minister's political agenda of normalizing Japan. Even though the optics and language changed, many analysts felt that the US-Japan alliance would climb to new heights under the new president. In other words, Prime Minister Abe had become the "Trump whisperer," one of the rare few leaders to have a personal rapport with the US president, or so it seemed.

This rapport unfortunately did not translate into much influence on an issue of critical importance to Japan and the premier himself. Prime Minister Abe had burnished his political credentials and made his early career advocating for a tougher line against North Korea, for its abduction of Japanese nationals and present nuclear belligerence. This position had not changed since he was deputy chief and chief cabinet secretary (akin to the US chief of staff) to Prime Minister Junichiro Koizumi in the early 2000s. The North Koreans have of course taken a hardline position against Prime Minister Abe. Yet, in characteristic Trumpian manner, the US president swiftly dealt three successive political blows to the Japanese prime minister in a short span of time.

On March 8, 2018, President Trump agreed to meet North Korea's Chairman Kim via a request conveyed by the South Korean national security advisor to President Moon at the White House, by-passing any discussions with Japan—in theory their principal ally in the Asia-Pacific region

(Landler 2018). On March 23, 2018, Japan was not exempted by the Trump administration from stiff tariffs on steel and aluminum imports, with one report gleefully announcing "for Japan, the hits keeps on coming." (*New York Times*, March 23, 2018). Brazil, Mexico, Australia and South Korea (the last two being allies in the region) were left off the list. Barely three weeks later, the US president gave his "good friend," the Japanese premier, a rather unpleasant surprise when he told him, on his visit to Mar-a-Lago, that Secretary of State Pompeo had met with Kim Jong-un over the Easter weekend in Pyongyang. He reiterated this again to the White House press corps with the Japanese premier standing by his side, and in his characteristic fashion tweeted about this on April 18, 2018. Prime Minister Abe's June 5 visit certainly did not secure what he needed from President Trump—namely an assurance that the US would not cut a deal with North Korea until a united position with regards to North Korea could be worked out. This saga of dealing with North Korea attracted much attention and commentary. Even though domestic opinion was relatively muted in Japan, critics of Prime Minister Abe had a field day and derided him on his choice of strategy (or lack thereof) and the ineffectiveness of his personal diplomacy. Others ridiculed President Trump, suggesting that he was as mad as the North Korean leader, unschooled in diplomacy and international politics. The most important questions, however, have little to do with President Trump's alleged recklessness and/or negligence, nor with Abe's effectiveness.

The escalating North Korean nuclear threat, from the waning years of the Obama administration to the present, represents one of the gravest periods in Japanese security since the Second World War. It raises certain questions about the basic long-held assumptions that Japan's policymakers and its people have cherished since the US-Japan security alliance was promulgated in 1951. The recent developments detailed above raise more questions than answers for those looking to "normalize" Japanese foreign policy.

The North Korea related events of 2017–2018 shocked many Japanese nationals. The world watched in awe as the combative rhetoric between the US and North Korea escalated between President Trump and Chairman Kim, fanning fears of an imminent war between the two nations. Situated at the frontlines of the US alliance network, and as host of US forces in Asia, Japan would definitely be targeted if hostilities were to break out between North Korea and the US. The escalation and war of words did not involve the Japanese leaders in a major way, but the US-Japan alliance could chain-gang Japan into a conflict that Japan was not prepared to fight. In initiating contact with North Korea and agreeing to meet its leader, the US exercised an autonomy within its rights as a sovereign nation, but from the perspective of Tokyo, two offensive elements stand out. First, the US had not given the proper consideration and reciprocity to Tokyo interests on this sensitive issue. Japan's primary concern was that the US might strike a deal with North Korea to decommission North Korea's long-range missiles only, leaving Japan well within the sights of its short- and medium-range missiles, even if North Korea stopped her missile and nuclear tests. Second, by arranging the summit without prior consultation with Japan, the US had taken steps to deviate from a united front on an issue that was critical to Japanese interests. This might be construed as a case of "abandonment," as Japan finds out after the fact, and certainly conveyed a particular message to Japan policymakers that the alliance might privilege American security and interests over Japan's.

The North Korea episodes raise broader and more important questions for Japanese foreign policy in general and for the US-Japan alliance in particular. First, it would appear that Japan as a significant economic power in the region is exasperated and helpless against a belligerent North Korea (USD 28.5 billion GDP in 2016—a fraction of Japan's USD 4.939 trillion GDP in the same year). Even with the militarization program and Japan's tightening of the alliance, Tokyo has little political or economic sway against Pyongyang's missile or nuclear threats. Second, it raises questions about the autonomy of Japan when its political elites bet Japan's security entirely on the US, particularly on a leader that both the US and Japanese public have little confidence in. This begs the question: are the solutions to US security problems necessarily suited to Japan all the time; and in the same light, can Japan reasonably expect that their interests would necessarily coincide with Washington's most, if not all of the time?

Third, is it acceptable for the Japanese people to continually accede to the US, even if requests to support the alliance are often at odds with, or at great expense to, Japan's national interests? The costs are not just defined in financial calculations, but also in terms of diplomatic flexibility, political opportunities, national pride and democratic progress. Japan's political loyalty to the US, and its perception of the alliance as a panacea to all its security and foreign problems, is problematic in a rapidly changing strategic environment where security issues might not be so clear-cut after all. How has the reaffirmation of the US-Japan security alliance affected Japan's relations with its closest neighbors in the long run, particularly if Japan is adamant on maintaining a lock-step diplomatic approach toward all others in order to remain a staunch ally of the US? (Magosaki 2009)

This leads to a further question: how has the development in Japanese foreign policy over the last two decades since the mid-1990s helped or hindered Japan's security? Such developments do not take place in a vacuum. From the perspective of planners in Tokyo, Japan's external environment has deteriorated rapidly and correspondingly, these changes have stoked changes in domestic political narratives and processes to adapt to these new challenges. Since the late 1990s, the neo-conservatives have seen their political fortunes rise, and their political agenda has come to define the mainstream political narratives. There are three key ideas behind neo-conservatism. The first idea is that Japan should bring to the fore of public discussions and consideration previously tabooed topics on security, particularly on how Japan could do more in order to fend for itself and also contribute to global concerns (Shinyo 1994; Nakanishi 2003; Ishizu 2006; Morimoto 2008). With the rise of China, much of this national conversation involves discussion on how to handle the "China threat," and related to this, the balance that needs to be struck between a strategy of an autonomous Japan and changes needed in the US-Japan alliance. The second key strand of conversation relates to the first. In their discussions about Japanese security, neo-conservatives in Japan perceive a key need to explain the necessity for having a national conversation on security in order to drag Japan out of a state of "peace senility or idiocy" (平和ボケ).

Pacifism, a key institution of postwar Japan, needs to therefore contend with strands of new thinking that the neo-conservatives regard as necessary for the younger generation in Japan. The neo-conservatives perceive the need for the Japanese people to reconsider how war history in its current form has created a stranglehold on the ability of the younger generation to take pride in their own country, and presents essentially a "victor's view" of justice, thereby taking away the necessary nationalistic gel for Japan to unite in the face of the precarious challenges ahead. Pacifism also allegedly provides an opportunity for Japan's neighbors to hold the moral high ground in their bilateral encounters, allowing history to be used in an instrumental manner to gain the upper hand in political negotiations, extract economic concessions or claim cultural and social superiority. The neo-conservatives therefore deem this a weakness, and that Japan needs to undertake normalization to rid itself of the abnormal status that it inherited as a legacy of the Second World War, and strive for a strategic-political status that is commensurate with its economic status (Singh 2002; Hughes 2009; Abe 2006; Aso 2007; Maslow 2015; Katada 2016). As the third largest economy in the world, Japan's quest for a political status that matches the influence of its economy suggests that normalization is essentially a rejuvenation that would restore Japan as one of the great powers in the world.

The third important element is the formal manifestation of the previous two elements in legal terms. Should the Japanese people codify changes in their thinking about security and Japan's world role, as well as their changing attitude toward the US-Japan security treaty, by making revisions to Japan's postwar peace constitution? Should Article 9 of the constitution be amended or revised to accommodate the necessary changes? An amendment to the peace constitution might be also be a bold identity statement that Japan is to be recognized not only as a "normal" power in all senses of the word, but also politically, and be accorded with an eminent status commensurate with her economic power and global contributions.

The processes of normalization and rejuvenation are essentially two sides of the same coin. The author argues that the processes involved are two dimensional—normalization being restorative, while rejuvenation allows Japan to become the nation-state par excellence. The overall process is of an ascendant trajectory, but faces resistance and obstacles both inside and outside of Japan. Despite this, the strategic direction in which Japan under the neo-conservatives is heading is clear, but the road ahead is not without pitfalls and challenges. This book seeks to explain and locate the difficulties that Japan faces in its rejuvenation process by examining the contradictory forces that drive Japan's foreign policy, and the challenges that lie ahead of the possible trajectories of its rejuvenation. One of the biggest challenges for Japan in its quest for rejuvenation is the prospect of eroding its democratic institutions, and falling into the trap of a hegemonic struggle between China and the US, where Japan faces a lose-lose prospect of either being entrapped in a conflict it has no desire to enter or being sidelined (abandoned) in the case of a grand bargain being struck between China and the US. Rejuvenation should have the overall effect of enhancing Japanese security, reducing the cost of defense and allowing Japan to build a conducive external security environment. Yet, after two decades of neo-conservative maneuvers, Japan is nowhere near establishing a better external security environment, and the costs of its remilitarization have increased. Relations with North Korea and China have grown increasingly tense. In the following section, a general survey of the conceptual literature on Japanese foreign policy is undertaken, before the chapter moves on to discuss the major challenge that Japanese democracy faces vis-à-vis the processes of normalization and rejuvenation.

Understanding Japan's Foreign Policy: A Conceptual Survey

Scholars and policymakers concerned with Japan's foreign policy have long debated the peculiarities, strengths and weaknesses of Japan's foreign policy, the study of which has been deeply influenced by developments in international history, international relations, political economy, and development studies. Given Japan's unique foreign policy position since the end of the Pacific War, it is no surprise that the literature on Japanese politics and foreign policy has taken on a unique characteristic too.

The first generation of literature mostly focused on the historical sources and the institutional structure that emerged in postwar Japan and its relation to Japanese politics and foreign policy. Scholars have written numerous volumes on how the Pacific War and its aftermath have influenced the making of contemporary Japan (Dower 1986, 1999; Barnhart 1987; Beasley 1987; Crowley 1966; Morley 1983; Nish 1966, 1972). Most of the literature outlined Japan's perceptions of and aspirations and expectations for their relations with China (Iriye 1982, 1999), Britain (Nish 1966, 1972) and the US (Morley 1983), illuminating how these relations were critical in driving imperial policies prior to the war. The influence of the US became all the more dominant in the postwar period as Japan's foreign policy was dictated (Agawa 1998) and influenced by the US (Schaller 1985; Dower 1979; Auer 1973; Weinstein 1971) as the Cold War set in.

As Japan's economy rises, the importance of cultural factors in explaining why and how Japan's policymaking began to help is important. In particular, the importance of *nihonjinron* (日本人論) and how this uniqueness tended to underlie much of Japan's success (or not) (Befu 2001; Katzenstein 1996, 1998; Davis and Ikeno 2002; Dale 2011). Other than the uniqueness of Japanese culture, much of the scholarly focus has been on the party and the state in Japan as the principal drivers of policy. Johnson (1982) has written on the importance of understanding how Japanese bureaucracy operates, in particular how the Ministry of International Trade and Industry (MITI) and the state have taken on a special dimension in planning Japanese economic activity and are instrumental in its success (Johnson 1982, 2001). Japan's political and economic model has therefore become the focal point of many scholars' efforts to understand and explain what lessons could be drawn it. This trend continued with Ezra Vogel's *Japan as Number One: Lessons for America*. This book was one of the bestselling English books in Japan since its publication in 1979, only to be followed about a decade later by Ishihara Shintaro's *The Japan that can say No*, another bestseller in Japan. Both books analyzed aspects of Japan's phenomenal success. The former discussed the strengths of the Japanese model that were instrumental to its rise, and the latter suggested that Tokyo should rethink and re-manage its relations with the US as a result of its newfound strength. The "Japan threat" period in the 1980s was fueled in part by xenophobia, in part by Japan's ascendant economy, where Japanese corporations were buying up large chunks of real estate in New York and Los Angeles. This naturally was deemed a threat by many US scholars and politicians, particularly when everyone felt that Japan was in fact free-riding on the US for defense. This trend of books advocating the ascendance of Japan took a respite in the 1990s when Japan's economy fell into deflationary growth.

However, this did not deter scholars working in development studies and political economy from trying to expound on Japan's relations to a new model of capitalism in East Asia. Japan is seen to be the inspiration for a new form of state–society relationship—not only for the greater East Asian "Tiger" economies of South Korea, Hong Kong, Singapore and Taiwan, but also for Southeast Asian economies and China. The "developmental state" model promises to provide an alternative to Western-based liberal capitalism (Woo-Cummings 1999) which could be a formula that countries outside Asia could emulate. There is therefore a widespread interest in the special role of the state and the party-system in Japan, as many perceive the key ingredient of success is the stability experienced by the voters in Japan. There is also much research interest in electoral systems and the dominance of the LDP in Japanese national politics (Curtis 1988, 1999, 2009). Factional politics was weakened by changes in electoral reform to a single-seat system. There are other reasons of course: US interference in the early years, the LDP's successful strategy of playing on the insecurities of the electorate, and the increasing marginalization of the leftist parties have also been attributed to why Japan's one dominant party state has lasted such a long time.

Toward the late 1980s and 1990s, Japan's related research blossomed for three reasons. First, Japan has stood out due to its exceptionalism, particularly in terms of the disparity between its economic prowess and its reliance on the US—in short because of its "abnormal" status created after the Second World War. Compared with the US, the term "exceptionalism" when applied to Japan has more of a cultural connotation. Second, by this time there has been considerable evidence for the buildup of empirical examples for theoretical innovation in terms of international relations theory, particularly for Japan's foreign policy making—in particular in the literature focusing on ideational influences in Japan's foreign policy. Third, empirical developments in circumstances prompted Japan's foreign policy community to embark on greater discussions and debates over the question of the "burden of history," as well as Japan's relations with its neighbors in Asia. To say the least, the difficulties Japan has had with its neighbors prompted much research on historical issues.

This is also accompanied by the emergence of a more assertive Japan, evidenced by increasing friction with its neighbors, notably with China and also with South Korea over a host of "history" related problems (Yoshibumi 1998; Midford 2011; Maslow 2015; Auslin 2016). From the 1980s' textbook problems to the comfort women issue with the South Koreans, the literature concerning what many scholars would call the "burden of history" blossomed. Buruma's (1994) *The Wages of Guilt: Memories of War in Germany and Japan* is probably one of the most recommended texts on Japan's war guilt alongside Berger's (2012) *War Guilt and World Politics*. This growing trend of literature attests to the perceived recalcitrant attitude of Japan over a host of political issues such as the Nanjing Massacre (Chang 1997; Fogel 2000; Igarashi 2000); the issue of apologies and atonement for its wartime transgressions, and its relationship with Japanese national identity (Lind 2008; Dudden 2008; Heine and Selden 2000; Hashimoto 2015); and the question of selective remembering (Dudden 2008; Seraphim 2008; Orr 2001; Gong and Teo 2010).

In terms of foreign policy, scholars debate the primary drivers of Japan's foreign policy from different perspectives in international relations theory. While it is not wrong to say that Japanese diplomats, like their counterparts elsewhere, are hard-nosed neo-realists, the scholarship on Japanese foreign policy is dominated by pieces pertaining to the impact of pacifism in particular, referring to the influence of anti-militaristic norms and how they have been the dominant guiding principles in Japanese identity, politics and foreign policy (Katzenstein 1996, 1998; Berger 1998, 2012). This category of writing fits squarely into the theoretical work done in international relations theory on constructivism in general and other ideational influences, such as techno-nationalism, on Japan's foreign policy mechanisms (Samuels 1994, 2007).

Even though there is discussion on how ideational factors influence Japan's foreign policy (Berger 1998, 2012; Cha 2000; Katzenstein 1998), structural realism cannot be discounted. Many scholars have argued that ideational matters play an important role in postwar Japan, but this does not negate the fact that the decisions undertaken by postwar prime ministers could be born out of neo-realist considerations rather than anything else. Prime Minister Shigeru Yoshida's decision to implement the Yoshida Doctrine, where Japan agreed to follow the US lead in foreign and strategic affairs, could be construed as a reasonable neo-realist move as it was the best play Japan had under the postwar circumstances, as he himself noted in his memoirs. To this day, many in Japan regard him as an old school liberal. The end of the Cold War ushered in more research on how various countries responded to the demise of the USSR and correspondingly to the possibility of a US retreat in the face of China's rise. These systemic changes have proved unsettling for most countries in the region, and held various implications for Japan's foreign policy. There are a few strands of research here.

The US-Japan alliance is one of the fundamental bedrocks of Japanese foreign policy, and in turn Japan is a critical component of the US strategy in Asia (Welfield 1988; LaFeber 1997; Green and Mochizuki 1999; Ikenberry 2003; Dian 2014). Since the end of the Pacific War, even though US-Japan relations have been relatively stable as the Japanese people wholeheartedly embraced all things American (Dower 1979, 1999; McCormack 2007), this set of bilateral relations has had its own fair share of challenges (Crowley 1966; Packard 1966; Dower 1999; Funabashi 1999; Nozaki 2008; Grimes 2008). Obviously, the most important question raised then was whether circumstances had changed so much that it meant the end of the US-Japan alliance (Funabashi 1999; Tsuchiyama 1995; Calder 2010). This would mean a departure from well-established practices of the US-Japan security policy that have underpinned Japanese foreign policy in place since the postwar period (Weinstein 1971; Scalapino 1977; Armitage and Nye 2012). The decision by Japan and the US to tighten the alliance and to ensure that Japan continues to play this exceptional role (Green 2003; Hornung and Mochizuki 2016) meant that for most part, the role of the US in Japan's foreign policy has become more salient, not less. The fundamental question is therefore how Japan should adjust its foreign policy to the new roles both Tokyo and Washington are playing while going forward, and if the stimulus for changes are endogenous versus exogenous (Hicks 1997; Hook et al. 2011; Samuels 1994, 2007; Santoro and Warden 2015; Green 2003, 2017).

The changes in Japan's external security environment and domestic politics have also led to a sea-change in Japan's foreign policy with regards to its immediate neighbors China and Korea (Cha 2000; Pempel 2003; Tanaka 2007; Wan 2008; He 2009; Bush 2013; Sohn 2010; Lam and Teo 2011; Rose and Teo 2013; Lee and Teo 2014; Calder and Ye 2010; Chien 2011; Glosserman and Snyder 2015; Rozman 2015), as well as in Japanese relations with the Southeast Asian countries (Graham 2006) and Japan's role in regionalism (Green and Gill 2009; Sohn 2010; Cioraci 2011; Chung 2013). Inevitably, all this research speaks to the fact that there is an increasing tension between a Japan that wants to institute a more neo-realist, "interest" based policy on one hand, and one that is deeply influenced by pacifist norms. While this might be true, over the last two decades more scholars have become convinced that neo-realism plays an increasing part in Japan's foreign policy, even though the debate on the extent to which ideological factors still influence Japan's foreign policy rages on (Lai 2013). There is a slew of literature that attests to this, particularly on the narratives surrounding the security debates on how Japan should act. At the heart of these narratives is the question of "normalization," and how Japan could or should act to best to define and/or protect its interests in the near future (Singh 2002; Inoguchi 2008; Soeya et al. 2011; Oros 2009, 2017; Welch 2011).

Today, Japanese foreign policy appears to be in a state of inquietude and exhibits contradictory tendencies. For most of the Cold War, the struggle between the right wing and the left wing was well documented. We see Japanese politicians debating and arguing about the best way forward to protect Japanese democracy from authoritarian regimes such as China or North Korea, but only to make and enact policies in a relatively anti-democratic manner to further their agenda. One need not look far, as for years Okinawa has complained about the US bases there, and recently young protestors lambasted the Abe administration for attempting to force constitutional reforms upon the Japanese electorate. Even though ordinary Japanese people living in Tokyo and Osaka pride themselves on being peace-loving, forward-looking democrats, they vote in right-wing nationalists such as Shintaro Ishihara (repeatedly) and Toru Hashimoto (as governors of Tokyo and Osaka respectively), whose remarks have often riled Japan's closest neighbors—China and Korea. The Japanese nation seems to reward nationalists and conservatives with political longevity—with left of center leaders such as Junichiro Koizumi and right of center politicians such as Shinzo Abe having the greatest public support. Even though the Japanese debate on whether they should become more autonomous in their foreign and security policies, the Japanese elites double down on their alliance with the US, thereby becoming more reliant on the US each day. Today, Japanese conservatives (or more accurately neo-conservatives) are more concerned with removing institutions (such as the constitution) put in place after the war rather than conserving them, while those who want to preserve these very institutions are regarded as "leftists" who are afflicted with "peace senility." Likewise, those who argue that Japan's interests should be placed above the US where they diverge are characterized as radicals, while those who argue in favor of the US-Japan alliance must be protected at all costs are known as nationalists.

The neo-conservatives arguably command the most attention for the way forward strategically for Japan. However, even though Prime Minister Abe does his best to mobilize the country behind his attempts to amend the Japanese constitution, fierce undercurrents move against his normalization and rejuvenation agenda. Domestically, he faces fierce protests from various quarters, particularly from civil society for his constitutional amendment. Even though the polity believes that something has to be done to secure Japan's future, there is evidence that voters who put the LDP in power did not vote Abe in because they supported the revision of the constitution, but rather because they wished to see a party with experience in power that would safeguard Japan's prosperity. Externally, the neo-conservatives seemed to have maneuvered Japan into a binary choice situation: either double down with the US or suffer a strategic future dominated by China. In short, Japan's strategic choices always invariably appear to be presented in a polemic manner. Japan is to choose between pacifism and remilitarization; to elect to bandwagon with the US against China or to become more independent.

Contradictory Tendencies, Democratic Resilience and Japan's Difficult Rejuvenation

This book examines the nature of Japan's attempt at normalization as a nation-state and its rejuvenation as a global power, arguing that these two dimensions are in fact two sides of the same coin—simply Japan is already an exceptional state in the world, given its natural geographic, demographic and strategic attributes. Chapter 2 will present some long-standing

Japanese political and philosophical ideas about statecraft, diplomacy and world politics. It will show among other things the tendency of Japan historically to constantly act in partnership with the prevailing global hegemon, and more often than not try and retain a number two ally position with the hegemon. Today, this is still true even when some scholars, such as Ezra Vogel (1979) who argued in his book *Japan as Number One*, the US has lessons to learn from the Japanese people and that Japan has the potential to become a global power in her own right.

The Westphalian notion of the modern nation-state assumes that all states, large or small, have certain attributes which make them similar, regardless of the political system that is instituted in the nation-state. Whether it is a constitutional monarchy, a military junta based regime or a communist regime, a nation-state is expected to have these basic attributes: (1) well defined territory; (2) a population that has similar shared cultural attributes, such as common history and language; (3) an effective central government with a monopoly on the use of force; (4) a functional and viable economy; (5) diplomatic recognition by other nation-states and hence an ability to enter into international treaties and wage war. The idea of "normality" implies that Japan would do what it takes to restore these attributes. In Japan's case, it is really because of its renunciation of the right to belligerence through Article 9 of the constitution after the Second World War that Japan today is regarded as an abnormality. This war-renouncing clause is both legal and political. It is legal because all decisions with regards to Japan's strategic and foreign policy, as well as the role of the military, stem from the constitution—technically the highest legal document in any given country. Hence in policies regarding the military—whether it is the decision to deploy the military for whatever purposes, or the status of the military within Japan itself for that matter, or the questions of what Japan can or cannot do within the ambit of the US-Japan alliance—Japan remains constrained by law because there is only so much latitude given to the prime minister for interpretation. It is political because today anti-militarism norms define the Japanese character deeply and Japanese domestic politics regard any changes to this pacifism as an affront to Japanese national identity. The angst is further accentuated given the exigencies of changing geopolitical circumstances—of a rising China, a belligerent North Korea and a US bent on unilateralism.

In theory, nation-states are "equal" under the UN Charter. However, in reality, countries possess varying degrees of strategic strength and political identities, and are at different developmental stages. Consequently, each country has their own preferred trading partners, political allies and international affiliations. Each nation-state has some countries that are extremely close or important to them, and some that they just cannot get along with—either out of competing interests or conflicting identity and values. Within the community of states, there will be some that are often therefore premised on realpolitik indicators, military strength, economic strength, ideological appeal and cultural supremacy.

Even though Japan eyes the idea of "equality," it is also well aware that in reality any social grouping, including the community of states, has a hierarchy. Japan's quest to seek normalcy therefore goes beyond just a restoration of the traditional attributes of a nation-state, it is also about becoming a nation-state par excellence. The Japanese people value equality and egalitarianism, but at the same time they have a strong social respect and national propensity to strive for excellence. This quest for excellence lies in the everyday attitude of the Japanese people and explains the country's phenomenal success. Known for their meticulousness, diligence and innovation, the Japanese undertake each task with exceptional vigor and expertise in everything they do—statecraft not excepted. Japan's ascendance as the second largest economy is not a confluence of luck, preferential access to the US market and Cold War conditions, but also largely due to the existence of this spirit of excellence, and at the same time a shrewd mastery of realpolitik. There is thus agreement that even though Japan seeks normalcy through restoration of the natural attributes of the Westphalian state, the process also naturally entails a search for a global role commensurate with its aspiration and the attainment of international reputation and respect. As a respected Japanese colleague said: "it's about status, status, status!"

Status is something that Japan has craved since the fifteenth century and continues to be one of the most important but understated drivers of Japanese political behavior. It is therefore important to look to history to understand the traditional drivers of Japanese foreign policy today. Japan seeks equality, but at the same time also excellence in its endeavors, and this necessitates the attainment of status in a hierarchical global order. Additionally, apart from the Second World War period, Japan has never sought hegemony in the international system, but instead has always relied upon establishing cordial relations with the hegemon, learning from the hegemon instead. This has always ensured Japan thrives in the existing system, and allowed Japan to develop to its modern-day form as a super developmental state.

Japan historically exhibited three important methods of achieving this goal. First, Japan has always leaned toward (some scholars prefer the term "hedged"), or bandwagoned with, the dominant power of the day, keeping cordial relations with the hegemon and benefiting from trading ties, while leveraging this relationship to maintain independence and latitude to act within the political system. In pre-historic times, Japan kept cordial relations with China and adopted technologies such as the writing system, Confucian philosophy, silk making to the operations of the tributary trade system. At the turn of the nineteenth century, Japan joined forces with one of the most powerful and successful colonial powers—Great Britain. First, Japan defeated Russia in the 1905 Russo-Japanese War, and later on during the First World War, balanced against Germany and seized its territories in the Pacific as spoils of the war. The alliance fell apart in 1920 due to racial tensions and realpolitik, as the British were not ready to accept a powerful and rising Japan (Vinson 1962; Nish 1972). By the 1930s, Japan found a new idol and ally in Nazi Germany, perceiving it then to be one of the most powerful countries in the world. The Japanese notion of Pan-Asianism was in fact dominantly inspired by the Germans (Hotta 2007). Japan perceived that the US was the single biggest threat to Imperial Japan's plans in Asia and conducted a pre-emptive strike on Pearl Harbor. In the aftermath of the Second World War, Japan aligned with the US to balance against the USSR, and in the post-Cold War world, balance against China. Second, Japan has always been able to learn and adopt from both friends and foes in the international system, particularly from the hegemon of the day. From ancient China, then Britain in the early twentieth century, to the US in the postwar era, Japan has always resisted hegemony to maintain its independence and adopted the strengths of the hegemons and improved upon them (Maruyama 1963; Peattie 1975; Shintaro 1991; Samuels 2003). From the tributary system, then imperialism and gunboat diplomacy to the building of a modern capitalist economy, Japan's ability to adapt to and innovate within the existing system is unparalleled. Some scholars have thus labeled Japan an "adaptive" state (Berger et al. 2007). Third, Japan has always been able to swiftly transform itself politically—from the feudal clans to the centralized Tokugawa Shogunate system to the Meiji State where the Samurais were swiftly disbanded, to Taisho democracy, to ultra-nationalism and the liberal democracy that followed, Japan has never seemed to have problems discarding or adopting institutions. Karel Van Wolferen alludes to the idea that "the most crucial factor determining

Japan's socio-political reality ... is the near absence of any idea that there can be truths, rules, principles or morals that always apply, no matter what the circumstances" (Van Wolferen 1989: 9). This might be overstating the character of the Japanese people. The Japanese nation has prized loyalty and excellence as two important attributes that generations of Japanese have striven to achieve, with great success. I would say that Japan's impressive shape-shifting abilities have more to do with its wholehearted quest in its tasks at hand—nothing more, nothing less.

THE IDEA OF NORMALIZATION AND REJUVENATION

Regardless of theoretical persuasion, there is no question among scholars of Japanese foreign policy that Japan's role in the international system has changed somewhat over the years. The question of "normalization" is no longer an "if" question or even a "when" question, but rather a question of "how" and "in what form." At the most basic level, the definition of "normalization" as understood by this book is the socialization of Japan as a power with political status and strategic capabilities that are commensurate with its economic achievements and the acceptance of the international community of the greater role Japan may play in international affairs. To that end, since the late 1970s, Japan has provided overseas development assistance to most of the countries in Southeast Asia and China. Japan has also strengthened multilateral trade agreements with its neighbors, dispatched peacekeepers (Tanaka 2007; Lam 2009) to Cambodia and East Timor, and helped in UN or ASEAN disaster relief efforts, such as in the aftermath of the 2003 tsunami that killed 230,000 in the Indian Ocean rim countries or Typhoon Nargis in Myanmar. Japan has supported peacebuilding diplomacy in Aceh and pushed for greater regional integration through ASEAN institutions. Yet, it is questionable whether these activities could really testify that Japan has "normalized" and even if so, to what extent can we say for sure that this is the case. The Asia-Pacific region has historically been considered to be Japan's backyard, while these activities do prove that Japan is becoming more assertive politically, they cannot attest to the restoration of political and security status proportionate to Japan's economic stature.

One would naturally assume that most of this literature from the 1990s onwards would be centered on Japan's "normalization." Surprisingly, this is not exactly the case. There have actually been very few books written exclusively on this subject matter (Oros 2009; Soeya et al. 2011; Hughes

2006, 2009, 2015), even though admittedly most of the scholarly literature does discuss this in part—whether it be the Japanese role in peacekeeping or Japan's relations with the US, China or Southeast Asia. What is evident is that when discussing Japan's normalization/rejuvenation, different politicians and scholars have radically different images of what this entails, even though the areas of discussions overlap. As Welch notes, how a state defines security and what it takes to achieve it are two very different things, and more importantly how a state defines its national interests might change over time, as in the case of Japan (Welch 2011: 17).

The former prime minister of Singapore, Lee Kuan Yew, said in the mid-1990s in a commentary that "to let an armed Japan participate in [peacekeeping operations] is like giving a chocolate filled with whiskey to an alcoholic." Such a view echoes the many discussions and debates that are located within the mainstream international relations theory on liberalism/realism. The dominant narratives put the "nature" of the Japanese nation under scrutiny. These policymakers and scholars (often from the vantage points of Japan's neighboring countries—China, Korea and Southeast Asia) often debate whether it is an inherent characteristic of Japan to seek power as an end in itself and, if given the latitude and opportunity to do so, whether a resurgent and militaristic Japan would ascend once again in Asia (Austin and Harris 2001: 137). On the flip side, there is a corresponding reaction on the part of many Japanese politicians and scholars who perceive things differently.

From their standpoint, the greatest impediment to the "normalization" of Japan stems from the misconceived ideas, discourses and narratives that exist both inside and outside Japan to the effect that Japanese people are "nationalistic" or "militaristic." It is the failure of these critics to recognize the significance of the nature of the Second World War (that the Japanese people were "misled" rightly or wrongly) and that Japan has since been reformed and is now one of the pillars of regional and global prosperity. These politicians and scholars perceive that in order to achieve normalization, a fundamental shift in mindset and worldview is necessary, and this change in mindset (i.e. eradicating pacifism) should emanate from the Japanese people themselves, especially from the younger generation (Nakasone 1999; Abe 2006; Aso 2007). Beyond that, Japan should use its political-economic and diplomatic influence to ensure that this new image of Japan is propagated worldwide, and in addition engage critics to ensure this erroneous misperception of Japan as a militaristic country not be left to stand. Emanating out of a desire to ensure that international relations theory becomes more "scientifically rigorous" and systematic, scholars working from the neo-realist perspective ground the debate differently from their realist counterparts. Unlike realism, where power is seen as an end in itself, neo-realist scholars often ground their debate on "normalization," by focusing on the concept of "national interests" in Japan's conceptualization of its foreign policy and on Japan's defense and security capabilities (or lack thereof). Invariably, these discussions on interests and/or capabilities would revolve around two fundamental pillars of Japan's strategy: the role of the US-Japan security alliance and nuclear weapons in Japan's strategic thinking.

Mochizuki (1997: 56–77) places the debate on normalization into three broad camps: Advocates for participation in collective security; advocates for the right to collective self-defense; and advocates for an independent strategy. Ichiro Ozawa, one of Japan's most influential politicians, and the man widely credited with having engineered the end of LDP rule in 2009, popularized the concept of a "normal" Japan through his book, *Blueprint for a New Japan* (日本改造計画, Nihon Kaizō Keikaku) in which he articulated his vision for Japan's participation in a collective security system under the mandate of the UN (Mochizuki 1997: 57–59; also see "Draft Report on Japan's role in the International Community" by the LDP Special Study Group, headed in 1991 by then LDP Secretary General Ozawa, *Japan Echo*, 1992 Vol. XIX, No. 2: 49–58). Even though it does not depart from the question of using force, this school of thought has come under attack from those advocating the "right to collective self-defense" because of the trust it puts in international bodies such as the UN. Most Japanese scholars would, however, fall within the "right to collective self-defense" camp. Unlike those who place faith in the UN system to maintain Japanese security, the advocates of collective security place their faith in the US-Japan security alliance. Hughes (2006) argues that Japan's normalization would be crucial to global security, as Japan's willingness and ability to support the US would be pivotal in maintaining US hegemony, at least in the Asia-Pacific region. The expected trajectory, however, is that Japan is likely to remain within the US-Japan security alliance for the time to come. Yet, no one should take for granted that the US-Japan relationship is trouble-free or that the alliance provides the best solution to all of Japan's problems. Green (1995) looks at the question of the US-Japan alliance from the viewpoint of military technology collaboration and highlights the dilemma facing the alliance—the question of strategic "abandonment" by the US versus the "entrapment" by the US into an unwanted military adventure. This vulnerability is especially crucial when it comes to Taiwan or the South China Sea, as one of Japan's strategic nightmares would be having to choose between the US and China. Therefore, there have been others who have examined Japan's normalization from a military viewpoint, arguing that the greatest impediment to Japanese normalization is Japan's inability to safeguard itself from attacks and its over-reliance on the US alliance for its military needs (Green 1995; Samuels 1994). One way forward to remove this impediment is for Japan to comprehensively re-evaluate its own military capabilities and ensure that it is able to meet the challenges to its security either alone or through the framework of the US-Japan security alliance. The more extreme group would of course advocate that Japan build up independent capabilities and even consider the abrogation of the US-Japan alliance (two prominent advocates being the former Tokyo governor Shintaro Ishihara and the late Shoichi Watanabe of Sophia University), and others would advocate that Japan acquire nuclear weapons under specific conditions (Nakanishi 2003). For instance, Nakanishi advocates Japan should acquire nuclear capabilities if (a) US commitment to Japan waivers; (b) China develops blue-water capabilities; or (c) North Korea acquires nuclear weapons. Fortunately, most Japanese analysts' positions do not fall at either extreme.

While neo-realists have a propensity to focus on material interests and power projection capabilities, neo-liberals focus on the role of institutions and regimes in their thinking on the normalization of Japan. One area of critical concern that neo-liberals share with neo-realists is the impact of the Japanese constitution (specifically Article 9, which renounces Japan's sovereign war-making rights) and the impact this has for the normalization of Japan. Many neo-realist scholars regard the limitations of Article 9 as an abhorrence to be altered or scrapped in order for Japan to have maximum strategic latitude and capabilities. Neo-liberals on the other hand would probably favor a more nuanced approach to the issue of the constitution. As they favor working within, reforming and strengthening existing institutions, they view constitutional and legal reforms as the best way forward. For example, they would consider cutting down the lengthy and protracted legal processes needed to secure support for the dispatch of troops abroad, and they feel that a reconstitution of Japan's domestic political and legal institutions would be necessary in order for Japan to withstand any political paralysis in the event of a crisis. They might also favor construction of a domestic consensus on how Japan should support the US in the event of crisis within the existing framework of Article 9. A group of scholars under the leadership of Yomiuri Shimbun established the Yomiuri Constitution Study Council in 1992 and actually proposed changes to Japan's constitution. A new "draft constitution" was published in the spring of 1994 in the *Japan Echo*. These efforts did not stop and Japan, under the leadership of successive prime ministers from Hashimoto onwards, put forward a series of legislation in order to facilitate Japan having more latitude to send troops abroad. Beyond the reform of the legal and political framework within Japan, neo-liberals might also see Japan's normalization through economic rather than military means. As long as Japan is able to maintain asymmetrical economic relations with other countries, and engage them through a complex web of economic interdependence, this would endow Japan with the necessary economic clout to be a great power, ceteris paribus. This thinking is not new, and essentially emanates from the Fukuda Doctrine promulgated in the 1970s that saw Japan developing its overseas developmental assistance (ODA) program. While Ozawa cannot be strictly classified as a neo-liberal, his idea of having Japan "normalized" and partaking in UN centered politico-military affairs is an indication of the faith he has in institutions.

As a result of left-wing ideology, there is a growing number of people who are working on or researching peace studies, but ironically this includes some who are interested in security studies, which cannot be funded at national universities. Despite this, there is still a number of Japanese scholars writing on security and foreign policy who subscribe to mainstream neo-realism and/or neo-liberalism, and there is a growing interest among scholars working in the field of constructivism concerning these questions. Constructivists are concerned primarily with the "ideational" in international relations—namely concepts such as identity, self-defined roles, norms and values of the nation and their linkages to the foreign and security policies of their countries (See Katzenstein 1996, 1998; Sato and Hirata 2008, for examples). For constructivists, the greatest impediment to the "normalization" of Japan lies not in the material interests or inadequate capabilities of Japan but rather the security culture and self-prescribed foreign policy roles that Japan has adopted since its defeat in the Second World War. While scholars in Japan might not use constructivist language or "terms" per se (in fact many of these scholars write in neo-realist language), many of them do conceptualize and debate Japan's role in global affairs. Inoguchi (2008), for example, put forward discussions involving Japan's role in global affairs. In the 2004 article, he debates whether Japan should emulate Britain, Germany or

France, and contextualizes Japan's linkages with the US in such a way that differs from the world role Japan has adopted since 1945. In another discussion, Inoguchi argues that Japan has readjusted and redefined its world role roughly every 15 years, and makes the case that since 2005, Japan has redefined itself as a "Global Ordinary Power" and readjusted its foreign policy accordingly. Soeya Yoshihide, a much respected Japanese scholar, has also argued that Japan must chart itself as a middle power and engage in neighborly policy as Japan's top foreign policy priority (Soeya 2008). Yet, there are others (Shiina 1991; Okazaki & Sato 1991; Ishizuka 2006) who perceive that Japan should take stock of the changes in the international system and act decisively to participate more confidently in world affairs, including among other things fulfilling its global responsibilities in the Persian Gulf in order to shape its future in the global community (Shiina 1991). Some scholars have argued that Japan is no longer an "abnormal" power in their foreign policy, as observed in Southeast Asia (Lam 2011: 93–209) while others argue that perhaps there are limits to what Japan can do, as in the case of Japan-Korea relations (Swenson-Wright 2011: 146–193). There is every evidence that Japanese policy in the post-Cold War world has begun to move beyond the reactive diplomacy of the Cold War years, and this is especially so in the Middle East (Rynhold 2002).

At a policy level, the "normalization" of Japan is thus not a recent phenomenon, but rather has been a political wish, if not actual projects, of almost all the postwar prime ministers. All of them have tried in their way to adjust, modify or interpret their policies in accordance with the latitude given to them to make the best use of the circumstances and the institutions they have inherited to maximize Japanese interests. The question of rejuvenation is to a large extent the result of a new phase of Japanese foreign policy. This in turn is a direct result of a new sense of mission and state power, beginning with Tanaka's normalization with China and the implementation of the Fukuda Doctrine in 1978 that saw the emergence of a more capable and confident Japan. Japan's success in its modernization project, the end of the Cold War and the inherent challenges that came with the era spurred on this rejuvenation trend. This book argues that it is vital to understand that efforts to rejuvenate Japan to normality run parallel with a desire for Japan to rise as a great power. Today, the processes of normalization and rejuvenation have come to define the agenda of the neo-conservatives in Japan. This agenda, however, has been interpreted by some commentators, particularly in Japan's neighboring countries, as little beyond raw remilitarization. There are also questions raised concerning the quality of democracy in Japan. First, critics argue that Japan ultimately has been a one-party state for most of its postwar history, notwithstanding two brief periods—under the Socialist led government (1993–1994) and the Democratic Party (DPJ) years (2010–2012). Second, liberal democracy is imposed, and Japan has not actually bled (in fought wars) for democracy. Third, Japan has always resisted "exporting" liberal democracy as its foreign policy goal, despite US governmental pressure. Fourth, there are competing ideas that detract the Japanese from their liberal democratic credentials: neo-conservatism certainly erodes Japan's liberal credentials, and grassroots nationalism erodes Japan's democratic credentials. In short, the ruling party LDP is not all that democratic in its statecraft, and much of Japan's democratization impetus appears to be emanating from the ground up.

Japan's strategy for rejuvenation, however, has entailed contradictory elements and results: as it seeks greater domestic support for a normalization agenda by reinterpreting its past, its security environment deteriorates because its neighbors in turn interpret this to be a sign of unrepentant remilitarism; as it seeks a greater role in international and global affairs, it piggy-backs on the US-Japan alliance as a strategy, resulting in greater dependence on the US. The Abe administration has purportedly wanted to build an arc of freedom and prosperity, ostensibly to contain China, a country identified as an authoritarian regime, yet Japan is keen to work with Myanmar, Laos, Cambodia, Vietnam and Russia—countries which are also known to have repressive regimes with human rights violations. In order for Japan to protect its cherished democracy, the LDP continually repressed the popular sentiments in Okinawa (McCormack and Norimatsu 2012), legislates security laws and eradicates the peace clause (Article 9) in the constitution to protect the very freedoms Japan says it cherishes.

Despite this, it is important to point out that despite all the lobbying the neo-conservatives have done, there is evidence from public opinion polls that Japanese democracy has had a much deeper effect than is commonly assumed by the critics (Eldridge and Midford 2008). Even though the Japanese public has supported the reaffirmation of the US-Japan alliance, they too cherish deeply the democratic values that Japan has acquired over the last few decades. To that extent, even though Japan goes forward, it is the democracy that is so engrained with pacifism in Japanese identity that will prevent the neo-conservatives from achieving what they want in a short time. The resistance to the prime minister's efforts to erode the constitution and to increase the power of the military remains relatively strong, and certainly these movements are an indication of the Japanese people's regard for the constitution and democracy, and the conscious efforts of these protestors to protect Japanese democracy. I term this phenomenon Japan's "democratic resilience."

Beyond Zero-Sum Games and Binary Choices: Transcending the US-China Divide

This same democratic resilience would also help balance the tendencies for Japan to take an extreme position in its foreign policy. Recent developments in Japan-US relations since the ascendance of President Trump have deepened a realization that it is essential for Japan to increase interactions with its neighbors—particularly China and North Korea—in order to insure long-term Japanese strategic interests. The rejuvenation of Japan thus becomes increasingly a major challenge simply because restoring normal attributes of a nation-state and achieving the kind of excellence that Japan aspires to is extremely difficult, not only because of the internal debates and contradictions between different Japanese elites and the people, but also because this is taking place in the shadow of the hegemonic competition that is being played out in the Asia-Pacific today, between the US and China. Japan is at risk of being perpetually locked into a subservient relationship, despite its strategy of tightly "embracing" the US to gain more latitude, and being chain-ganged into a conflict it does not want to be involved in. This is particularly so in its management of its relationship with China.

Even though Prime Minister Abe has time and again articulated that Japan's foreign policy is not just about China, but rather that Japan's outlook should really be global in nature, the very fact that this is articulated often suggests China still remains a significant factor in Japan's strategic calculations. Repetition speaks for itself. This theme will be further developed in Chaps. 2 and 3.

This phenomenon is likely to see two important trends as Japan searches for a way forward. The first is an increased tightening of the US-Japan alliance, thereby increasing Japan's dependence on the US in all aspects, even though it seeks greater "independence." This however is against the respect of Japan's early leaders; from Yoshida to Kishi to Nakasone, most of these leaders were obsessed with the international status that stems from greater international contribution, as well as independence from the

US. Also, this process would almost guarantee the accentuation of US-China competition and Japan-China tensions as Japan seeks to do its "part" in achieving alliance goals.

The second trend is that this reaffirms the narrative of the China threat within Japan, thus preventing the prospect of Japan being able to work sustainably with China in any manner. This is most manifested today in East and Southeast Asia. That the South China Sea has been militarized is probably one of the most important and frightening episodes of US-China hegemonic competition. At first glance, this might seem a good idea. It would at the very least prevent the possibility of the US and China working out a partnership of sorts that might relegate Japan to a secondary position vis-à-vis the US. This is particularly so, as some commentators have suggested, because China is a more natural partner to the US in resolving of many of the global problems (White 2013). This is not because China is better than Japan, but rather because many of the pressing problems of our time originate from or involve China: Diseases, intellectual property thefts, transnational crimes, food safety problems, counterfeiting industries. This sort of rhetoric, however, is often misinterpreted and/or rejected by Japan—for this is unthinkable. Beyond that, such intense focus on China as a threat is self-perpetuating and self-fulfilling.

For a longer term, the benefits of an extremely tight embrace with the US might not necessary outweigh the benefits. The US could undertake policy changes that leave Japan surprised and in a bind. This is not beyond the realm of impossibility. Trump's about-turn on the Trans-Pacific Partnership (TPP) and his conduct of unconventional diplomacy with North Korea without consulting with Japan are the clearest indications of the fallacy of Japan's assumption yet. Taking an explicit position out of loyalty to the alliance at all costs, including sacrificing the possibility of engaging and working with Japan's closest neighbors, is of an extremely high cost. Japan should reconsider and rebalance its priorities to ensure its own interests are always taken care of first and foremost. Today, even though this strategy makes sense to the LDP's leaders, the question of whether this is truly the case is actually a moot point—simply because none of the leaders who have actually considered viable alternatives have put their vision in place. A Japanese colleague and good friend Sugita Yoneyuki argued that political and military cooperation with China might be possible the day China catches up or even overtakes the US as the regional hegemon. There is no guarantee of course that such a day will come, but at the same time, the assumption that closer Sino-Japan relations can be had at will, particularly after the tensions over the years, is problematic. Beyond that, treating China as an enemy from the get-go will often effectuate this materiality. However, this attests to the model put forth in this book that Japan would always seek cooperation with the strongest power to hedge against systemic challengers and disruptors.

If Japan seeks normalcy and rejuvenation, a possible strategy might be for it to consider working on a parallel track with China—maintaining good relations with the US need not come about at the expense of Japan's relations with China. This could be a viable political choice. Instead of demonstrating "alliance" credentials vis-à-vis China, Japanese politicians could seek an alternate track of working with China outside of the Asia-Pacific region without being detrimental to its existing relations with the US. There are geographical regions and issue areas that China might have more influence over than the US (such as North Korea), and recent developments in Japanese foreign policy might retard rather than enhance Japanese interests. It would help Japan gain greater credibility and shake off its international image as just a US ally.

Particularly if Japan wants to play a greater role, and to that extent a possible leadership role in some fields, Japan would need the support of its Asian neighbors in both US-led camps and the non-alliance group. Until Japan receives this support (from both the US-led camp and those outside of this camp), it will have a hard time achieving its aspirations. Its close association with the US might work well in East Asia, but this comes at a cost, particularly as Japan seeks to broaden its role abroad beyond the Asia-Pacific. The association with the US might cause friction for Japan's policy goals in certain geographical areas and with certain countries, and limit greater goals that it could achieve that might be commensurate with its status in the region.

Japan therefore needs to exhibit some resolve that it cares for its Asian neighbors' security as much as it does for the alliance. Even to this day, there is still certain tension in Japan-South Korea relations, and one might question if these relations can actually function normally without friction without the US. Their relationship, characterized as a 'quasi-alliance," suggests the vital mediating role of the US is marred by historical friction and varying degrees of understanding of mutual support (Cha 2000).

During Koizumi's era, it would almost certainly appear that while the US was engrossed in fighting the War on Terror, China and Japan could not handle their bilateral relations independently as Sino-Japanese relations deteriorated to a new low. While one might attribute the deterioration of this relationship to the negligence of the Bush administration, there is a sense that this might be intentional. By the end of the tempestuous period, not only did Japan resolve to tighten its alliance relationship with the US, but Beijing also wanted the same, as it felt that only the US could handle the politicians in Tokyo, and that Sino-Japanese relations could be better managed through Washington D.C. This is not to say that Japan's foreign policy agenda had not advanced during Prime Minister Koizumi's term. Koizumi had not only begun to centralize the Prime Minister's office over both foreign policy and domestic politics (Shinoda 2007), but had also managed to send a clear message to China that historical issues would be factored into Japan's foreign policy decisions.

From China's and South Korea's perspectives, there is certainly room for their relations with Japan to be improved. From Tokyo's perspective, the Koreans and the Chinese have been unreasonable, particularly in not recognizing the gestures and development aid that Japan has provided in the postwar era. Those contributions toward national development ought to count against the demerits of the Second World War. A normal and rejuvenated Japan, therefore, should not continue to bear the cross of war responsibility in perpetuity. This "emotional" stalemate is what inhibits Japan's closer relations with its neighbors.

Japanese politicians, therefore, have always found it easy to exploit these sentiments—as they are deeply felt across the nation, and ingrained in grassroots nationalism in Japan. Yet, the hardest thing for any politician to do is the opposite—to rally the nation not only to have excellent relations with the US, but also with its closest neighbors. A Japan which aspires to regional and global leadership would have the support of not only its allies, but also of its closest neighbors in its own backyard.

The normalcy and rejuvenation Japan seeks should not be confined to narrow definitions of military revival. Japan is already an economic superpower with tremendous soft power. Japan is extremely popular in the West, and perceives itself to be a member of the First World bloc. Japan's normalcy and rejuvenation should come about from a genuine re-evaluation of its priorities vis-à-vis the US and China, possibly rising above the US-China hegemonic struggle to become a genuine global power that is commensurate with its existing status.

The democracy movement today is more important than ever to prevent the radicalization of Japanese politics in the widest sense. Ironically many Japanese youths, particularly those of school-going age, are determined to ensure that the LDP and the Abe administration do not completely eradicate the pacifism and democratic culture of yesteryear. Their concern, however, is more about the preservation of democracy and how the government is strong-arming their political agenda through Japanese parliament without seeking a compromise. These youths have been criticized as misunderstanding the geopolitical dimensions of Abe's strategy.

At the same time, popular opinion of China is at an all-time low. Anyone mentioning the possibility of closer Japan-China relations in Tokyo would be politely dismissed at best, at worst laughed at or risk being ridiculed as a "China" or "Korean" sympathizer most of the time. However, this sentiment is not new—nationalism in China, Japan and Korea has all but inoculated the respective nations against any suggestions of working with their neighbors as being unpatriotic and/or foolish. In Japan's case, the protestors resisting the government attempt to "normalize" Japan are doing so because of democratic inclinations—most feel that the government has ignored public opinion regarding the use of force and deployment overseas. There is less discussion of the revisionist version of history that the Abe administration articulates.

The Japanese nation's instinct to protect the constitution is a major statement against revisionism. There is no stronger apology than to maintain the constitution, and that accepting that the Japanese constitution, particularly the Article 9 "No War Clause" is the most formal apology that the Japanese nation can make to its neighbors. Japan therefore has every reason to let the constitution stand as is, rather than amend it. Japan has done well to adjust to security challenges so far, particularly through minute administrative and legal measures to subvert the constitutional constraints. Japan's security problems must be dealt with, and certainly Japan needs to take measures to ensure certain parities with China, but constitutional revisionism need not make Japan more secure—in fact, it might make Japan less secure in time to come, should the external security environment deteriorates as a result of this.

Chapter Overview and Synopsis

Chapter 2 examines the historical roots of Japan's idea of resurgence and rejuvenation, and locates its quest for normalization within Japan's philosophical and political thinking from ancient times.

This chapter puts forth the argument that it would not be possible to understand the nuances and undertone of Japan's foreign policy today without historicizing Japan's relation with China and the West. This chapter provides a philosophical and historical context toward the understanding of how Japan has always striven to remain a nation-state par excellence in the tempestuous international relations of the region. The chapter illustrates the contradictory values of egalitarianism and the quest for excellence that is embedded in Japanese political philosophy and social thinking, and argues that since the late fifteenth century, the principal country Japan has always been concerned about in its strategic thinking is China, despite statements to the contrary. The chapter outlines the adapting strategy Japan has used in its historical international relations, particularly through its cultivation of the dominant hegemon of the day, its adaptive learning and its consummate quest for exceptionalism. Shifting its analysis to a more contemporary focus, the chapter examines the rise of the idea of "abnormal" Japan against the traditional philosophical political thinking of the Japanese elites. The chapter then maps out the central tenets of Japanese postwar conservatism before scrutinizing the major differences of the neo-conservatism that drives Japan's normalization and rejuvenation today. The chapter then seeks to unpack the three major tenets that Japan's neo-conservatives are concerned with: (1) revising the constitution; (2) managing the US-Japan alliance and (3) eroding the pervasive pacifism that is found in Japanese society. The chapter concludes by examining the ironical linkage on how Japanese democracy and historical revisionism may co-exist, and on how neo-conservatism today drives the paradoxes in Japanese politics and society. In presenting these narratives and discussions, this chapter unpacks some of the contradictory tendencies we see in today's Japan. This chapter argues that the "irrationality" and paradoxes we see in Japanese foreign policy today in fact conform to the long-term pattern in Japan's external behavior historically.

Chapter 3 examines the tensions Japan faces in its Asia-Pacific policy, and overall raises the question whether Japan's security is best served by over(t)ly relying on the US-Japan alliance while making a perpetual enemy out of China and North Korea. The principal target of Japanese "normalization" and rejuvenation of its foreign policy is China. Prior to 1998, China had never explicitly been cited as a threat to Japan. Yet as Chinese power grew, the People's Republic became the primary rationale and motivation for Tokyo elites to drive the rejuvenation of their country. Despite this, in official narratives before 1998, Japanese neo-conservatives only highlighted the dangers of a belligerent North Korea to justify their platforms and policies. As Prime Minister Junichiro Koizumi's chief cabinet secretary, Shinzo Abe was one of the first politicians to highlight and emphasize the North Korean threat. Their real concern, however, was not so much North Korea, but China. However, by the early 2000s, both North Korea and China have come to play a crucial and important role in Japan's strategic imagination and narratives. Thus, the period saw Japan doubling down on its alliance with the US, effectively orientating all efforts to harmonize its foreign and security with the US. This chapter explores whether Japan's normalization efforts have paid off in terms of ensuring a more stable outlook for Japan's security in view of tensions with China and North Korea in recent times, and argues that the greatest security problem for Japan stems from an overt belief in the sanctity of the US-Japan alliance. There have been critical junctures at which Japanese expectations as an ally have not been met (e.g. the US rapprochement with China in 1972 and recently in 2018 with North Korea).

Japan's normalization and rejuvenation therefore currently hinges on the strengthening of the US-Japan security alliance, the revision of the constitution, and the socializing of the Japanese people to reframe their historical perspective and social norms away from pacifism to support Japan's military reorientation. Prime Minister Shinzo Abe has been moderately successful in strengthening and deepening Japan's ties with the US, and has been extremely adept at advocating for Japan's rejuvenation as a global power by persuading the Japanese people to support his agenda of ensuring that Japan lives up to its global responsibility, alliance commitment and democratic spirit at home. Yet, Japan's plan for this rejuvenation faces serious challenge at home from different political factions and societal groups. Tokyo faces resistance and inertia from the nation's pacifist traditions and democratic culture that prevents the revision of the constitution or the sustained support of Japan Self-Defense Forces (JSDF) deployments abroad. Externally, Japan risks falling into the trap of being chain-ganged right into the center of a hegemonic struggle between the US and China. There is a big difference between being a good ally and getting entrapped in a position where one's foreign policy posture is severely curtailed. Japan's rejuvenation must be built on utilizing US-Japan relations to further its interests in the Asia-Pacific and beyond. In doing this, Japan's security cannot be worse off than before, because that simply defeats the purpose of the exercise of having an alliance. Likewise, Sino-Japanese relations must be advanced to the point where Japan can leverage and benefit from this relationship for economic growth and security rather than becoming a permanent security liability. Thus leaning to one side at all costs might be politically expedient in the short term, but ultimately self-defeating and detrimental to Japan's interests in the long run.

This is exemplified in the contestation between the US and China in the South China Sea. For Japan to achieve the status commensurate with its economic power, which it has been seeking arguably since the 1970s, it needs the support of its neighbors in both East and Southeast Asia. While *some* Southeast Asian countries welcome the presence of a stronger US-Japan alliance in the region to balance Chinese influence, competition between the US (with Japan) and China would cause consternation for ASEAN, as none of the countries would want to choose sides. Japan's rejuvenation should therefore transcend this "with us or with them" divide. Furthermore, Japan's attempt to revise its constitution may appear to be a normal course of action to the neo-conservatives, but it does hurt its image with its Asian neighbors. As political scientist Chalmers Johnson notes, the peace constitution is the sincerest apology that Japan can make to its Asian neighbors, any amendment to this constitution would have tremendous implications for Japan's soft power and image abroad, particularly in Asia. Japan's rejuvenation as a global power cannot come without substantial support from its own neighborhood. If Japan is able to secure this, then prospects for its regional and global leadership would be substantially enhanced.

Chapter 4 discusses Japan's involvement in peacekeeping activities in the Middle East. Even though the rejuvenation of Japan calls for a greater role for Japan in international affairs, the extent to which it is able to do this in the Middle East is still relatively constrained. Over the last two decades, Tokyo's principal concern with the Middle East is the extent to which Japan can support the US in the Gulf. Japan's focus seems to be on the traditional dimensions of "peacekeeping," with its efforts concentrated on traditional elements of military support and humanitarian intervention efforts. This is closely tied to the normalization agenda of having the Japanese military extend its operating range and scope from the Japanese shore, and at the same time enhancing interoperability with the US forces in the region. Such a focus facilitates the incremental erosion of the limits of Japan's constitutional constraints, as there is great public support for Japan contributing significantly to world affairs and strengthening its alliance with the US. Such single-minded focus, however, appears to stymie the realization of a potential role that Japan could be well equipped to play. The limited vision has not gone unnoticed in Japan, as it raises the question as to why Japan is unable or unwilling to play a greater role in the mediation of the Arab-Israeli conflict, as Japan's national interests are closely tied to the Middle East. Throughout the postwar period, Japan's interests in the Middle East have been largely protected by the US, given Japan's fidelity to the Yoshida Doctrine. In an age where Japan seeks normalization and rejuvenation, particularly after the Cold War, there is no question that Japan's interests in the Middle East might not necessarily be aligned with the US anymore. This chapter explores and assesses Japan's past and recent efforts, particularly since Prime Minister Abe came to power, to become a dominant political power in its own right as a peacemaker. The chapter suggests that Japan should consider building a coalition with China and other powers such as the EU to play a moderating influence in the Middle East process, particularly during the Trump administration where the US has zealously leaned toward Israel. In doing so, it might require Japan to rise above its own preference to privilege US goals, and work together with other actors in the international community toward peace between the Arabs and Israelis.

The chapter raises questions as to whether the alliance is indeed an asset to Japan's aspirations to greater political role in areas outside the Asia-Pacific. The book argues that if Japan is able to adopt a more independent strategic stance away from the US orbit, it would be able to find greater traction politically and diplomatically in the Middle East, as the image of Japan held by the people in the Middle East is one where it is capable of playing a greater role in international affairs and being a possible reasonable counter-voice to the US. Any such "normalization" efforts, such as Japanese activities in support of UN sponsored (or otherwise) peacekeeping, peacebuilding and reconciliation in the Palestine-Israeli issue, might be resisted not by China or the Middle Eastern states, but rather by the US. However, this is only possible if Japan privileges US goals to its own interests, and Japan may find that the country that poses the greatest impediment to its rejuvenation could very well be itself.

Chapter 5 examines Japan's deployment to the Gulf of Aden to fight pirates. Compared with Japan's cautious and incremental approach to other Middle East policy issues, the anti-piracy deployment is one of the most obvious and high profile deployments of the Japanese military to date. The nature of the mission—to protect Japanese and international assets and join an international US-led coalition with a clearly defined mandate to fight a non-state threat—has provided the Japanese government with a strong justification to deploy troops. This chapter illustrates how the anti-piracy deployment has been positive as a whole for Japan's rejuvenation as a global power. Additionally, this chapter also illustrates that it is entirely possible for China and Japan to collaborate on security matters if there is no political intervention or competitive elements involved. Tokyo could consider working more closely with Beijing on other security projects beyond the Asia-Pacific (such as in the area of provision of international public good), to foster more goodwill and confidence in their mutual bilateral relations. Beyond that, Japan might find that having Beijing roped in on projects where both countries have common concerns would be beneficial for two reasons. First, Beijing has sway in some areas that the US does not (e.g. Iran) and might be more helpful than the US in getting traction in important issue areas. Second, closer Japan-China cooperation might help moderate the vagaries of international politics and the excesses of US unilateralism. This would pave the way for Japan to rehabilitate and become the true and respected global political power that it so richly deserves to be.

Chapter 6 consolidates the arguments put forth in the book. The book argues that the US-Japan security alliance both facilitates and hinders Japanese normalization and rejuvenation in different ways. With the Asia-Pacific region, the alliance provides both strategic and tactical advantage for Japan's normalization vis-à-vis its principal strategic rival in the region, China. Japan's tight embrace of the US-Japan alliance stems not only from competing interests, clashing identities and nationalism, but also from deep insecurities. This insecurity stems not only from the threat that China poses (whether existential, ontological or material), but also from how the rise of China might affect Japan's standing in the world and in the region, and most importantly the implications this has for the US-Japan alliance. In short, Japan has a security paranoia that it would be "abandoned" by the US, as the latter seeks to build a new regional architecture with China. Most, if not all, Japanese cannot live with the fact that some other country rather than Japan would play a more important, instrumental role as the alliance partner to the most powerful country in the world. This is in line with the historical model presented in Chap. 2.

Yet outside of the Asia-Pacific, it is questionable whether Japan needs to be so reliant on the US. In some issue areas, Japan's interests are not consistent with those of the US. If the neo-conservatives in Japan are so keen to elevate Japan's status and rejuvenate Japan as a great power, then surely it would be in Tokyo's interests to chart a different course in accordance with Japan's national interests rather than those of the US. From Iran to North Korea, from the Persian Gulf to Africa, Japan could actually reconsider whether cooperation with China (as opposed to the US) in these third countries or issue areas might bring greater traction to the achievement of Japanese interests. True rejuvenation brings forth a latitude of freedom, and if anything this should confer upon Tokyo a new way of interpreting events and geopolitical realities. Working hand-in-hand with China on issues such as the provision of international public goods or co-investment in third countries could bring a reduction in tensions, and more constructive bilateral relations. It might even achieve a win-win solution, not only for Tokyo and Beijing but also for Washington, as Japan could further tighten the US-Japan alliance for the foreseeable future as it seeks to improve its relations with China. In that respect, Japan might achieve greater political status commensurate with its economic power, and find that its strategic choices are not as polemic as it assumes them to be. A "beautiful Japan" could well be a reality in the near future.

References

Abe, S. "*Utsukushii kuni he*" (Towards a Beautiful Country). Tokyo: Bungei shunju, 2006.

Agawa, N. "Japan as the Fifty-first State." *Japan Echo*, 1998, 25(6): 7.

Armitage, R., & Nye, J. "The US-Japan Alliance CSIS 2012." Second Armitage-Nye report, http://csis.org/files/publication/120810_Armitage_USJapan Alliance_Web.pdf

Aso, T. "*Totetsumonai kuni*" (An Extraordinary Country). Tokyo, Shinchosha, 2007.

Auer, James. *The Postwar Rearmament of the Japanese Maritime Forces, 1945–1971*. New York; Praeger, 1973.

Auslin, M. "Japan Gets Tough: Abe's new Realism," *Foreign Affairs*, vol. 96, no. 2, March/April 2016, pp. 125–134 (9).

Austin, G. & Harris, S. Japan and Greater China: Political Economy and Military Power in the Asian Century. London: Hurst, 2001.

Barnhart, Michael. *Japan Prepares for Total War: The Search for Economic Security, 1919–1945*. Ithaca, NY: Cornell University Press, 1987.

Beasley, William G. *Japanese Imperialism. 1894–1945*. Oxford and New York: Clarendon Press, 1987.

Befu, H. *Hegemony of Homogeneity: An Anthropological Analysis of Nihonjinron*. Melbourne: Transpacific Press, 2001.

Berger, T. *Cultures of Antimilitarism: National Security in Germany and Japan*. Baltimore, MD: Johns Hopkins University Press, 1998.

Berger, T. *War, Guilt and World Politics*. Cambridge: Cambridge University Press, 2012.

Berger, T. U., M. Mochizuki, et al., eds. *Japan in International Politics: The Foreign Policies of an Adaptive State*. Boulder & London: Lynne Rienner, 2007.

Buruma, I. *The Wages of Guilt: Memories of War in Germany and Japan*. New York: Farrar, Straus and Giroux, 1994.
Bush, R. *The Perils of Proximity: Sino-Japanese Security Relations*. Washington D.C.: Brookings Institution Press, 2013.
Calder, K. *Pacific Alliance: Reviving US-Japan Relations*. Yale University Press, 2010.
Calder, K., & Ye, M. *The Making of North East Asia*. Stanford University Press, 2010.
Cha, V. *Alignment despite Antagonism: US_Japan_Korea Triad*. Stanford, C.A.: Stanford University Press, 2000.
Chang, I. *The Rape of Nanjing: the Forgotten Holocaust of World War II*. London and New York: Penguin, 1997.
Chien, C.P. "Japan's Involvement in Asia-Centered Regional Forums in the Context of Relations with China and the United States." *Asian Survey*, vol. 51, no. 3, 2011, pp. 407–428.
Chung, C. "China and Japan in 'ASEAN +3' Multilateral Arrangements: Raining on the Other Guy's Parade." *Asian Survey*, vol. 53, no. 5, 2013, pp. 801–824.
Cioraci, J. "Chiang Mai Initiative Multilateralization." *Asian Survey*, vol. 51, no. 5 2011, pp. 926–952.
Crowley, J. *Japan's Quest for Autonomy*. Princeton: Princeton University Press, 1966.
Curtis, G. *Election Campaign Japanese Style*. New York: Columbia University Press, 2009.
Curtis, G. *The Japanese Way of Politics*. New York: Columbia University Press, 1988.
Curtis, G. *The Logic of Japanese Politics*. New York: Columbia University Press, 1999.
Dale, P. *Myth of Japanese Uniqueness*. Oxford & New York: Routledge, 2011.
Davis, R., & Ikeno, O. The Japanese Mind: Understanding Contemporary Japanese Culture, Vermont: Tuttle Publishing, 2002.
Dian, M. *The Evolution of the US-Japan Alliance: The Eagle and the Chrysanthemum*. Oxford: Chandos Publishing, 2014.
Dower, J. *Embracing Defeat*. New York, W.W. Norton, 1999.
Dower, J. *Empire and Aftermath: Yoshida Shigeru and the Japanese Experience, 1878–1954*. Cambridge: Harvard University Press, 1979 & 1988.
Dower, John. *War without Mercy*. New York: Pantheon Books, 1986.
Dudden, A. *Troubled Apologies Among Japan, Korea and the United States*, New York: Columbia University Press, 2008.
Eldridge, R. D. & P. Midford, eds. *Japanese Public Opinion and the War on Terrorism*. (The Palgrave Macmillan Series in International Political Communication). New York: Palgrave Macmillan, 2008.
Fogel, J. ed., *The Nanjing Massacre in History and Historiography*. Berkeley and Los Angeles, CA; University of California Press, 2000.

Funabashi, Y. *An Alliance Adrift.* New York: Council on Foreign Relations, 1999.
Glosserman, B., & Snyder, S. *The Japan-South Korea Identity Clash.* New York: Columbia University Press, 2015.
Gong, G., & Teo, V. *Reconceptualising the Divide: Identity, Memory, and Nationalism in Sino-Japanese Relations.* UK: Cambridge Scholars Press Publishing, 2010.
Graham, E. Japan's Sea Lane Security, 1940–2004: A Matter of Life and Death? London & New York: Routledge, 2006.
Green, J. *Arming Japan: Defense Production, Alliance Politics, and the Postwar Search for Autonomy,* New York: Columbia University Press, 1995.
Green, J. *By More Than Providence: Grand Strategy and American Power in the Asia Pacific Since 1783.* New York: Columbia University Press, 2017.
Green, M. *Japan's Reluctant Realism.* New York and London: Palgrave, 2003.
Green, M., & Gill, B. eds. *Asia's New Multilateralism: Cooperation, Competition and the Search for Community.* New York: Columbia University Press, 2009.
Green, M., & Mochizuki, M. *The U.S.-Japanese Alliance in the 21 Century.* New York: Council on Foreign relations, 1999.
Grimes, W.W. *Currency and Contest in East Asia.* Ithaca, NY: Cornell University Press, 2008.
Hashimoto, A. *The Long Defeat: Cultural Trauma, Memory and Identity in Japan.* New York: Oxford University Press, 2015.
He, Y. *The Search for Reconciliation: Sino-Japanese and German-Polish Relations since WW II.* New York and Cambridge: Cambridge University Press, 2009.
Heine, L., & Selden, M. eds., *Censoring History: Citizenship and Memory in Japan.* Germany and the United States, Armonk, NY; M.E. Sharpe, 2000.
Hicks, G. *Japan's War Memories: Amnesia or Concealment?* Aldershot: Ashgate, 1997.
Hook, G., Gilson, J., Hughes, C.W., & Dobson, H. Japan's International Relations: Politics, Economics and Security, Oxford and London: Routledge, 2011.
Hornung, J., & Mochizuki, M.M. "Japan: Still and Exception US Ally," *The Washington Quarterly,* vol. 39, no. 1, 2016, pp. 95–116 (21).
Hotta, E. Pan-Asianism and Japan's War 1931–1945, London: Palgrave, 2007.
Hughes, C. *Japan's Reemergence as a "Normal" Military Power.* London and New York: Routledge, 2006 (paperpack) / 2017 (hardcover).
Hughes, C.W. *Japan's Remilitarization.* New York and London; Routledge, 2009.
Hughes, C. *Japan's Foreign and Security Policy under the "Abe Doctrine": New Dynamism or Dead End?* London: Palgrave, 2015.
Igarashi, Y. *Bodies of Memory: Narratives of War in Postwar Japanese Culture, 1945–1970.* Princeton: Princeton University Press, 2000.
Ikenberry, J. "America in East Asia," in Pempel et al. *Beyond Bilateralism.* Stanford, CA; Stanford University Press, 2003.

Inoguchi, T. "Japan as a Global Ordinary Power: Its Current Phase." *Japanese Studies*, 2008 vol. 28(1): 3–13.
Iriye, Akira. *Power and Culture: The Japanese-American War, 1941–1945.* Cambridge, MA: Harvard University Press, 1982.
Iriye, Akira. *Pearl Harbor and the Coming of the Pacific War: A Brief History with Documents and Essays.* New York: St., Martin's, 1999.
Ishizu, T. "*21 Seiki no Eapawaa - Nihon no Anzenhoshou wo Kangaeru*" (The Airpower of 21st Century - Thinking about the Security of Japan). Tokyo: Fuyoushobo, 2006.
Ishizuka, K. "Japan's New Role in Peace-Building Missions." *East Asia*, 2006, 23(3): 19.
Johnson, C. *Blowback: The Costs and Consequences of American Empire.* Owl Books, 2001.
Johnson, C. *MITI and the Japanese Miracle: The Growth of Industrial Policy 1925–1975.* California: Stanford University Press, 1982.
Katada, S. "At the Crossroads: TPP, AIIB and Japan's Foreign Economic Strategy." East-West Center Perspective, 2016, (8) http://www.eastwestcenter.org/system/tdf/private/api125.pdf?file=1&type=node&id=35659
Katzenstein, P. *Cultural Norms and National Security: Police and Military in Post War Japan.* Ithaca: 1998.
Katzenstein, P. *The Culture of National Security.* Columbia University Press, 1996.
LaFeber, W. *Clash: U.S.-Japanese Relations throughout History*, New York: Norton, 1997.
Lam, P.E. *Japan's Peace-building Diplomacy in Asia: Seeking a more active political role*, London and New York: Routledge, 2009.
Lam, P.E. "Japan's Relations with Southeast Asia in the Post Cold War Era: "Abnormal" No More? in Soeya, Y., Tadakoro, M., & Welch, D.A., *Japan as "Normal Country"? A Nation in Search of its Place in the world.* Toronto: University of Toronto Press, 2011.
Lam, P.E., & Teo, V. *Southeast Asia Between China and Japan*, UK: Cambridge Scholars Publishing, 2011.
Landler, M., "North Korea Asks for Direct Nuclear Talks, and Trump Agrees", *The New York Times*, 8 March 2018.
Lai, Y.M. *Nationalism and Power Politics in Japan's Relations with China: A Neoclassical Realist Interpretation.* (The University of Sheffield/Routledge Japanese Studies Series) Oxford and London: Routledge, 2013.
Lee, G., & Teo, V. The Koreas Between China and Japan, UK: Cambridge Scholars Publishing, 2014.
Lind, J. *Sorry States.* Ithaca: Cornell University Press, 2008.
Magosaki, U. "*Nichibei Domei no Shoutai - Meisou suru Anzen Hosyo*" (The Truth behind the US Japan Alliance - Unclear Path of Security). Tokyo: Koudansha, 2009.

Maruyama, M. *Thought and Behavior in Modern Japanese Politics*. Editor Ivan Morris. London and New York: Oxford University Press, 1963.
Maslow, S. "A Blueprint for a Strong Japan? Abe Shinzo and Japan's Evolving Security System." *Asian Survey*, vol 55, no. 4, 2015, pp. 739–765 (26).
McCormack, G. *Client State: Japan in the American Embrace*. London and New York: Verso, 2007.
McCormack, G., & Norimatsu, S.O. *Resistant Islands: Okinawa Confronts Japan and the United States*. Maryland: Rowman and Littlefield Publishers, 2012.
Midford, P. *Rethinking Japanese Public Opinion and Security: From Pacifism to Realism?* Stanford, CA; Stanford University Press, 2011.
Mochizuki, M. M., ed. *Toward a True Alliance: Restructuring U.S.-Japan Security Relations*. Washington, D.C.: Brookings Institution Press, 1997.
Morimoto, S. "*Nihon Boei Saikouron - Jibun no Kuni wo Mamoru toiu Koto*" (Rethinking the Defense of Japan - Protect our Own Nation). Tokyo: Kairyusha, 2008.
Morley, James ed., *The China Quagmire: Japan's Expansion on the Asian Continent, 1933–1941*. New York; Columbia University Press, 1983.
Nakanishi, T. "Nuclear Weapons for Japan" Japan Echo, Oct 2003, 30 (5).
Nakasone, Y. *The Making of the New Japan: Reclaiming the Political Mainstream*. Surrey: Curzon Press, 1999.
Nish, I. *Alliance in Decline: A Study in Anglo-Japanese Relations, 1980–1923*. London: Athlone Press, 1972.
Nish, I. *The Anglo-Japanese Alliance: The Diplomacy of Two Island Empires, 1894–1907*. Athlone Press, 1966.
Nozaki, Y. *War Memory, Nationalism and Education in Postwar Japan, 1945–2007*. Oxford and New York, 2008.
Okazaki, H. and S. Sato, "Redefining the Role of Japanese Military Power." *Japan Echo*, 1991, 18(1): 6.
Oros, A.L. *Japan's Security Renaissance*. New York: Columbia University Press, 2017.
Oros, A.L. *Normalizing Japan: Politics, Identity and the Evolution of Security Practice*. Stanford, CA: Stanford University Press, 2009.
Orr, J.J. *The Victim as Hero: Ideologies of Peace and National Identity in Postwar Japan*. Honolulu: University of Hawai'i Press, 2001.
Packard, G. *Protest in Tokyo: The Security Treaty Crisis of 1960*. Princeton, NJ: Princeton University Press, 1966.
Peattie, M. *Ishiwara Kanji and Japan's Confrontation with the West*. Princeton, NJ: Princeton University Press, 1975.
Pempel et al. *Beyond Bilateralism*. Stanford, CA; Stanford University Press, 2003.
Rozman, G. *Asia's alliance Triangle: US-Japan-South Korea Relations at Tumultuous Times*. New York and London: Palgrave, 2015.
Rose, C., & Teo, V. The United States Between China and Japan, UK: Cambridge Scholars Publishing, 2013.

Rynhold, J. Japan's cautious new activism in the Middle East: a qualitative change or more of the same?. *International Relations of the Asia-Pacific*, 2002, 2 (2): 245–263.

Samuels, R.J. *Machiavelli's Children: Leaders and Their Legacies in Italy and Japan*, Ithaca: Cornell University Press, 2003.

Samuels, R.J. *"Rich Nation, Strong Army": National Security and the Technological Transformation of Japan*. Ithaca, NY: Cornell University Press, 1994.

Samuels, R.J. *Securing Japan: Tokyo's Grand Strategy and the Future of East Asia*. Ithaca: Cornell University Press, 2007.

Santoro, D., & Warden, J.K. "Assuring Japan and South Korea in the Second Nuclear Age." *The Washington Quarterly*, vol. 38, no.1, 2015, pp. 147–165 (19).

Sato, Y. and K. Hirata, eds. *Norms, Interests, and Power in Japanese Foreign Policy*. New York: Palgrave Macmillan, 2008.

Scalapino, Robert ed, *The Foreign Policy of Japan*. Berkeley: University Of California Press, 1977.

Schaller, Michael. *The American Occupation of Japan: The Origins of the Cold War in Asia*. New York: Oxford University press, 1985.

Seraphim, F. *War Memory and Social Politics*. Harvard University Press, 2008.

Shiina, M. "Japan's Choice in the Gulf: Participation or Isolation" *Japan Echo*, 1991: 18(1): 6.

Shinoda, T. *Koizumi Diplomacy: Japan's Kantei Approach to Foreign and Defense Affairs*. Seattle: University of Washington Press, 2007.

Shintaro, I. *The Japan that can Say No*. London and New York: Simon & Schuster, 1991.

Shinyo, T. "The Conditions of Permanent membership in the U.N. Security Council." *Japan Echo*, 1994, 21(2): 10.

Singh, B. "Japan's Post-Cold War Security Policy: Bringing back the Normal State." *Contemporary Southeast Asia*, 2002, 24(1): 24.

Soeya, Y. "Diplomacy for Japan as a Middle Power." *Japan Echo*, 2008, 35(2): 6.

Soeya, Y., Tadakoro, M. & Welch, D.A. *Japan as "Normal Country"? A Nation in Search of its Place in the world*. Toronto: University of Toronto Press, 2011.

Sohn, Y. "Japan's New Regionalism: China, Shocks and Values," *Asian Survey*, vol. 50, no. 3, 2010, pp. 591–615 (24).

Swenson-Wright, J. The Limits to "Normalcy": Japanese-Korea Post-Cold War Interactions, in Soeya, Y., Tadakoro, M. & Welch, D.A., *Japan as "Normal Country"? A Nation in Search of its Place in the world*. Toronto: University of Toronto Press, 2011.

Tanaka, A. (Translated by Hoff, J.), *Japan in Asia: Post-Cold War Diplomacy*. Tokyo: Japan Publishing Industry Foundation for Culture (JPIC), 2007 (2017 edition).

Tsuchiyama, J. The end of the Alliance? Dilemmas in the U.S.-Japan relationship," in Peter Gourevitch et al., eds, *United States-Japan Relations and International*

Institutions after the Cold War. San Diego: Graduate School of International Relations and Pacific Studies, 1995, pp. 3–34.

Van Wolferen, K. *The Enigma of Japanese Power*. New York: Knopf Publishing, 1989.

Vinson, J.C. "The Imperial Conference of 1921 and the Anglo-Japanese alliance." *Pacific Historical Review* 31, no. 3 (1962): 258.

Vogel, E. *Japan as Number One: Lessons for America*. Cambridge: Harvard University Press, 1979.

Wan, M. *Sino Japanese Relations: Interaction, Logic, Transformation*. New York & London, Routledge, 2008.

Weinstein, M. *Japan's Postwar Defense Policy, 1945–1968*. New York: Columbia University Press, 1971.

Welch, D.A. "Embracing Normalcy: Toward a Japanese "National Strategy" in Soeya, Y., Tadakoro, M. & Welch, D.A., *Japan as "Normal Country"? A Nation in Search of its Place in the world*. Toronto: University of Toronto Press, 2011.

Welfield, J. *An Empire in Eclipse: Japan in the Postwar American Alliance System*. London and New Jersey: Athlone Press, 1988.

White, H. *The China Choice: Why We should Share Power*. Oxford: Oxford University Press, 2013.

Woo-Cummings. *The Developmental State* (Cornell Studies in Political Economy). Ithaca: Cornell University Press, 1999.

Yoshibumi, W. *The Postwar Conservative View of Asia: How the Political Right has delayed Japan's Coming to Terms with its History of Aggression in Asia*. Tokyo: LTCB International Library Foundation, 1998, (originally published to Japanese in 1995).

Open Access This chapter is licensed under the terms of the Creative Commons Attribution 4.0 International License (http://creativecommons.org/licenses/by/4.0/), which permits use, sharing, adaptation, distribution and reproduction in any medium or format, as long as you give appropriate credit to the original author(s) and the source, provide a link to the Creative Commons licence and indicate if changes were made.

The images or other third party material in this chapter are included in the chapter's Creative Commons licence, unless indicated otherwise in a credit line to the material. If material is not included in the chapter's Creative Commons licence and your intended use is not permitted by statutory regulation or exceeds the permitted use, you will need to obtain permission directly from the copyright holder.

CHAPTER 2

Japan's Rejuvenation: Origins, Debates and Concepts

It is said that heaven does not create one man above or below another man. Any existing distinction between the wise and the stupid, between the rich and the poor, comes down to a matter of education.

Gakumon no Susume [An Encouragement of Learning] (1872–1876)

Once the wind of Western civilization blows to the East, every blade of grass and every tree in the East follow what the Western wind brings… We do not have time to wait for the enlightenment of our neighbors so that we can work together toward the development of Asia. It is better for us to leave the ranks of Asian nations and cast our lot with civilized nations of the West… We should deal with them exactly as the Westerners do.

"*Datsu-a-ron*" [On departure from Asia], *Jiji Shimpo (1885-03-16)*.

Fukuzawa Yukichi (福澤 諭吉)

Japan's Political and Philosophical Traditions: Equality, Hierarchy and Exceptionalism

The China Dilemma

Widely regarded as one of the founders of modern Japan, Fukuzawa Yukichi's (福澤 諭吉) thinking and philosophy register the angst of the dilemmas that contemporary Japan faces today (Fukuzawa 1875, 2007). Fukuzawa, born into a Samurai class was an opponent of elitism and feudal thinking, particularly disliked the ideas of Confucian hierarchy that pervaded Japan. His disdain for the way Japanese politics, steeped in traditional order where many leading Samurais were not responding to economic decay and social ills of the day was only matched by his disappointment in Japan's inability to deal with the challenge of Western infringement and colonialism. As part of Japan's first embassy to the United States, he travelled widely in not only the United States but also to Europe, where he absorbed, crystallized and translated his thinking into guiding principles for Japanese politics.

The roots of Japanese enlightenment during the Meiji Restoration stemmed from Japanese reforms privileging equality over hierarchy and choosing self-determination over divine destiny. Capitalizing on Westphalian ideals, the Meiji elites saw the future of the Japanese nation emerging as a modern sovereign state in the fraternity of Western colonial powers. Japan's destiny lied in casting off the constraining shackles of her feudal Confucian past and the embracement of the prevailing imperialistic logic then. Fukuzawa's famous thesis "only when the individual is independent can the nation of such individuals be independent (一身独立して 一國独立する / *isshin dokuritsu shite ikkoku dokuritsu suru*) could be loosely transposed to Japan's understanding of how international politics worked. Needless to say, the illusion that the Westphalian international system where nation-states are equal (in principle at least), and in their relations independent (in principle at least) was hardly the international system Japan and her East Asian neighbors found themselves being transposed into as they entered the twentieth century.

Fukuzawa's enlightenment ideas are not new. For centuries, Japanese intellectuals have struggled with ideals imposed by Chinese inspired Confucianism (Watanabe 2012). The influence of Confucianism in Japan has been widespread, but over the course of time, Japanese thinkers and philosophers debated the virtues of their national development vis-à-vis the developments of their closest neighbor in the continent. China figures prominently in ancient and contemporary Japanese political philosophy and thinking for two natural reasons. First, until the arrival of the West via colonialism and modern technology to Asia, and for that matter, Japan did not come into contact with a credible alternative set of philosophy, thinking and social system. The primary reference for East Asian societies including Japan remained China and Chinese civilization. Second, by this time, the influence of the Chinese Confucian thinking has over the course of centuries permeated into the way how other East Asian societies structured themselves and conducted their daily affairs. The Confucian model in short informed the basic infrastructure of their society and provided the basis for these societies to debate about the merits or demerits of what worked and what did not for their society and the differentials in development trajectory as well as strategies for their future.

One natural but key development in Chinese and Japanese society is the development of the Samurai class in Japan. Feudal Chinese society has always been divided into four classes: Confucian literati and landlords, peasants, artisans, and merchants. Japanese society mirrors this stratification—with one important exception. Samurai warriors, not Confucian literati and landowners, stands at the Apex of this stratification. This social structure has largely been in force since the twelfth century, with the Emperor revered as the sovereign. Viewed from today's prism, this might seem ironic, but pre-modern Japan is very much a warrior nation, setting herself apart from China in this respect. This is exemplified by the Japanese idiom, "Cherry blossom stands out amongst flowers, and the warrior stands out amongst men" (花は桜木人は武士; *Hana wa sakuragi, hito wa bushi*). This contrasts against the Chinese idiom that states good quality men will never be soldiers just like good quality metal would not be cast into nails (好男不当兵,好铁不打钉, *Haonan budang Bing, Hao tie bu dading*). This idiom of course is not representative of Chinese attitudes on military force throughout Chinese history. The Chinese version of medieval pacifism was prevalent during Song dynasty (960–1279) as Chinese civilizational attainment and economic prosperity reached a peak, and also in later Ming dynasty (1368–1644). Tang China (618–906 A.D.) and Han dynasty (206 B.C.–220 A.D.) was more militaristic due to government structure and the way the military was raised and incorporated.

Many members of Japanese warrior class therefore did not think that Confucian learning could or would be able to help Japan resolve their existing social and political problems. The conceptualization of Japan as a nation to compete with China led many to move towards "National Learning" (*Kokugaku*) with an emphasis on the martial arts element.

> Our nation is a nation of arms. The land to the West [China] is a nation of letters. Nations of letters value the pen. Nation of arms value the sword. That's the way it has been from the beginning ... Our country and theirs are separated from one another by hundreds of miles, our customs are completely different, the temperaments of our people are dissimilar – so how could we possibly share the same Way? (Nakamura 1843 cited in Watanabe 2012: 285)

The question of what is a viable strategy for Japan for the future and how this relates to China has been a central question for Japanese elites since the sixteenth century. China became the primary reference to compare and contrast, to emulate and distinguish (but eventually to discard during the Meiji era). Japanese exceptionalism therefore has its roots from this period onwards. During the eighteenth century, Japanese scholars ruminated about the peace and relative prosperity of Tokugawa Japan in comparison to continental China (Maruyama 1975) and the Warring States (Sengoku period 1467–1586) of the past. Matsuzaki Kankai (1725–75) suggests that compared to the Xia and Zhou dynasties, the great peace Japan enjoys far surpasses China (Watanabe 2012: 186–187).

Ota Kinko, suggested in that in [*Hogen Monogatari*], Japan's reign of twenty-seven emperors in a period of at least 340 years did not see a single official put to death. This model of benevolent government was one that dynasties of the Tang, Song and Ming could not hope to emulate, arguing this is not something that "even the rule of the sages of the Three Dynasties could not be better …. thus our country is more easily governed than China, whether under centralized rule or under feudal rule".

Another noted scholar, Hattori Nankaku, a contemporary of Ota Kinko suggests that this could be due to the superior nature of the Japanese people:

> In China, sages and emperors stand below their deified ancestors, while the various lords arrayed throughout the land acknowledge the emperor, and then below them there are a bunch of dukes and such … it is enough to make you think that the character of the people of that country is really quite awful. And this is why the sages ruled through rites and music. But in Japan it appears peaceful rule can be effected without rites and music, so the character of our people must be better than that of the Chinese (Nankaku in Yuasa 1993 cited by Watanabe 2012: 188)

Japanese thinkers suggest Japan is superior to China because of the Japanese allegiance to the traits of honesty and faithfulness (Ota 1823 cited in Watanabe 2012: 188). Japanese people were seen as more substantial and less deceitful, and truly blessed by divine powers among early Japanese thinkers (Watanabe 2012: 283–291).

Second, this illustrated the reverence that both Japanese sovereign and subjects had for each other. Motoori Norinaga (born 1730) a prominent political thinker in the eighteenth century employed by the Tokugawa House in Wakayama, argued Japan's long peace was a result of this relationship, and it helped Japan avoid the turmoil and difficulties experienced in China. Norinaga believed in universal truths, and argued against relativism—that peoples of their land should only believe in the myths of their land for this would result in people only believing in fiction (political myths). Therefore, Norinaga argues that the peace that prevailed in Japan was possible because of the deep respect that the subjects had for the sovereign, and Japanese subject would never think of overthrowing the sovereign as to replace them. In the context of pre-modern Japan, the concept of Government (*matsurigoto* 政), is a "service rendered to the sovereign by the subjects" (Watanabe 2012: 244). Therefore "whether a country was well governed depends on whether inferiors respect superiors. If the members of the ruling class show deep respect for superiors, the lower classes in turn will show similar respect for those above them, and the country will naturally be well governed" (Brownlee 1988: 56 cited in Watanabe 2012: 244). This thinking is similar in logic to the Confucian ideals of "Five Cardinal Relationships" (五倫 or *Wu Lun*) where political and social cosmology consists of five principal type of relationships: between rulers and subjects; parents and offspring; husband and wife; among siblings and among friends. These relationships are defined in terms of a set obligations that each party should carry out in order for the cosmological universe to function properly.

Unlike in China, subjects in Japan would unlikely think of overthrowing their sovereign and assuming the Emperor position for herself, and thus Japanese exceptionalism lies in the unquestioning loyalty of the subjects to the sovereign. The importance of the continuity of Japan's imperial lineage thus becomes the ground for asserting Japan's superiority over China and Korea. China was often referred to disparagingly as *Seido* (land to the West), *Seiju* (western barbarians), *Shin'i* (Qing Barbarians) or *Shina* (China) (Watanabe 2012: 289). By the Edo period, Japan was so decentralized with nearly 300 fiefdoms, it was therefore a wonder that such a decentralized system was able to enjoy the long period of stability.

Japan's Exceptionalism

Japanese exceptionalism therefore is premised upon the rejection that China should be construed as the Middle Kingdom. Some early Japanese thinkers considered that Japan herself could be construed as the Middle Kingdom as well. From the mid-fifteenth century onwards, Japan sought to improve upon their conditions through both adapting to Chinese institutions and indigenizing the practices to suit their circumstances. The question of national development and social learning is therefore critical. Japanese intellectuals of modern times acknowledged the centrality of Chinese contributions but premised Japanese exceptionalism on Japan's ability to mount a challenge to the China model that could therefore be made on improving existing innovations made in China (Katsube 1785 cited in Watanabe 2012: 282). In this sense, there is every confidence that adapting innovations and intellectual advancements to indigenous conditions is key to reconciling domestic needs and Japan's place in the wider world.

Within Japan, the reverence of the institution of the Emperor thus became the pride and the foci for the elites to show both the equality of Japan vis-à-vis China, and to offer a competing universe and frame of reference for the Japanese worldview. This was critical for Japan's subsequent empire building efforts. The Japanese court, like the Chinese, instituted a parallel system of tributary-vassal relations. The Kingdom of Ryukyu (present day Okinawa), situated between China and Japan consequently had to present tribute to both the Chinese Court (from Ming China in 1372), the Satsuma Daimyo (from 1590 onwards) and subsequently to the Japanese Emperor when Japan was unified (Leung 1978: 7–24). The Satsuma Daimyo had incorporated Ryukyu ostensibly because they did not help them in their War against Korea, but more so because the Satsuma Daimyo wanted to strengthen against their domestic rivals and share in the Ryukyu trade with Southeast Asia and China.

This ability to learn from the existing hegemon, and at the same time resist her influence is a signature hallmark of Japan exceptionalism in pre-modern East Asia (Paine 2017). This duality underpins Japan's thinking in pre-modern era vis-à-vis China, at the beginning of the twentieth century vis-à-vis Britain and in the postwar era with the United States. Japan would not accept another power's presumed superiority—particularly when the power is the hegemon of the day. This is the basis of Japan's quest for equality. The "peripheral" and isolated nature of Japan's geography help with the notion of the centrality of Japan too exemplified by the letter Prince Shotoku (Asuka period) wrote to Emperor of Sui in 607 referring to himself as the "Son of Heaven" in the "Land of the rising Sun".

Another important attribute that made Japan exceptional was her capacity to learn and adopt from stronger nations, particularly existing hegemon to adapt the institutions that would help strengthen her power vis-à-vis her external foes and friends. Thus, for Meiji thinkers such as Fukuzawa, Japanese exceptionalism expressed in terms of progress achieved through a complete and thorough learning and adaptation of Western methods, philosophy and thinking. Western learning is more practical compared to traditional Chinese way, and in essence, critical for Japan because Western knowledge provides an alternative basis for Japanese society to utilize in its everyday application. The value was not in the things or knowledge acquired, but how they were used (Blacker 1964: 63). Therefore, there was no contradiction for Meiji elites in Japan's quest for exceptionalism in International Relations and egalitarianism in domestic politics. Meiji and Taisho elites did not see a contradiction in adopting and learning from the West and at the same time resisting the Western colonial powers which brought ships or guns.

The concern for egalitarianism i.e. the idea not to be seen as a "secondary" power, pushed Japan in earlier centuries to grow her domestic institutions while active debates on the nature of Confucianism was seen again in this era. Intellectuals, such as Fukuzawa, changed their perceptions over time over the question of equality and egalitarianism between individuals in society and nations. In the initial years, he felt Japan should open up not due to fear of the Western colonization, but because he felt Japan has a sense of moral duty and self-interest as nations have equal rights. Japan was fascinated by the development of international legal jurisprudence, (萬國公法) in the late Edo period onwards. The solution to prevent the colonization of Japan and to ward off the attempts to colonize Japan was for Japan to learn from the West. In his later years, he became particularly worried about the prospects of how Japan can withstand colonization, particularly in her intercourse with the West.

Thus, the problems that the Meiji elites faced were not so different from their predecessors in the era before. In undertaking reforms to open up and learn from the West, the elites at this juncture came face to face with the difficult question of how Japan could strive for and maintain her independence whilst learning from the dominant hegemon at hand.

As the external environment was changing rapidly, particularly in East Asia, the Meiji elites felt even more compelled to ensure that even as Japan strove for her best during this era, Japan needed to remain free and independent.

By 1878, Fukuzawa was disillusioned as he believed that international relations were not governed by reason but by the principle of strong devouring the weak (*jakuniku-kyoshoku*) (Blacker 1964: 172). Japan had to seek Civilization, not only through the perfection of human condition domestically through new learning and adaptation to allow this enlightenment but also ensure that it survived the Hobbesian International Political system (Fukuzawa 1875 [2008 Retranslation]: 225–260). Neither divinely-bestowed legitimacy nor Confucian ideals of hierarchy translate into power in international politics. Realpolitik indicators such as military attributes, state coffers, and political-economic influence mattered much more. In short, liberalism was insufficient alone to guarantee Japan's well-being, rather it had to be enforced with realpolitik calculations. It is not surprising therefore to find Japan once again evolved to change their national character—to quickly assume, adapt and innovate various elements of their society to become a first rate colonial power—the prevalent ideology at a time of European expansionism in order to maintain a sense of egalitarianism with them, and at the same time learn from these countries to further enhance Japan.

At the turn of the nineteenth century, Japan did indeed learn and adopt the ways of foreign adversaries in earnest (Samuels 1994). The British were invited by the Japanese during this era to assist in the construction of Japan's transportation system (hence the Japanese drive on the left like the British rather than the Americans). Japanese elites learn the wonders of modern steam-engine and ship building technology from the Americans and Britain (which they later used to assemble one of the largest naval armada for the Second World War). Drawing from the Prussian and British models, Meiji elites wrote the Meiji Constitution (明治憲法). Tokyo learnt the principles of Constitutional monarchy and sent delegations of students and officials to Europe and America. During Taisho period, Japan boldly emulated the institutions of liberal democracy even though to a large extent, it was questionable if the Japanese people then had truly embraced the spirit of liberalism and democracy at home.

True to Japan's national character, the nation did extremely well not only to reform her domestic structures but also were able to calibrate and craft her external policies effectively, positioning Japan to do extremely well in the age of imperialism. Beginning with a victory in the 1895 Sino-Japanese War and the 1905 Russo-Japanese War, Japan achieved strategic pre-eminence that was absolutely necessary to her aspirations to be "equal" to the Western powers in the region. Ironically, in her quest to achieve parity with the colonial powers, Tokyo subordinated the rest of Asian neighbors to her imperialistic ambitions.

Japan did earn a seat among the Western powers but not earn the commensurate respect and power Tokyo craved. International reactions to the 21 Demands levied upon China in 1915, the limitations imposed by the Washington Naval Treaty in 1922 and the enactment of the Japan Exclusion Act in the United States were interpreted negatively by Japan as both a security problem, and also a racial discrimination one. Thus, despite decades in learning, adapting and applying, Japan did not secure the requisite respect and security she sought. Tokyo was plagued by insecurities with good reason. This insecurity led Japan to reinterpret events and frame her options to preempt subjugation, and led Japan to a series of disastrous decisions that set her on the road to War.

Japanese expansionism into Manchuria in 1931 was mandated by a belief on the part of the Japanese elites in the Nazi Germany's concept of Lebensraum (living space), which was essential for the continued prosperity and logical expansion in the realization of the nation's logical next steps in her Manifest Destiny. As part of her larger strategy, Japan encouraged the colonial expansion of settler colonies in Manchuria, with over 850,000 Japanese subjects moving to the region (O'Dwyer 2015). The settlers themselves had tremendous motivation in settling in Manchuria, and showed tremendous "determination and initiative (O'Dwyer 2015: 4) in urbanizing the new lands in Manchuria, becoming a development force in their own right and negotiating their own territoriality, space and existence vis-à-vis the Japanese state and other imperialist powers. By 1940, Japan entered into the Axis Pact Alliance with Nazi Germany and Italy, endorsing an alliance that designated Asia as Japan's primary sphere of influence. As the war raged on, Japan mistakenly believed that it was necessary to pre-empt the entry of United States into the War through a pre-emptive strike on Pearl Harbor.

Like today's China, many Japanese elites at the turn of the twentieth century, viewed these developments as little more than racist containment of a rising Japan, being denied her rightful place in modern East Asia. The contradiction between Japan's domestic social concern for egalitarianism and her foreign policy ambitions widened as liberalism gave way to military radicalism and ultra-nationalistic mood at home, setting her on a disastrous course to war. This shift of the tame nationalism of Meiji and Taisho Japan to the ultra-nationalism of the Showa Era grew in part due to insecurity, in part from imperial ambitions but also from a genuine sentiment to eradicate the shame and disrespect that the other colonial powers had shown Japan despite her achievements. In short, it was a fight for honor as much as it was for ambition and insecurity. Ironically, it was Japan's quest for a better human condition, independence and equality with the Western powers that saw the rise of Japan in pre-War East Asia, and ultimately down the path for War (Shimazu 2006). This remained the basis for Japan's quest for status and power in pre-War and arguably postwar International Relations.

The San Francisco System and the Making of an "Abnormal" Japan

With the surrender of Japan after the bombing of Hiroshima and Nagasaki in 1945, the dynamics of the security landscape changed drastically. Japan, as the rising hegemon in East Asia had not only been thoroughly vanquished by the United States, but for the first time in history, has had a foreign power occupy mainland Japan. Japan's quest from the Meiji era onwards to learn from the West and become a respectable power in East Asia has now ended in tragedy, as United States deliberated on the fate of Japan. With the treatment of interwar year Germany in mind, the Occupation authorities in Japan needed to ensure that militarism in Japan did not emerge again, and that Japanese society needed to be thoroughly disarmed. From the Japanese perspective, it was a period of great uncertainty and insecurity. The great project that the Meiji elites started, and subsequently Taisho and Showa elites had promised had ended with a nation exhausted and stripped of her sovereignty.

The Occupation brought about a shock arguably greater than the defeat, as for the first time, the autonomy and the question of national self-determination has been taken away. The great project of building Japan into a great power since the Meiji Restoration was resulted in a nation exhausted and sapped, and sovereignty lost. Even more horrifying for most Japanese is the possibility that the Sovereign of Japan, the much-revered Emperor would be held responsible for the war. Given the pride of the Japanese people in the uninterrupted lineage of their Sovereign, this was extremely untenable. The pre-war propaganda of the savagery of the American race did not help either. Thus when confronted with an enemy who had fought and defeated the Emperor's Imperial Army, who acted in such unexpected manner—many Japanese were in awe. Not only did the Occupational authorities requested aid from Washington D.C. to feed the starving civilians, there was no massacres as many expected. The American troops that arrived had behaved professionally. Most importantly, the decision of President Truman's administration not to hold the Japanese sovereign responsible for war was a political masterstroke, as it engendered the gratitude of the Japanese nation, laying the firm basis for cooperation between the United States and Japan ever since.

From the inception of the Occupation to the signing of the Treaty of San Francisco (サンフランシスコ講和条約/*San-Furanshisuko kōwa-Jōyaku*) and the Security Treaty between the United States and Japan (日本国とアメリカ合衆国との間の安全保障条約 *Nipponkoku to Amerikagasshūkoku to no aida no anzen hoshōjōyaku*) in 1951, Japan unwittingly found once again faced with drastic changes in her external environment. These two treaties laid the foundation of what is now known as the San Francisco system. With the onset of the Cold War, the United States instituted a system of alliance from this period, signing a series of bilateral alliances with Japan, South Korea and to a lesser extent, entering into arrangements with Singapore, Thailand and Taiwan to confront the Soviet bloc. Japan had little opportunity but to participate as a primary member of the United States' alliance bloc.

The domestic mood in Japan in the 1950s was one of great trepidation and hope (Richardson 1974). The six years of occupation heralded a new era where the Japanese adopted elements of American popular culture. Japan transformed domestically, picking off the democratic experiment they left off during the Taisho era, with two important differences. First, the United States with over two centuries of democratic experience was actually then an active domestic actor in Japanese politics, designing and imposing institutions within Japan. Such close proximity not only imbibed Japan with democratic institutions, but endeared Japanese people to all aspects of American culture. Replicas of the Statue of Liberty and Mount Rushmore were erected in Tokyo's "America Fair", baseball games were held between Boston Red Sox and Yomiuri Giants and students of Waseda and Keio Universities, and live models were parading in modern swimsuits in Tokyo's department stores (Taylor 2014).

Second, the Americanization of Japanese society, alongside the onset of the Cold War and the Korean War did not automatically led to the complete domination of the United States in Japanese politics with no room for local elites. In fact, many of the pre-war elites were still functioning as official intermediaries—the best example is that of Nobusuke Kishi. Despite the change of heart in Washington D.C. to turn and rearm Japan for the Cold War, the institutions that the Occupation authorities had built turned out to be resilient enough to withstand American pressure for remilitarization.

Third, the postwar period ushered in a new ideological framework. Japanese people celebrated both pacifism and democracy, and saw these two ideational influences as facets of the same coin. With the Japanese preference for egalitarianism, the Japanese pursuit of social democracy sits extremely well with Pacifism, and enabled the postwar Prime Ministers (starting with Yoshida Shigeru) to withstand demands from the United States to rearm by referring to the widespread public dissatisfaction as well as the Constitution put in place. The popularity of left-wing parties such as the Japan Communist Party (JCP) and the Japan Socialist Party (JSP) certainly help limit political appeal of American strategic agenda in the initial years.

Japan instituted a system of economic realism for the next four decades, with the LDP practicing a very narrow interpretation of Article 9 of the Constitution that limited remilitarization. This strategy was realpolitik, and did not make Japan anomalous as it reflected the changing realities of competitiveness in the global system in the postwar period. Economic power rather than concrete military strength mattered more than anything (Pyle 2007: 259; Dower 1988: 315). This system sat very well to the dominant political development in Japan as there was some sympathy within the country for Russia and China, probably because Japanese were familiar with the egalitarian ideals. Egalitarianism is deeply embedded in Communist and socialist political thinking, and this is compatible with Japanese perchance for social justice for all. The success of Japan's economic realism however did not stifle discussions of restoring normalcy of the Japanese state and the prospects of Japan gaining the respect and status it deserves in the international system.

The origins of what is the discourse on Japanese "normalization" have their earliest roots in narratives, thinking and institutions built during this period. Ichiro Ozawa, a dominant LDP politician wrote the bestseller "Blue Print for a New Japan" in 1984 was the first to use the idea of a "normal" nation even though these ideas have been discussed as early as the 1950s. The 1980s has seen the emergence of a new and more confident Japan, as indicated by the rush of intellectuals, policymakers and politicians who publicly argued that Japan should become more assertive vis-à-vis the United States. Some scholars have argued that it is mandatory for Japan to become "normal" at the expense of the Pacifism that she had built up over the years (Middlebrooks 2008). In the previous decades, even though the sentiments with regards to constitution revisionism and strengthening Japan in the alliance relationship, these grouses are usually articulated more subtly. However, by the 1980s, Japan's ascendance as the world's second largest economy has raised the confidence of many Japanese commenters, coinciding with the "golden" age of postwar Japan. Table 2.1 below captures the essence of Japan's foreign policy posture vis-à-vis the dominant hegemon and the rising power, as well as the technology and acquisition pattern of Japan historically.

Mainstream Conservatism in Japanese Politics During the Cold War

The LDP's dominance in Japanese politics provided much political stability for Japan's economic development both internally and externally. For much of the Cold War, the LDP advocated for conservatism, which has come to be known as "postwar conservatism" since the administration of Hayato Ikeda to Keizo Obuchi. This Conservatism is defined by LDP as a party that did not abandon the weak, pursue enlightened self-interest based on the principle of international cooperation and a preference for fiscal health that provided for inter-generational fairness in terms of assets and opportunities (Funabashi 2016). Japan's social policies very left wing, very socialist and in effect, Japan pursued what was termed as "social democracy" at the very outset (Satoh 2018, Personal Communication).

The dominance of the LDP was due to a few factors: the institutional advantage that the "first past the post" electoral system conferred the incumbent party; the traditional Japanese culture that rendered acquiescence with the ruling party, and the pork-barrel politics phenomenon and System support explanation by which people voted in favor of the system but not the LDP (but in the process viewing that there were no other choices other than the LDP) (Schneider 2006; Tanaka 2007). The LDP cultivated exceptionally strong ties with the bureaucracy (Richardson 1974) with many senior bureaucrats leaving to serve in the Diet, and

Table 2.1 Evolving Japanese strategic posture over the centuries

Period	Regional hegemon (or First among Equals)	Japan's acquisition(s)/learning from dominant Hegemon	Rising powers to challenge dominant Hegemon at that point	Japan's Foreign policy posture
Pre-modern East Asia	Imperial China	Writing System; Confucian system & Worldview Everyday technologies e.g. Silk making; Urban Design; metalworks technology; agriculture etc.	Colonial Great Britain (alongside Dutch, Spanish, Portuguese, American colonial presence)	Ran parallel tributary trading system to prevent subordinate (or achieve comparable) status to China Sakoku policy (closed door) until 1853; similarities to the Canton Trade system ran by China When forced open by Commodore Perry through unequal Treaties, Japan opened her doors to learn from the West
Meiji & Taisho Japan (Arrow war–Mid-1930s)	Colonial Great Britain	Steam Engine Technology Transportation Westminster Parliamentary System & Constitutional Monarchy (Choshu Five sent to study at UCL)	Germany & Russia	Balanced against Germany in World War One Establishment of Anglo-Japan Alliance to balance Russia after World War One

Showa Japan (1930s–1945)	Nazi Germany	Totalitarian ideology Fascist Expansionist economic plans; military technology	United States	Tripartite Pack (Japan, Germany & Italy in 1940) against the US dominantly & Attack Pearl Harbor to pre-empt US from entering the War
Cold War (1945–1990s)	The United States	Dominant One Party State with Liberal Democracy Capitalistic System Technology R & D	USSR	US-Japan Security Alliance and working with PRC to contain the USSR
Post Cold War World	The United States	Diplomatic Engagement & strategy Alliance Management & Coalition Building High Tech & Weaponry Influence through coalition building & IGOs like UN Institutions & Developmental Assistance	PRC	Globalizing US-Japan Security Alliance & "normalization" of Japan Sought to "balance" against a rising China Seek rejuvenation of Japan as global power (e.g. UN Security Seat; independent political actor beyond Asia

served as an incubator of sorts to match emerging political talents with local power politics and interests—all rallying around variants of the same conservative political ideology. One might even suggest the LDP actually constitutes five to six different parties, if one assumes that each faction is a party in itself. The factional horse-trading enables the exchange of interests and considerations, rendering the LDP a party machinery that is often able to coopt agendas and aspirations across a large spectrum of the Japanese political universe. To that end, the LDP has been called an oxymoron as it is arguably neither truly liberal nor democratic in her practice of politics. Lastly, the dominance of the LDP is also largely a function of the support of the United States. The shift from US goals in rehabilitation to containment meant that handpicking certain Conservatives to govern would ensure Japan stay staunchly anti-Communist and pro-American. The subtext meant the difficult understanding/interpretation of history between the United States establishment and these rehabilitated Japanese warriors would need to be swept under the rug.

Japan's relative political stability and economic prosperity since the 1950s has been underpinned by three important pillars that have been put in place since the 1950s. First, Japan adopted a new **Constitution** in 1947 that has guided Japanese politics, social development and foreign policy since 1947. The Constitution was widely seen as an instrument that was hoisted and imposed upon Japan, and was highly resisted by many Japanese officials at the time of its conceptualization. This resistance gave way to grudging acceptance but has since evolved into a wholesale embrace by most Japanese people. Second, the Japanese adopted **Pacifism** as the dominant political philosophy and worldview for politics and international relations. In mainstream Japanese politics, this is enshrined not only in the Article 9 of the Constitution, but materialized in the ideational framework by which Japanese people view the world and successive generations of Japanese administration have premised their policies upon. The Yoshida doctrine, enacted by the Shigeru Yoshida mandated that Japan followed the lead of the United States in strategic affairs, whilst focusing her efforts on economic development and national reconstruction. This principle provided guidance to Japanese politicians and nation with regards to her domestic and foreign priorities, and ascertain the amount of resources, attention and efforts be given to global affairs and international commitments versus domestic priorities e.g. the building of the Japan Self-Defense Forces. Third, the **US-Japan Security Alliance**, embodied by a Treaty signed in 1951, (reinterpreted and updated in 1960), became the single most important instrument to reconcile the exigencies of national security concerns with the demands of pacifism. The 1951 Treaty saw Japan regaining sovereignty and the 1960 Treaty decisively instituted the alliance as a central pillar in Japanese politics and foreign policy. The Yoshida doctrine and the US-Japan Security Alliance taken together allowed the flourishing of a genuine pacifist democracy at home in Japan, and enabled Japan to maintain an asymmetric relationship with the United States, relying on the US for nuclear protection, security protection and a privileged position in US grand strategy in Western Pacific.

These three pillars—the Constitution, Pacifism and the US-Japan Alliance provides a powerful cocktail for the making of a prosperous and forward looking Japan. Utilizing an export led economic growth strategy, Japan achieved double digit growth throughout the 1970s and 1980s. Japan's innovation in manufacturing, particularly in sectors such as electronics, automobiles and consumer goods, and her preferential market access to the United States, Europe and Asia, saw her economic and trade linkages intensified across the world. Japan overtook West Germany as the second largest economy by 1967, and Japan's economic growth continued growing at a double-digit growth rate in the 1970s. With this new found economic prosperity, Tokyo sought to increase her political clout through the application of Fukuda doctrine in 1977. Japan built a program of Overseas Developmental Assistance (ODA) to engage regional countries in Southeast and East Asia in order to improve her security in a comprehensive security. This growing political and economic importance is reinforced by a corresponding rise in Japan's soft power as her traditional and popular culture became extremely popular across the world. By the late 1980s, Japan entered into an era of renaissance, cementing her position as the de-facto leader in Asia. Her evolvement from a subjugated defeated military power to a modern peaceful democratic economic superpower was complete.

The rise of a more confident and assertive Japan was however not without problems. The 1980s saw the emergence of unprecedented friction in Japan's foreign relations with the United States and China (Hoppens 2015; Koga 2016). As Washington and Tokyo quarreled over trade deficits, technology co-operation and transfer (Green 1995), alliance management in areas of risk distribution and burden sharing, nationalistic narratives began to emerge in both the United States and Japan. Even though decades have passed since the Second World War, the burdens of the war related issues lingered on. The Chinese reaction to Japanese Prime

Minister Nakasone's Yasukuni Shrine visits (1983 and 1985) and the controversy over history textbooks took the Japanese by surprise. After all, Prime Ministers Ohira Masayoshi, Suzuki Zenko and Nakasone Yasuhiro had visited the shrine a total of 21 times but it was a non-issue with the Chinese government until 1985 (Sakamoto 2014). Tokyo learnt that Japanese aid and assistance cannot completely eradicate memories of Japanese Imperial Army's conduct and sins during the Second World War—be it in Philippines or Korea, China or Indonesia. Domestically it is also difficult to do so, as social memories are increasingly contested even up till today (Tamanoi 2009; Takahashi 2006, 2010). Diplomatic difficulties aside, the Soviet threat however provided the strategic clue to ensure that China, Japan and the United States remained stable.

Notwithstanding these difficulties, Japan's relations with the Reagan's United States and Deng's China in the 1980s still looked to be the "Golden Age" in recent Japanese diplomatic history. During this time, Japan has grown strong, and domestic rhetoric has encouraged many in Japan to think of themselves as being somewhat as a challenger (or alternative) to the United States herself, besides the Soviet Union. At the same time, China-Japan relations were entering into a new phase. As Chinese society emerges out of two decades of political excesses into an age of reform and openness, Chinese civil society began debating the issues of war responsibility vis-à-vis Japan while China was benefiting directly from Japanese help and assistance. The Land of the Rising Sun, in short was back at a leadership position in East Asia regional system.

Foreign diplomatic difficulties and rising domestic confidence therefore led to the emergence of a new and virulently nationalistic discourse in Japan. The 1980s saw the emergence of a few of these politicians who argued explicitly for an end to Japanese exceptionalism of being a pacifist super-economic power. In short, Japan should reconsider elements that had rendered her "abnormal" and seek to "maximise" Japan's power and international status. Japan's prestige can be enhanced through the lifting of her reputation through the reconsideration of Japan's international contributions and commitment to the San Francisco system principally through the modification (or eradication) of the three central pillars: the Constitution, the US-Japan Security alliance and the wider framework of Pacifism and the role of the military in Japanese society.

The Rise of Neo-Conservatism: From Normalization to the Rejuvenation of Japan

The 1990s heralded systemic changes that fundamentally affected the positive outlook for Japan and challenged the foundations of her strategic outlook. First, the collapse of the USSR meant not only the loss of a common strategic enemy with the United States, but also the raison d'être for the existence of the US-Japan alliance put in place in the 1950s at the start of the Cold War. Second, the economic rise of China presented a sense of ontological threat to Japan, particularly so as Japan had undergone a decade of deflationary growth. Third, the relative stability of the Cold War years had been replaced by an era of escalating security challenges that directly or indirectly involve Japan—from the Taiwan Straits Crisis, the dispute over Senkaku islands to the North Korea threat. Fourth, there were extra-systemic factors. Japanese elites and people were shell-shocked after forking out $13 billion USD in contribution to the first Iraqi war, the Kuwait government did not include Japan in the vote of thanks recorded in the New York Times it took out. This was ostensibly because Japan had not contributed personnel, but in reality was because the Japanese Foreign Ministry had asked the Kuwaitis not to acknowledge Japan. Even though Japanese funds contributed to the War effort, and contributed mine clearing operations in the postwar era, there was a deep sense of outrage i.e. the MOFA's plan had backfired spectacularly. The overchange in the domestic narratives led to the passage of the 1992 International Peace Cooperation Law that saw the dispatch of Peacekeeping troops to United Nations Transitional Authority in Cambodia following the conclusion of the civil conflict.

The origins of the shift of the mainstream politics towards the right of center in Japanese politics have been a long time in the making. This correction is partially a result of generation change coinciding with the systemic changes in the Northeast Asian security environment and a domestic slump in the confidence of Japan's future, partially a result of the erosion of pacifism as the elderly generation in Japan dies out. The efforts to rethink Japan's politics and foreign policy in accordance to a new kind of Conservatism really set in with a change in both domestic and foreign policy circumstances and were in a large part facilitated by rise of internet and social media in politics.

The LDP's mainstream conservatism did not really change until the tenure of Junichiro Koizumi. As the fourth longest serving Prime Minister,

PM Koizumi is one of the most well-known Japanese Prime Ministers in recent times. He built a formidable reputation for being maverick in Japanese politics. During his tenure, he redefined the role of the *Kantei* (Prime Minister's Office), and the Office's relationship to the traditional media, the bureaucracy and the LDP party machinery.

Koizumi's very shrewd advisors, in particular his principal secretary, Isao Iijima played an extremely important role in helping Mr. Koizumi craft his image and manipulate the media, in turn allowing him to command a popularity unprecedented in postwar history of the LDP. Through reaching out to gossip magazines and tabloids, and through his direct messages to the Japanese electorate on social media, Koizumi's image as a reformer in resisting traditional LDP politics empowered him as an agent of change. His ability to direct his political messages and received support for them is unprecedented, and to that extent enabled him to secure the support to undertake his political agenda.

The Prime Minister was also insistent on naming his own liaison officers to the powerful Ministries, rather than have the Ministries assign their own preferred officials to the Kantei. This move to rein in the bureaucrats has continued to this day by the Abe administration with marked success (Winter 2016).

As a politician who was relatively clean during his 30-year-old career, Mr. Koizumi was always careful about accepting courtesy calls from patrons and backers, as well as cautious about the sources of political donations—and in the words of Mr. Iijima himself, Koizumi is one of the "cleanest and most scrupulous politicians in Japan" (Strom 2001). He sought to enforce the law punishing politicians who receive money to act as go-between in arrangements between private and public parties, and to prevent collusive bidding for government projects, and political neutrality of public servants. This provided him with a legitimacy that enabled him to reduce the influence of lobby groups and special interests, "end the power of vested interests and old-fashioned customs, including the privileged circle of journalists" and eradicate the ability of the bureaucrats who dictate to the Kantei (Strom 2001). Koizumi wanted to end the consensual and moderate forms of politics and politicking which policies were implemented step by step through persuasion and compromise (Funabashi 2016).

The ferocity and the unconventional methodology by political strategies took on the traditional LDP machinery by surprise. This change was most exemplified by Koizumi's attempt to reform Japan Post. This is an institution revered by both the ordinary Japanese as well as much of the LDP elites. Japan Post was said to be the world's largest financial institution, with 24,700 branches and banking and insurance assets of $3 trillion. Koizumi regarded Japan Post acted as a slush fund of sorts for political elites and piggy bank for bureaucrats who often relied on it as a source of cheap capital for wasteful projects (Will 2006). Faced with opposition from his own ranks, Koizumi recruited and fielded 37 candidates against his LDP opponents (many senior politicians) in the 2005 election, defeating most of these party elders in the process. The Japanese people's penchant for a strong leader was exemplified by their love for PM Koizumi as he put up new signals and symbols (visits to the Yasukuni Shrine), resistance phrases (let's destroy LDP), not to mention fielding a host of political assassins to kill off his opponent (Faiola 2005; Will 2006).

At the same time, it must be pointed out that Koizumi's success during this period could be attributed to the electoral reforms in Japan. One should not assume the increase in interest in a particular policy area such as national security to be driven by changes in candidate or voter preferences, but rather that there is a possibility that it is driven by candidates' efforts to survive under new electoral rules or new political institutions (Catalinac 2015: 14). Koizumi's politics have made it possible for the first time that national security and foreign policy have become platforms by which candidates could compete on during elections.

Koizumi's populism unfortunately was contemporaneous with a rabid nationalism that drove the LDP conservatism in a different way. Koizumi adopted a nationalistic posture that explicitly identified China as not only the "other" in Japanese nationalism, but as an existential security threat that Japan was destined to stand up to. This is one important differentiating aspect of the neo-conservatism from the previous generation of conservatism during the Cold War era.

This had had two important effects. Koizumi's ignorance of warnings from China not to visit the Yasukuni shrine drove Sino-Japanese relations to deteriorate rapidly over the period he was in power. From the perspective of the Chinese (and some Japanese), Koizumi is known for his mishandling of Sino-Japanese relations. The period of his administration saw the outbreak of some of the worst protests in contemporary Sino-Japanese relations (Chen-Weiss 2014). From the Japanese perspective, the political effect of Koizumi's practice is to desegregate the burden of history from Japan's China policy. By constantly ignoring China's political rhetoric and diplomatic pressure, Koizumi desegregated historical issues from bilateral relations, and seize the political advantage from China. Even though this set back Japan's relations with China, it also meant that Japan could chart her own path over issues like the East China Sea disputes where critical national interests are at stake. It also meant that Japan could effectively enhance the US-Japan alliance with vigor without worries, particularly with the neo-Conservatism that he was advocated became mainstream both within and outside of China.

The second important effect is that from the early 2000s onwards, neo-Conservative elites sought to revisit the ideas of postwar system in Japanese domestic politics and the central pillars of Japanese foreign policy with vigor. The neo-conservatives is a reactionary movement against the post-war leftists and liberals, and the elements of traditional culture and national pride are being used to rebuke liberals and leftists, as the latter are being accused of denying Japan's traditions. In terms of foreign policy, even as the Japanese elites looked to reaffirm the US-Japan Security alliance (Dian 2014), the new LDP elites undertook a series of administrative measures to sidestep the Constitutional constraints in order to legitimize/legalize the actions. This pragmatism appeared to reconcile the exigencies of the moment but did not stop the Japanese elites from wanting to move ahead with more substantial legislation to effect this normalization process. Supersizing threats and effectively managing the media content therefore was one of the most important ways forward for the LDP elites to gather the support and moment needed for this.

Shinzo Abe built on Junichiro Koizumi's "reactionary" conservatism in a different way. Compared to Abe, Koizumi is seen as theatrical, liberal maverick. Even though Abe's methodology is not nearly as populist as Koizumi's, he was certainly far more methodological. Without the flare Koizumi exhibited with his openly flamboyant "resistance", Abe has been nothing if not coldly calculating in the advocating of his political agenda, moving away from the traditional way of politics and known brand of trusted postwar Conservatism. Despite this, it is still questionable if Abe would be able to capitalize on his time in the office to centralize and run foreign policy "*Kantei*" style like his two most popular predecessors—Nakasone and Koizumi. Abe took to abstract ideology and nationalist imagery (Mark 2016), something which Koizumi had not done a lot on. Hence starting with Koizumi right up to the present, Japanese politics took a relative sharp turn as both the Japanese elites and the people started to debate seriously as to the possible remedies that are able to lift the country out of its economic slump and also to recalibrate so her policies could face the challenges of the future. To that extent, three most important pillars of postwar Japanese politics and foreign policy need to be reconsidered.

First, Japan needs to rethink her role as a Pacifist power. This essentially is a question of rethinking and reinterpreting her political and diplomatic identity. Tokyo has to consider what kind of international contributions it should and could possibly make in relation to her pacifist identity and to what extent should this change and if so in what direction. In particular, how should the Yoshida doctrine and Japan's military fit into the overall current trajectory of Japanese foreign policy. At the same time, how should this pacifism speak to the concerns of the younger generation of the Japanese, particularly as they search for their place in the world and their views on the future as well as on the past.

Second, how could and should Japan overcome the constraints of her foreign policy vis-à-vis the Japanese Constitution, particularly with regards to Article 9. The challenges are both political and legal in nature. They are political because in essence, the Japanese Constitution is a deeply cherished statement of apology extended to Japan's neighbors as much as it is an important maker in Japanese national identity. They are legal because the Constitution of any country should be considered as "higher law", even as many Japanese regard that the Constitution was a document hoisted and imposed by the occupation authorities. Even as the Japanese people have over the last two generations gone out to embrace this document, should the Japanese people continue this as both a higher law and an institution or should it be amended and changed with times?

Third, Japan needs to understand how to position and recalibrate her alliances to meet the challenges of the changing times. In particular, how should the US-Japan alliance be handled, and how should this alliance be calibrated in relation to the rest of her foreign relations, particularly with Japan's closest neighbors? Should domestic institutions, even important ones such as the Constitution be changed to fit the exigencies of the alliance? How should the Alliance evolve to accommodate Pacifism and the Constitution?

The Contours of the Debate on Japan's Rejuvenation

Ichiro Ozawa, one of Japan's most prominent politicians, was one of the first persons to have suggested that Japan needed to consider making political change to become a "normal" nation (*futsu no kuni*). His book published in Japanese in 1993 (English 1994) "Blueprint for a New Japan; the Rethinking of a Nation" (*Nihon Kaizo Kei Kaku*) (Ozawa and Gower 1994), argued that Japan need to increase international contribution, security cooperation with the United States and participate actively to build a new international order. There are parallels drawn between Ozawa and Koizumi, with both politicians suggesting they want to destroy the LDP to reform the parties, with Ozawa wanting to seek principled political reforms using old school reforms and Koizumi keen to bring about economic reforms via domestic restructuring (Mulgan 2015).

There are of course different ways to think about Japan's foreign and security postures using different typologies or categories (Soeya et al. 2011). Soeya Yoshihide, one of the foremost intellectuals in Japan today have advocated Japan should travel down a path towards what he calls "middle power diplomacy" (Soeya 2011: 22–97)—a characterization that exhibits the typical Japanese modesty that understates both Japanese achievement and abilities. As much as this idea might appeal to many Japanese, it is also true that Japan's wanting to join the UN Security Council and contribute to international community might not sit well with such political and diplomatic modesty. For most part, the security and foreign policy narratives today are very different from yesteryears (Vosse et al. 2017). Cheol-Hee Park has divided and placed noted intellectuals and politicians in Japan in a four-quadrant diagram where one axis represents the view of international commitments (from important to unimportant) and another axis measures the degree of militarism (i.e. from anti-military to pro-military). Most of Japanese politicians such as Nakasone, Ozawa, Koizumi and Abe will fall into the quadrant which is pro-military and regard international community as important. Only ultra-nationalists would be pro-military and disregard international commitments as unimportant (such as Shintaro Ishihara). Politicians of the previous generations are generally anti-militaristic even if they regard international commitments as being unimportant. Park notes that for most politicians (Ozawa, Ishihara, Nakasone, Koizumi) there is a general consensus that Japan needs to strengthen her political leadership, tweak her Constitution, implement some sort of crisis management and increase Japan's international commitments. In essence, Japan's normalization/rejuvenation would require increased westernization of Japan and an emphasis on institutional engineering (Park 2011: 98–121).

Richard Samuels, one of the world's most respected Japan specialists, argues that security narratives within Japan can be split into four different worldviews (Samuels 2013). First, there are those who distrust foreign entanglements prefer Japan acquire and sustain an independent military capability and domestic technological base. From their perspective, Japan should be autonomous and self-reliant with equidistance from both the US and China. Japan would and should pursue an active international agenda only if it is able to do so. Samuels argue that Pacifists and Gaullists who prize sovereignty above all else, and a modern posterboy of this narrative will be Shintaro Ishihara. The second worldview are those that advocate a bandwagoning strategy with the rise of China. They lean towards the Chinese as they discount the China threat at the risk of alienating the United States. In this sense, they see greater democratization and pluralization of global power in a multilateral world. This category would probably include the links of former DPJ President Yukio Hatoyama and Ichiro Ozawa. The third worldview are those who seek to balance China. There are less attracted to China's economic rise and perceive that it might be better to hedge by balancing China militarily through a robust US-Japan alliance. They perceive Japan would be the best off and safest when US is the dominant player, and Japan is tightly entwined with the United States. This worldview is shared by the more center-right politicians of the LDP, such as Kishi Nobusuke, Nakasone Yasuhiro, and today's Abe Shinzo. Koizumi Junichiro is however more nationalist than right of center even though he is associated with the neo-Conservatives.

The fourth category are "integrators", who believe that there is no trade-off between growing stronger relations with China and maintaining a tight alliance with the United States. In Samuel's words, they "fear China betrayal and Washington decline in equal measure" and they wield both a "shield and a sword". Samuels argue that the "pragmatic wing" of the LDP during much of the Cold War belongs to this camp. Needless to say, the last two decades has seen the dominance of worldview three in Japanese public narratives, where politicians and officials all call for a more muscular US-Japan alliance. But as Samuel notes from the study, it is ironic that despite the high conflict over Senkaku islands, few Japanese view the rise of Chinese military power as a key problem in bilateral relations (Samuels 2013: 1–6). The succinct typology encapsulates the positions on the three major challenges that actors across the political spectrum might hold—Constitutional Revisionism, US-Japan Alliance and Pacifism, Global Engagement and the use of force. Understanding how these three important pillars or challenges are being addressed across the political spectrum by different politicians and scholars are critical for narrowing down our understanding of the contemporary discourse on Japan's rejuvenation. The following section unpacks the central ideas and debates in each of these themes.

The Central Pillars of Rejuvenation

Theme One: Constitutional Revisionism

Compared to the 1889 Meiji Constitution, the 1947 Constitution made major progress in a few respects. First, the sovereignty of the 1947 Constitution rests with the people, as opposed to the Emperor. Second, it offered universal suffrage for women and third, it emphases human rights, equality before the law and non-discrimination on the basis of race, social status or family origins. The Meiji Constitution provide a stipulation of rights within the confines of the law as dictated by the Meiji Emperor, in particular listing out the duties and responsibilities of the subjects (See in particular Chapter two of the 1889 Constitution) during peace time.

The initial ideas of the 1947 Constitution shocked many members of the Japanese elite and the people. The elites, manifested by the bureaucrats were most worried about the prospects of how the institution of the Emperorhood related to the Constitution, particularly if sovereignty rested with the people, but not the Emperor. The real issue for many in the right-wing faction of the Liberal Democratic Party was (and still is) the existence of Article 9, which removes the war making power of the Japanese nation. As the following passage published in the Japanese newspaper shows, the Japanese response did not see the necessity or the merit of Article 9 in the draft of the 1947 Constitution made public:

> Nor are we without some misgivings concerning the other focus of this constitution, the eternal renunciation of war. We are convinced, to be sure, that an aggressive war should be banned for all time, but should we not be left with the right to fight a war of liberation, in case a foreign power should commit aggression against us and attempt to subject us to a state of slavery? If the right to wage a war should be totally given up, then the nation should have a status of permanent neutrality recognized, as is the case with Switzerland, and guaranteed by the United Nations, by force if necessary. While we would be the first to vote for the perpetuation of peace and abolition of war, we would also defend our nation's life and independence even at the cost of our blood . . . (Yomiurihochi, 8 March 1946)

The reaction of the Japanese society to this Constitution was diverse. There were complaints about the language of the draft being imprecise and repetitive. The reaction of the Conservatives was naturally aghast, with more radical wing of the Conservatives asking for the Article to be dropped, along with others mounting legal challenges to Article 9 in the Japanese courts. The Japanese judiciary avoided ruling on these political challenges, preferably sending these requests back to the political process. (Fukui 1970). The Conservatives saw the Constitution as a foreign imposed document capable of "weakening the nation" with 'the unwarranted suppression of the ideal of the state and patriotism and excessive fragmentation of the powers of the state'.

Even though the Conservatives (alongside the leftists) lead the criticisms against this abhorrent development, the Constitution was adopted nonetheless. In embracing this Constitution, the LDP, led by Shigeru Yoshida was perceived to be making a neo-realist decision as it allowed Japan to maximize her interest and latitude, and accorded Tokyo the maximum power that Japan could muster in such a situation. Subscribing to the Constitution allowed Japan to realign the political priorities and foreign policy vis-à-vis the United States, channeling resources and strategic attention to domestic priorities such as rebuilding the economy. The Japanese elites quickly discovered that the Constitution provided an extremely efficient shield ironically against the United States who had by the Korean War changed her mind about the expectations of what Japan should or should not do. Yoshida was extremely adept at using the Article 9 of the Constitution to barricade against US demands for Japan to remilitarize, and the LDP successfully use this narrow interpretation for a good four decades (Pyle 2007: 236). At the same time, in his memoirs, Yoshida argued that the Constitution is entirely "foreign imposed". General MacArthur, he revealed, had told him that the Far Eastern Commission had come to the decision that the Japanese people were free to adjust in a year or two after the Constitution come into effect as the Allies wanted to show that this was entirely born out of the will of a free Japanese people (Yoshida 2007: 117–118). In Yoshida's eyes, Article 9 need not be revised, but he did not preclude that it could be revised, but it has to be a decision of all the people's careful deliberation (Yoshida 2007: 119).

Hatoyama did initiate moves towards Constitutional revision through the submission of the Constitutional Revision Committee but was forced to abandon due to opposition in the Diet. Nobusuke Kishi followed in Hatoyama's footsteps by also commissioning a research group on the revision of the Constitution, and this finding of the research group in 1964 were shelved by Prime Minister Hayato Ikeda to avoid antagonizing public opinion that was fiercely anti-militaristic. The debate was particularly intense during the 1950s as the dominant theme of Japan's domestic politics tittered on pro-amendment and anti-amendment of the Constitution (Nagai and Toshitani 1986). In 1955, when the Liberal Democratic Party was founded, Nobusuke Kishi, insisted that the LDP sought constitutional revision be adopted as one of the founding objectives (Fukui 1970: Chapter 8; Johnson 1995; Schaller 1995, 1996).

The peace constitution sits uncomfortably with the Conservatives in few respects, providing the principal reasons for the Conservatives to push for its amendment. First, the Constitution is viewed by supporters, including its architects as the principal mechanism to prevent Japan from ever going down the "slippery slope of militarism", but to its detractors it is both a hallmark of shame and a permanent chastisement on Japan, despite her postwar achievements and rehabilitation efforts. Second, the Constitution, particularly Article 9, hamstrings Japan's sovereign choices to use force, particularly in a rapidly declining security environment. It therefore unfairly constrains successive generations of Japanese to fend for themselves. Third, Article 9 sits uneasily with the existence of Japan's security apparatus, particularly the Japan Self-Defence Forces and the attendant supporting institutions, apparatus and legislations. Amending it to acknowledge the existence of the JSDF is the right move as it provides legal mandate and remove this contradicting hypocrisy as one of Japan's most important public institutions. Fourth, it provides legitimacy to the historical narratives that the Conservatives have been hawking since the end of the Second World War, and lends legitimacy to the over exercise and rightwards push in mainstream politics. Fifth, removing Article 9 also helps facilitate Japanese aspirations of "globalizing" her strategic reach and geopolitical influence. This has two dimensions: first, it is born out of a genuine altruistic sense of wanting to contribute to global peace and humanitarian missions and second a desire to support US-operations globally to upgrade the US-Japan alliance per se, so as to provide a global dimension to Japanese Foreign Policy.

The strategy by which the LDP is advocating the changes is straight forward. The goal of revising the Constitution has been central to LDP and Japan's politics during the 1950s and 2000s but it has never materialized. The 2012 Senkaku dispute provided the golden opportunity for the new Abe administration to push for its rejuvenation agenda and advocate for Constitutional change. The Conservatives had suggested that the current Constitution is not a Japanese Constitution since it was imposed during the Occupation Period and suggests that a new Constitution should be made by Japan itself. The second strategy is to suggest that the Constitution has outlived its utility and does not meet the exigencies of modern Japan's needs, and suggest that additional clause be introduced into the Constitution. Revision of the Constitution to meet the requirements of the present is not only important but necessary. A third strategy is to suggest that any revision can only come about as a result of democratic will of the people as the ultimate sovereignty rests with the people, not the government. Employing this narrative would mean that the focus has shifted on how to amend the Constitution as opposed to whether or not amendments should be undertaken. Thus, the narrative suggests that it is people of Japan, rather than the LDP that decides on the Constitution amendment (Takahashi 2013). In Prime Minister Abe's first term, he successfully managed to pass a law that paved the way for Japan to consider the prospects of Constitutional Amendment. In his second term, he has undertaken a series of step towards Constitution amendment.

Theme Two: The Nature and Tone of the US-Japan Alliance

The US-Japan alliance stands as one of the three important pillars in Japan's quest for rejuvenation. One of the most interesting aspect of the US-Japan alliance is how much the Japanese elites at the beginning of the postwar years all wanted to sought greater independence from the United States—albeit their very different political platforms and ideologies.

When Prime Minister Yoshida resisted the pressures for the remilitarization of Japan from Washington, the result was the signing of the San Francisco Treaty and the 1951 Security Treaty between the United States and Japan. This treaty was highly unequal and carried a tremendous price for maintaining the pacifist stance. It preserved many of the prerogatives of the US military, and in effect made Japan a military satellite state of the United States—giving US basing rights, power to quell domestic disorder, right to project power against a 3rd country without prior consultation, extra-territoriality in relation to the American servicemen, and compelled to recognize the government of Taiwan, thereby sacrificing any relations with the mainland Chinese government (Pyle 2007: 234). The resistance of the Japanese elites to aid in the American goal of spreading democracy worldwide led American elites to conclude that Japan has "no basic convictions for or against the free world" (Pyle 2007: 236). Yoshida believed that citing public opinion and narrowly interpreting Article 9 would shield Japan from the increasing demands made by Washington regarding militarization. This strategy was a realist one—in doing so and utilizing the pacifist shield, it allowed Japan to recuperate and refocus her efforts on domestic reconstruction. The terms of the 1951 Treaty were not ideal, but it allowed Japan at least to move one step away from having completely to do what it was told during the Occupation years.

One particular aspect that troubled Yoshida was the question of equality. His view of the US-Japan Treaty at the inception was that it should be viewed from an equitable perspective. In return for Japan's obligation to host US forces, the United States should therefore agree to defend Japan. Yoshida therefore felt that the US position that US forces are there simply because "Japan cannot defend herself" was a problematic gesture (Yoshida 2007: 215).

As a political arch rival of Yoshida, Prime Minister Hatoyama too sought a certain independence from the United States, even had he come to power at a time when there was intensifying domestic struggle within and between the Conservative and the Socialist camps. This of course led to the consolidation of the Liberal Party and Democratic Party, and of the socialist parties into the Liberal Democratic Party and the Japan Socialist Party respectively, known today as the 1955 system. Hatoyama was instrumental in normalizing relations with the Soviet Union. To some extent, this did help moderate the influence of the United States within Japan.

When Yoshida's arch rival Nobusuke Kishi was rehabilitated by the United States and subsequently elected as the Prime Minister, it was a boon for the US-Japan alliance. It is common enough to find narratives among critics of US-Japan relations that Kishi, in gratitude for his rehabilitation to the Occupation authorities has sought to decisively push for a renewed version of the US-Japan Security Treaty against popular wishes. This however needs to be qualified. First, American attempts to influence Japanese politics faced increased obstacles because there was widespread sympathy Japanese people have on the ground for left wing politics during the 1950s. Kishi faced tremendous obstacles in trying to push through the bill for the revised US-Japan security alliance. Second, one of Japan's most critical observers of Japanese politics and foreign policy Magosaki Ukeru observes that Kishi is seen as an extremely pragmatic politician who is always striving for Japan's interests vis-à-vis the United States. In pushing for the revised Treaty, Kishi wanted to eliminate the unequal aspects of the Alliance, including the elimination of the clause that empowered US authorities to quell domestic disturbances, a voice in the deployment of Japanese troops, and an explicit security guarantee from the United States in the event of an attack (Pyle 2007: 237–238). To this extent, Kishi shared Yoshida's vision: to rebuild Japan, economic reconstruction and restoration of independence would be necessary. Unlike Yoshida, Kishi viewed rearmament as necessary, but regarded Yoshida leaning too much towards the United States, and Hatoyama in leaning too far away from the United States. Kishi saw a more "balanced" and nuanced policy, and recalled that he spent 70% of his energy devoted to the revision of the US-Japan Security Treaty (Kitaoka 2016: 106). Prime Minister Abe argued that his grandfather's goal was indeed striving to have more independent relationship with the United States. The renegotiated US-Japan Security Treaty is a perfect case of Japan trying to obtain greater political leeway and independence from the United States rather than pliantly accept diplomatic subservience to the United States.

Japan's alliance with the United States grew more difficult towards the latter half of the 1960s. The single biggest issue facing US-Japan alliance was not the perceived aggressiveness of Khrushchev or a radical China detonating nuclear weapons, but from the deepening involvement of the United States engaged in an escalating war in Vietnam. A public opinion poll found the number of Japanese people who viewed the US positively had declined rapidly from the 45% in 1965 to 18% in 1974, to the extent that US Ambassador Reischauer was spat upon during an engagement in Japan (Kosaka 2016: 153). The biggest challenge for the Sato Administration was the negotiation of the reversion of Okinawa and the negotiation of Japan's Three Nuclear principles (i.e. no manufacture, possession or introduction of nuclear weapons) with the United States (Hoey 2015). There is of course much skepticism, for it is an open secret that United States military in Japan did have nuclear weapons on board their warships for a better part of the Cold War.

The reversion of Okinawa (McCormack and Norimatsu 2012) brought about an important but understated development for the US-Japan alliance at that time—that of the transfer of control of the Senkaku/Diaoyu islands.

Instead of transferring the islands back to the Republic of China (an US ally), the effect of transferring the islands control to Japan has created advantages for the United States: it awoke Chinese nationalism against Japan, and sowed the seeds of discord between Japan and China, and Japan and Taiwan, adding a point of contention between these East Asian countries. It bound Japan more tightly to the United States that ever before as a client state (McCormack 2007). By enacting a policy of "not taking sides" on the sovereignty and at the same time, suggesting the islands control are covered by the US-Japan Alliance, it creates a permanent role for the United States in the region's security architecture.

With domestic and international opinions turning against the Vietnam War as well as the cost of the operationalization of the Containment policy, President Nixon campaigned on the promises of bringing the United States troops home in a bid to achieve "peace with honor" in his Presidential Campaign. The United States also cut the dollars link to this goal as they realized they cannot honor this commitment. All these spoke to the relative decline of an over-extended country. In introducing the Guam Doctrine in 1969, the United States recalibrated their strategic outlook to achieve détente and arms control with the USSR. In particular, Nixon introduced the Vietnamization aspect of his doctrine, which essentially meant that the United States would extend the protection of her nuclear umbrella, but respective allies would have to shoulder their own defense. Even though Nixon's message was principally meant for South Vietnam, the effect of these US policies brought shocked Japan (known as *Nixon shokku*) (Frankel 1971).

This was not surprising, as Japan's role in the US grand strategy has almost always been taken for granted by Washington. Henry Kissinger had little interest in Japan as his found his counterparts "not conceptual" and that "they have no long-term vision, that they go for decisions by consensus", and that they were "prosaic, obtuse, unworthy of sustained attention", and regarded them as "little Sony salesmen" (Kissinger 1979: 321–25; 1982: 735–46). For Japan, the move was both insulting and demeaning. The United States undertook secret overtures to the Chinese whilst preventing the Japan from speaking to the Chinese.

The US-Japan Security Alliance did not provide the kind of equality that the Japanese had hope. Tokyo realized from Washington's perspective, Beijing was the key, not Tokyo. The United States had hoped that the change in strategy would enable the United States to do more with less. A planned withdrawal from Vietnam, the operationalization of Guam

Doctrine, and détente with USSR will change the strategic perspective in China. Beijing would face a declining United States, a growing Soviet threat and the prospects of a Japan rearming—that would prompt Beijing to welcome the US presence in Japan, not otherwise. The United States hopes that this alone would be sufficient to pull China towards the United States, and outweighed her desire to regain Taiwan, protect her Communist allies in Vietnam, and the ideological aversion for capitalism. Even though Nixon was an admirer of Kishi, who was Prime Minister Sato's half brother—there was limited respect that the United States gave to the Sato's administration insofar when the Alliance was concerned. Prime Minister Sato was also a protégé of Yoshida Shigeru, and sought a harmonious and cooperative stance with the United States, even though the rapprochement effectively ended the political career of Sato (Iokibe 2016: 232).

The dynamics of the 1970s was however quite different from the previous decade. Tanaka Kakuei strove to normalize relations with China, and Miki Takeo as his successor was keen to sign a Peace Treaty with China—even though it did not materialize until 1978 during Prime Minister Fukuda's reign. The interest of Prime Ministers Tanaka and Miki were to insure that Japan was not left out in the Cold, but also proactively to engage China. As renown Japanese scholar Iokibe Mokoto noted, the practice of Japanese Prime Ministers visiting the United States as the first foreign visit is akin to feudal lords paying respect to the Shogun in ancient times. It is indicative of the importance of US-Japan relations and Japan's as a dependency—as Prime Ministers Tanaka, Miki, Fukuda and Ohira did in the 1970s, albeit for different reasons (Iokibe 2016: 231). Prime Ministers Ikeda and Sato went because of the privileged position of the United States, Tanaka and Fukuda went because of other plans they had for the Alliance (Iokibe 2016: 231). Tanaka's visit was to sought Nixon's blessing for Japan's normalizing relations with China, and Fukuda's visit was to build on expanding Tanaka's diplomatic initiative to reach out to China and expand it into an Asian wide initiative (Iokibe 2016: 232). Notwithstanding this, neither Tanaka nor his successor Prime Minister Miki undertook steps to expand Japan into a strategic power—as Japan's defense policy at that time was premised more upon détente and autonomous defenses whilst not seeking to become a military power (Shinkawa 2016: 194–195).

Japan's foreign policy took an increasingly "autonomous" streak during this decade. Prime Minister Fukuda Takeo had personal experience of the Tokyo Air Raids that that almost killed him during the Pacific War, and experienced the "unreasonableness" of the Occupation authorities whilst working at the Finance Ministry (Iokibe 2016: 217). Whilst growing up as an ardent nationalist, he deeply revered Prime Minister Kishi, and was particularly enamored with his ideas on Constitution revisionism and rearmament. He had recalled that it was important for Japan to "construct a political system that is completely free of reliance on the occupation forces", perceiving Yoshida and Ikeda served the Occupation authorities too much, and that it was wrong to have a Constitution not made by Japanese themselves and have relied on the Americans entirely for Japan's national defense (Iokibe 2016: 217). Yet, overtime Fukuda evolved, and even though he remained a nationalist, he also acquired an internationalist outlook, and had put in place the most forward looking foreign policy that Japan has seen in the postwar era. The Fukuda doctrine builds on what Tanaka has achieved with China, and undoubtedly the first-time postwar Japan expanded its diplomacy to focus on Southeast Asia. Fukuda's "Omni-directional foreign policy" should be seen as an attempt to reinforce the US-Japan relations as the cornerstone of Japanese foreign policy and use it as a base to further develop relations with Asia, and in Iokibe's words—this is not the "flipping of US to Asia" (Iokibe 2016: 232).

Over the course of the two and half decades, the US-Japan alliance has seen incremental changes to the power relations between the United States and Japan. By the 1970s, issues regarding burden sharing and allegations of Japan's free riding cropped up in Japan's bilateral relations with the US. Japan's rapid economic rise had made some in the United States question the degree of which Japan was shouldering the burden of defense arrangements. The United States not only demanded Tokyo to shoulder more of the cost of operations, but Japan had consistently refused to spend more than 1% of her GDP on defense. The United States also wanted Japan to participate in technology transfer arrangements. The United States under President Carter also wanted to ensure Japan did not get to repossess her own nuclear fuel (Iokibe 2016: 232). To that extent, Prime Minister Ohira Masayoshi and Suzuki Zenko took the traditional interpretation of the Constitution and the US-Japan Alliance, and by the beginning of the 1980s, the relationship of the US-Japan alliance was at a low.

Prime Minister Nakasone was arguably one of the more successful Prime Ministers in the postwar era. The US-Japan relations thrived during this period despite Japan was becoming economically richer and politically more powerful. With Japan's economic strength, he was able to steer Japan to greater heights in terms of her diplomacy in Asia and with the

United States. He was also able to redeem Japan's image in the eyes of the South Koreans and the United States through cultivating close personal relations with not only President Reagan but also the South Korean leader Chun Doo-wan. Nakasone agreed to a technology transfer protocol with the United States, ignoring Japan's "Three Principles of Arms Exports". The Nakasone government interpreted that the transfer was legitimate because of the US-Japan Security Treaty, overrode the Cabinet Legislation Bureau and demanded that the defense budget be raised from 1% to 5% (Kusano 2016: 278).

During Nakasone's tenure, he increased trust between US and Japan, helped Japan establish a global presence and stepped up Japan's confrontation against the USSR after the drowning of the KAL Flight 007 (Kusano 2016: 278). The narrative debating the issues surrounding the US-Japan Alliance had changed remarkably in this decade. It reflected the changes in the capabilities, status and economic relationship that Japan had built over the last three decades, as well as the change in Asia-Pacific's security environment. Japan in the 1980s was a lot more confident and assertive than the Japan was in the 1950s and 1960s, and dealing with the United States from a position of strength, not weakness. Her relationship had in short morphed into one of "equal" at least from the Japanese point of view, as the asymmetricities that had so marked the relationship in the 1950s was now completely reversed, at least in the economic and technological spheres. This improvement brought on increased friction in the management of alliance matters as the alliance partners began wrestling over the question of the alliance cost, technology transfers and spillover effects from the tensions both countries faced in their bilateral relations.

Most interestingly, this period also coincided with a period of strong relationship with China at the same time. The 1980s is known today as a period of Gold Age for Sino-Japanese relations. This indicates that strong Japan-US and Japan-China relations can co-exist if conditions are right. As the USSR commits to *Perestroika* and *Glasnost* under Gorbachev, East Asia became a much more amicable place politically as relations between China, the USSR, the US and Japan improved, alleviating the tensions that the Cold War had instituted in the region over the past thirty years. This however did not last very long, as by the 1990s, Japan once again found herself at odds with her neighbors, particularly China over issues to do with history and other realpolitik concerns, creating a downward spiral in the bilateral relationship. These developments however had the important effect of reaffirming and boosting the US-Japan alliance to unprecedented heights, making their relations perhaps better than the decades before.

Theme Three: Pacifism, the Use of Force and Global Engagement

The Fusion of Democracy and Pacifism

It is debatable if democracy was an organic element in traditional Japanese political thinking and system as after all Taisho democracy and Freedom Rights Movement (自由民権運動 *Jiyū Minken Undō*) are parts of recent Japanese history. What is not debatable however was the speed and ability of the Japanese to totally transform and adapt to democratic practices immediately after the Second World War, particularly if we consider democracy as an import that was hoisted upon the Japanese polity by the Americans.

Likewise, Pacifism as a belief was not organic prior to the Second World War as local conditions did not provide the incentives for people to embrace such a belief and there was no war from the start of Meiji which had significant popular movement opposing it (Yamamoto 2004: 2–5). There are however others who argue that Pacifism in Japan can be traced to earlier intellectual thinkers such as Kitamura Tokoku, Kinoshita Naoe, Uchimura Kanzo, Kotoku Shusui (Bamba and Howes 1978; Matsuzawa 2016) Admittedly, protests against the state in favor of peace is a modern postwar phenomenon. The onset of Pacifism in Japan during the late 1940s and 1950s therefore stemmed from a genuine desire of the Japanese people to consciously avoid war and bloodshed in the name of development and progress, and an attempt to prevent the ability of the State elites, whether the Cabinet Ministers or the Military from being able to mobilize the nation towards war time effort. The strength of pacifism in postwar Japan is therefore backed by the democratic will of the Japanese people to effectively marginalize (not eradicate) the remaining strands of right wing ultra-nationalism and conservatism residual in Japanese society in the postwar period.

This pacifism stems from institutions and practices introduced at a few levels. First and foremost, it draws its legal and political status from the Constitution, particularly Article 9 that renounces the option of War making as a sovereign right of the Japanese people to the way the Japanese elites interpreted the law. The Constitution is a conscious decision of the people, and in the words of John Dower, it is one of the most profound statements of apology that the Japanese people could make to her neighbors. The Constitution also rests the sovereignty of the nation in the name of the people, establishing the democratic institutions that make up contemporary Japan as we now know it. Second, the establishment of the US-Japan Alliance, and the implementation of the Yoshida doctrine removed the necessity of Japan as a sovereign country the need to upkeep an active military force when the responsibility for Japan's security was effectively outsourced to the Americans. Even as Japanese society eschewed militarism and war, the role of the military in Japan's control became one of the most important pillars of this pacifism. Third, the idea of peace is something that is deeply held by postwar generations as something they would practice as individuals. Japan's grassroots peace movements, usually made up of union or women groups, were often resisting the government, not so much because of defending personal moral belief than an collective act of advocacy calling on the government to oppose nuclear weapons and rearmament and not to sign partial peace or Japan-US treaties inimical to peace (Yamamoto 2004: 213–214). Peace and pro-Constitution activism stimulates the emergence of a new kind of citizenship, eradicating feudal remnants and promoting a new relationship between the state and the individual (Yamamoto 2004: 214). In short, pacifism had fused with democracy and the new Constitution and embedded deeply as important elements in Japanese national identity.

From Truman's "containment" policy to Eisenhower's "rollback Communism" initiative, the exigencies of the Cold War put United States at odds with the tendencies of Japanese politics. The American effort to remilitarize Japan was kept in check largely by a confluence of factors. First, the institutions that the United States imposed upon Japan by the Occupation authorities before Washington changed their mind i.e. the Constitution and the multi-party democratic system allowed the Japanese elites to use them to fend off American pressure to remilitarize. Second, the existence of principally the left-wing socialist movements and the nascent liberal democratic forces coincided the general mood among the civilians that made up much of the pacifist base—all add to the strength of the pacifist State. Third, the neo-realist nature of postwar politicians like Yoshida Shigeru who saw the Constitution and general public opinion as a shield to fend off US pressure and enable Japan's economy to recuperate.

The Subjugation of the Military

One of the most revered and respected institutions in ancient and pre-war Japan is the military. As a political and social institution, the importance of the military's role in Japan cannot be overstated. Like many States in Asia, Japan has a praetorian culture in the sense that her Statesmen have always had linkages to the military—even the first generation of Meiji elites were samurais. By the end of the Pacific War, the status of the military had become drastically reduced, and the anti-militarism that had set in have perhaps for the first time in modern history completely negated any positive image of the military.

Postwar Japan had a clear and defined role mission for Japan's military—to stay hidden in plain sight. The idea of the military was different from that of other society have about their military. Japan's forces will be used only for self-defense, never for offensive capabilities. It would not have the right to come to the aide of her allies in any scenario for collective self-defense, and its deployment will be strictly for the defense of the Japanese homeland. The aversion to the use of military force in the postwar period was so strong that in 1958 Oe Kenzaburo (the 1994 Nobel Laureate) described those sitting for the JSDF entrance exam as the "shame of their generation" (Sado 2017). Overall the image of the military is one that is extremely negative, and is looked down upon by the politicians, journalists and civilian population.

To that extent, the idea of subsuming military to civilian control is a strange and new concept for Japanese people. There are two important strategies to ensure this is so. The first is for the control of the military was for the postwar authorities to completely oversee the military via civilian staff, second, was to ensure that the budget of the military is constrained and independently checked. Taken together the way the military is constituted and positioned within the Japan is that it is a force that remained "unseen" and is being relegated as "non-use" (Sado 2017: 205–208). Various veteran politicians such as Yoshida Shigeru, Fukuda Takeo and Ichiro Ozawa have on different occasions lamented on the importance of the role Japan could play in global affairs and spoke with regret on the inability of Japan to play a more global role with regards to United Nations affairs. Their responses were of course in hindsight natural given the exceptional rise of postwar Japan. Even as the Japanese subordinated the military to civilian control and disregarded the use of force, the institutionalization of democracy did not mean that Conservatism and right-wing nationalism disappeared from Japan. There was often an element of

Conservatism and right wing nationalism that belied Japanese democracy. These two strands of ideological influences are conceptually different in nature, and will be explained later on in this chapter.

Hiding in Plain Sight: Nationalists and Conservatives in Postwar Japan

In the postwar period, even as Occupation authorities tried to eradicate or suppress all nationalist movements, they never completely disappeared. In particular, the ultra-nationalist groups with pre-war linkages had to survive by either disappearing into the rural areas or modifying their programs (Morris 1960: 160). For most part, nationalist parties across the spectrum did support the United States in their open narratives adopting a pro-US, anti-Soviet position (*Shimbei Hanso*), what they really wanted was for Japan to rearm and to adopt a more independent posture. As Morris put it, the "*shimbei*" [support the US] for the nationalists is [preferable] to "Japan's present enfeebled condition, [and] the American alliance must be accepted as the lesser of two evils ... ...", and that nationalists regard that if they "sit back, they will fall prey to the Communist invasion; if [they] stand up, [they] will become the catspaw of American imperialism" (Morris 1960: 170). Nationalism is however not the sole domain of the political right, and left wing groups such as the Communists employed it too in Japan. The Japan Communist Party and the Social Party in the postwar era was only able to use nationalism to a limited effect in Japan, unlike the Chinese communist simply because in Japan, traditionally Japanese nationalism is being mobilized from reformist or revolutionary channels into that of national unity and military expansion which for all intents and purposes not useful for the Communists in Japan (Morris 1960: 399). Likewise for the extreme right in Japan, their weaknesses are: (1) nationalists are generally strong in critique, but lack concrete solutions; (2) they are reactionary politically but are unable to concrete material wealth and livelihood issues and (3) they are heavily clique-based, and rely heavily on the personalized ties with the leaders that have little mass appeal (Morris 1960: 402–403). Thus, Japan's political system has been locked in a struggle between liberals and conservatives, and from the extreme end, between the Communists and the Ultranationalists on the right. That being said, the right-wing (and also the Conservative) factions are far more in tune than the left wing will ever be in terms of its commensurability with traditional Japanese culture as well as with the employment of nationalism as a tool for statist political mobilization. This is particularly true of rural agrarian areas. Additionally, Conservatives are more likely to act in concert with rightwing groups than with Communist groups, and this is the reason why many tend to confuse Conservatives with Nationalists in Japan.

When the Occupational authorities changed their minds and began to ask the Japanese elites to reverse course and remilitarize because of the Cold War, they were met with resistance from groups across the political spectrum, particularly from the left wing and civic groups (Yamamoto 2004; Morris 1960: 386). The switch to move the emphasis from reform to stabilization, from democratization to anti-Communism only suited the Conservatives in Japan. The opposition to this was a strange coalition made up of leftists—socialist leaning politicians, grassroots activists and liberals.

The United States' preference for staunchly anti-Communist LDP conservatives to helm Japan of course is a conscious decision to ensure that Japan remains firmly in the United States orbit. Beyond the realization of the unpopularity of the American attempts to remilitarize Japan, Washington is also keenly aware of the popular sympathies the Japanese people have for leftist parties and ideology, even though they might not necessarily translate into support for the Soviet Union and China. The support for right of center Conservatives naturally however is to ensure that Japan remains firmly supportive of the United States and the alliance with her, as well as to prevent the USSR or China from making inroads into the domestic political process in Japan. Yet, ever so often, Japanese politicians, regardless of their political ideologies sought to resist the United States when they felt the policies of the United States were not advocating in the country's best interest. It explains why Yoshida, Hatoyama or Kishi (the former two never saw eye to eye) could interpret their own political choices and actions that put Japan's best interests first and foremost.

This however has an unintended consequence as the Liberal Democratic Party, housing the remnants of the pre-War cabinet politicians became very much the embodiment of US foreign policy in East Asia. The exigencies of the Cold War meant that Washington had not rehabilitated these pre-war politicians, but elevated them into positions of authority to foster illiberalism and revisionist views that American servicemen who have fought during the Second World War would neither recognize nor endorse (Overholt 2007). There is no contradiction here—as politicians worldwide would try and mold themselves into an image they imagine that would enable them to get the most votes.

There are of course differences between Conservatives in Japan and their nationalist counterparts even both largely use the reverence for the institution of the Emperor and pay homage to traditional Japanese culture to lay claim to the fact that their agendas and actions are inspired by the values of the Japanese nation. There are similarities between the groups as they are often skeptical of foreign influences, thus the Occupational authorities' plans for democratization, Constitutional constraints are in fact unwelcomed by both groups, so does the Chinese or Korean references to war issues. As Winkler notes (2011: 4–5), it is important to understand that there is a certain amount of ideological flexibility among the Conservatives in Japan, and the factionalism has helped to maintain the longevity of the Conservatives. There are important differences between the two groups. Right Wing groups consider that all people are equal before the Emperor, and thus they tend to side with the people, whilst Conservatives distrust the common man, and have little positive to say about egalitarianism unless it is the legal or spiritual kind. Despite these differences, right wing groups tend to side more with the Conservatives than other groups, including the left-wing groups who purport to be nationalist too.

Pacifism and Spectator Democracy: Becoming Peace-Loving Global Citizens

For average Japanese citizens, the struggle between the left leaning parties such as the Japan Socialist Party versus the Liberal Democratic Party, or the LDP elites versus the United States policy group or the politicians versus the bureaucrats, or citizenry versus the government has become somewhat of a normality in Japanese politics. This is seen as democracy at work—a democracy that has been imposed by the United States in the postwar period but has grown to be embraced by the Japanese people very quickly over a generation. Even though the US wanted to rearm Japan for the Cold War, pacifism quickly became entrenched in postwar Japan, as political doctrine, as an ideology and as a way of life and provided much resistance to prevent this from materializing.

In particular, pacifism became intertwined with the ideals of democracy—that every Japanese citizen to a large extent assimilated both pacifism and democracy that the two sets of ideas became conflated and subsumed in the beliefs and outlook of the average Japanese person: Japan was pacifist democracy; Japan did not and had no military—all they had was a small, defensive self-defense force and Tokyo followed the lead of the United States in all strategic matters. Japan and the Japanese people will never consider using force to resolve disputes or stake their interests. In short, pacifism has infused into Japanese national identity and influence almost all aspects of life and guided Japanese foreign and strategic perceptions as the influence of anti-militaristic norms was very real (Katzenstein 1996, 1998; Berger 1998, 2012). It had bearing on the way politics was conducted in Japan. For much of the postwar period, foreign policy issues and strategic direction were not dominant in domestic political campaigns, with the exception of US bases in Okinawa. The LDP's dominance was in part because voters wanted a party that will preserve "stability" in Japan, focused on economic reconstruction and prosperity. LDP's staunch support for the United States, and singlemindedness in preserving power and the capitalistic system made it the party of choice for both the Japanese people and the United States.

The dominance of the LDP however has led some to suggest that Japan was a "spectator democracy" that allowed Japanese citizens to watch world developments on the sidelines. This "non-participatory" mode also ensured that the central government is a father figure and that needed to be trusted and revered (Tominomori 1993: 83–84). This "paternalism" therefore forms the basis of government-people relations in Japan. Consequently even though there is a profession for egalitarianism among grassroots group, there is also a contradictory preference for hierarchy and elitism in Japanese politics. There is therefore an inherent tension between Conservatism and democracy (Winkler 2011: 6; Kitaoka 1992: 89–90), and this tension is most observed in the way Japanese talk and think about politics and foreign policy and the actual implementation. The result is a clear trend of hypocrisy in Japan's defensive posture.

This creates two different spheres of influences in Japan's public sphere—the pragmatic conservatives/nationalists who want Japan to rearm and attain a military that befits her economic clout, and ultranationalists who will deny any wrong doing in Japan's past (Yamamoto 2004: 216). The presence of the US-Japan forces negates Article 9, and casts doubts on Japan's pacifism. For the United States perspective, often it would look like that the Japanese were selfish in that they were not pulling their weight behind their own defense. From the perspective of Japan's neighbors, the pacifist democracy and the profession of "3 Nuclear principles" on one hand and the existence of nuclear weapons hosted on US warships made Japan looked particularly hypocritical.

In the postwar period, Japan thus evolved into a democracy with certain special characteristics that provided the stability which both the Japanese people and Washington sought in the region. The first and most important facet is the dominance of the Liberal Democratic Party. The LDP currently led by Abe Shinzo came about as a merger of the Liberal Party led by Yoshida Shigeru and Democratic Party led by Hatoyama Ichiro in 1955. The LDP's longevity is unparalleled in East Asia, only to be outdone by the Communist Party of China and the Workers Party of Democratic People's Republic of Korea (DPRK). The LDP reign's was only briefly interrupted in 1993–1994 where two Socialist prime ministers (Hosakawa and Murayama) came to office.

The recipe for LDP's electoral success was simple: LDP politicians were effective in building pork-barrel relationships with their Constituents and other stakeholders. This included the powerful bureaucracy and close relationships with the multinational companies *Zaibatsus*. The LDP was also extremely adept at electoral manipulation, among other things the co-option of the agendas of the opposition and smaller parties (starting as early as during Hatoyama Ichiro's period where he co-opted the Socialist Parties agenda of normalizing relations with the Soviet Union). The LDP was also extremely creative in the implementation of the multi-seats district zones, effectively reducing the ability of smaller parties to organize and fight the campaign because of the constraints of their smaller sizes. The smaller interruption when LDP lost power in 1993–94 however allowed the Socialist party to address by reinstalling more single seat wards in the electoral process. Among the Japanese people, there is a constant fear any elevation of the leftist party would destroy the US-Japan Security Alliance and the good that the Japanese economy has done would be disrupted and Japan would become poor (Ogawa cited in Onishi 2005).

Japan's democracy was also for a large part marred by a weak civil society. Even though Japanese democracy is described as "vibrant" or "vigorous" by various commentators, the way civil society has developed remains lopsided. Despite the flourishing of private organizations in the fields of welfare or international aid, organizations that scrutinize government working and functions, human rights and other information still have little influence (Onishi 2005). This is not surprising, since many civil society organizations are still relying heavily on government funding, and this stands in consonance with the Japanese tradition that social organizations should exist for community solidarity and helping each other out so long they do not challenge the absolute feudal authority of the Tokugawa Shogunate (Pulsford et al. 2011).

For most part, Japanese electorate during the Cold War did not take the socialism very seriously simply because they were more worried about the possible destruction of the Japan-U.S. relations and that Japan would become poor (Oguma cited in Onishi 2005). This fear is not extraordinary—almost all the regimes in East Asia which were in the US led-bloc had seen authoritarian regimes holding onto power with varying degrees of similarity to the LDP during the Cold War. Chiang Kaishek's Kuomintang (KMT) in Taiwan, Lee Kwan Yew's People's Action Party (PAP) in Singapore and Park Chung Hee's Democratic Republican Party are all examples, although the United States has for a better part of the Cold War comfortable with an identifiable candidate in East Asia which is sympathetic to her causes (Hastings 1988: 32–34).

Thus, even though Japan's democratic progress vis-à-vis its Asian neighbors is admirable, Japan's pacifism is derived from a population dissuaded from socialism by fear of economic decline and maintained by a strong state whose Conservative politicians rely on a variety of non-democratic means to keep the system going. As Japan's economy grew, and a new generation comes to the fore in Japan, the result is the emergence of a more confident generation devoid of war memories. This means the genuine sense of pacifism that has so motivated the postwar generation has been eroded increasingly. By the 1970s, the impetus for Japan to attain a political status commensurate with her political status is clear, and that Japan should indeed be allowed to contribute more to the United Nations. The Fukuda doctrine provided Japan with an Asian focus diplomatic focus, and by the 1980s, Japan has started for the first time to reconsider all the things that the nation has not undertaken previously. First, Japan began to utilize her economic influence to undertake Overseas Development Assistance to assert her political influence across China, Southeast Asia and elsewhere. Japan also became an increasingly influential contributor to the United Nations, requesting that she be made a permanent member of the UN Security Council as early as 1973. Nonetheless, it was only in 1992 that Japan joined the first peacekeeping UN Mission (Cambodia), signifying the reconsideration of a greater political and military role to come in the following decades. Japan also began to consider what sort of power it could evolve into by the 1980s as her economic prowess grew to a considerable degree. By the mid-1990s, Japan started considering to transform her military into a "post postmodern expeditionary army" (much like what the US Army has evolved during the War on Terror) (Hunter-Chester 2016: 9, Chapter 8).

The Erosion of Pacifism: Can Democracy and Historical Revisionism Co-Exist?

The emergence of the neo-Conservatism in the post 1990 can only be explained by a coincidence of factors: the collapse of the USSR, the rise of China, the backlash against Japanese checkbook diplomacy exhibited in the first Gulf War and the general loss of strategic direction after the end of the Cold War. For the first few years of the decade, the strategic debate within Tokyo with regards to Japan's strategic direction was contemporaneous on the possible isolationism of the United States and the rise of China. Japan faced an increasing number of issues across all fronts with China ranging from PRC's nuclear test in 1995 and a dispute over the Senakaku/Diaoyu islands. As Japan began to debate the question of the utility of the US-Japan alliance domestically, a contemporaneous debate regarding the rise of the China threat was taking place. By 1996, President Clinton and Prime Minister Hashimoto agreed to reaffirm and reinvigorate the US-Japan alliance. The price of doubling down on the US-Japan alliance can only be done with popular support—that was the beginning of shift of public opinion against China contextualized against greater domestic and international reports regarding China's development. The 1998 DPRK missile tests that saw North Korean missiles overfly Japan (whom the North Korean says is a satellite test) provided Tokyo, particularly their neo-conservatives the perfect opportunity to advance their agenda. By supersizing the DPRK threat, the neo-Conservatives were able to rally the support for their agenda.

By Koizumi's tenure, the traditional way of conducting politics was undergoing a sea-change. Koizumi capitalized on the frustration of the voters who were concerned about the way traditional politics were conducted in Japan. Coming up in a political system where he did not have the prestige from a brand-name political family (like Abe Shinzo or Hatoyama Yukio), he was nonetheless singularly successful because he was able to do three things that were different from his predecessors. He was able to handle the bureaucracy by insisting on handpicking the liaison officers to the different ministries instead of relying on the Ministries' to send him the candidates. Koizumi had a very talented media advisor, Issao

Nakajima who was able to sidestep the control of the traditional broadsheets by reaching out to the tabloids. Beyond that, there was also very careful usage of social media to help with the calibration of Koizumi's image and positions on issues. Koizumi was projected to be a leader of Japanese people, a force for change—whether it was confronting the Chinese, reforming Japan's postal system or vowing to "destroy" the traditional LDP by using female "assassins" to run against his political opponents. The visual politics portrayed him as a politician of strength, as a strong leader and a man of the people—and above all, someone who resist tyranny, power politics and corruption.

The success of Koizumi is also aided by his foreign policy success (or failure depending on one's perspective). First, Koizumi's September 2002 visit to DPRK was a tremendous success, when Kim Jong-il admitted "rogue elements" had abducted Japanese nationals in the past, and successfully having five abduction victims out of seventeen returned in May 2004. This however raised expectations of the Japanese people for the return of the rest of the abductees and for them to take a harder line against the DPRK. Second, US-Japan relations were amicable during his tenure, particularly because of Japan's support for the United States' War on Terror. Third, even though the United States was accused of "neglecting" Asia, resulting in the downward spiral of Sino-Japanese relations, an alternative interpretation is that the United States and Japan gained strategically in a big way during this period. By letting Japan "act" autonomously, it enhanced Japanese self-awareness of her security posture. Prime Minister Koizumi did not heed the calls of the Chinese and Koreans not to visit Yasukuni shrine. Acting defiantly, he visited the Shrine six times in his capacity as Prime Minister even as China and Korea, Singapore, Hong Kong, Taiwan and even Australia protested (Onishi 2006). One of Koizumi's advisors communicated to the author: "The Prime Minister believed that even if he had caved in to China and Korea on this matter [Yasukuni Shrine], they [China and Korea] still would not treat Japan with the respect she deserves … it therefore did not matter what he did or did not do since no amount of reconciliation would get him [or Japan] any leeway with China or Korea". Instead, the protests from China and Korea boosted his popularity at home (except with the business community) and his ratings provided him with a political longevity that most of his LDP predecessors can only admire whilst at the same time help him with the political situation.

Photo: Mr. Nakatani, Director General of the Defense Agency, embarks on the Japan Maritime Self-Defense Force destroyer Kurama (DDH-144) during a homecoming reception of MSDF ships, Kirisame (DD-104), Kurama, and Hamana (AOE-424), March 16, 2002. Japan's MSDF have been in the Indian Ocean providing vital logistical support, including supplying fuel, to U.S. and coalition ships in the fight against terrorism. (By Jonathan R. Kulp, U.S. Navy [Public domain], via Wikimedia Commons)

Sino-Japanese relations had deteriorated to one of its lowest point in postwar history. There is however no question that by 2005, neo-conservatism had become a central element in Japanese politics, ending the dominance of pacifism as an ideology in Japanese society. Public opinion supported a tougher stance against China (Hoshino and Satoh 2012), and increasing cooperation with the United States. Even though a significant portion of electorate had doubts about the politicians' intent and capability, the surge of emotive nationalism became the basis of a true democratic force which Japanese harnessed against China. This provided Japan an opportunity to advance her strategic interests and give a big boost to the US-Japan alliance (Lai 2014). In this respect, Koizumi had managed to put forward the neo-Conservative agenda in a big way. The United States gained because by the end of Koizumi's tenure, many

Chinese believe it might actually easier for US to handle Japan rather than do it by themselves. Like the Japanese, the Chinese too eased up on the US-Japan relations.

The support for this neo-conservative focus on security is not irrational nationalism. For the average laymen, whether the person lives in Tokyo, Hanoi or Manila, the rise of Chinese economic power and the reported irredentist agenda China is allegedly undertaking is usually enough to stoke a strong reaction. At the same time, this is often magnified by their own economic malaise and stagnation, accentuated by China's rise and the closing of the gap between their countries' comprehensive national strength. This of course is worsened by the fact that China is also set to overtake the United States as the World's largest economy in the near future, and represents a real chance that the United States might seek to drive a grand bargain with China by entering into a real comprehensive strategic partnership with the PRC. In other words, Japan faces the prospects of strategic abandonment which she has feared since the early 1970s (Frankel 1971; Schaller 1996). This double impetus therefore pushes Japan to undertake policies which would forestall or at least slow down the prospects of that happening as Japan seeks out a more independent and calibrated strategic policy.

Thus the erosion of pacifism in Japan is accompanied by a grim reality of grudging acceptance by the Japanese nation that it is time for Japan to undertake a greater sense of responsibility for her own defense as well as for global commitments worldwide (APH20C 2017). Japan's UN and international contributions will be discussed in depth in Chap. 4. Even as pacifism has imbued Japanese with a strong sense of liberalism and democracy, it is questionable if this has truly imbued deeply into the Japanese psyche. While Japanese people might have responded enthusiastically to universal concepts and ideals such as liberty, equality and human rights, their outlook imbued with fresh moral zeal, their moral compass did not extend much beyond the country's borders (Yoon cited in Yamamoto 2004: 219). Japan's quest for normalization and rejuvenation is therefore promising to change this.

By the time Abe Shinzo came to power in 2006, he laid the important ground work for the neo-conservative shift for Japan to play a greater part in her defense. The strategy was to hasten and build on the achievements of Hashimoto-Clinton agreement as well as the achievements under Koizumi-Bush on the US-Japan Alliance even as Japan tried to seek out a way to work with China. Abe's strategy lied in laying out the groundwork for greater public support for Japan's normalization and rejuvenation as a political power (Smith 2014, 2015; Tanaka 2017).

There are four central elements. First, Abe wanted to build a national education program to ensure that future generations of Japanese would have the "correct" historical understanding of events and feel "proud" of the country. This of course is aimed at negating the prevalence of the anti-militaristic norm that is so prevalent in the country and which Abe views as the fundamental barrier to Japan's normalization and rejuvenation. Linking this national education which in theory is supposed to transmit "traditional" culture, necessitates the definition of all things quintessentially "Japanese", and creates an in/out group dynamics that makes any criticism of this security policy look "unjapanese" and unpatriotic. The ideational concept of "face" is central to East Asian nationalism, and this element cannot be underestimated (Chien and Fitzgerald 2006). Second, given the Constitution is both a political and legal instrument, any attempt to reorient Japan's security posture would necessitate a legal maneuver. Abe has three sub-strategies to do incrementally erode the legal constraints and to pave the way for an eventual referendum on amending the Constitution. Taking his service as Koizumi's Chief Cabinet Secretary and as Prime Minister for the two separate terms, Abe Shinzo has: (i) increased the neo-conservative presence in the Diet, by coopting members, or forcing political opponents to adopt this policy orientation by persuasion, coercion or co-option; (ii) implemented gradual changes through administrative decrees and incremental legislation to continually erode the Constitutional constraints; (iii) using Prime Ministerial discretion to reinterpret and expand what is permissible under the US-Japan Alliance (such as the right to collective security). Third, since the early 2000, the Japanese government, including the DPJ governments of Hatoyama, Kan and Noda has tried to garner greater public support by highlighting through the media the dangers posed by the People's Republic of China and the Democratic People's Republic of Korea. In particular, they have sought to promote the wisdom of political moves to normalize the usage of force through the Japanese military. In short, the JSDF is now promoted as a force that can be deployed and used rather than one that should remain inconspicuous and not used. Since the March 11 disaster, the JSDF has become more accepted and been highly regarded in and outside of Japan. Fourth, the Japanese government has sought to raise the status of the

JSDF and its actual fight capability by remedying its perceived inadequacies particularly in terms of how the JSDF is constrained and how it connects to the US forces in Japan and beyond.

Neo-Conservatism and the Paradoxes of Japanese Democracy

Conservatism, in its natural form are technically not antithetical with pacifism necessarily. The problem is that today, neo-Conservatism speaks to a trend that is deeply related to the belief that postwar institutions that had served Japan so well in the decades after the war is no longer a viable to meet the needs of Japan in the Post Cold War era. Neo-Conservatives therefore call for the overhaul if not removal of two of these institutions—that of Pacifism and the Constitution. This means out of the three pillars that are being explored here: Constitution, US-Japan Alliance and Pacifism, the neo-Conservatives are asking to change the two of them. What can we make of the relationship between neo-conservatism and democracy, and of nationalism and pacifism?

To begin, it is important to distinguish between conservatism and neo-conservatism in the Japanese context. The pre-dominant difference between today's neo-Conservative politicians from their predecessors during the Cold War is the neo-conservatives organizing principles and their evaluation of Japan's current responsibility for the Second World War, and Japan's position in East Asia vis-à-vis China and Korea and the general security environment. Neo-conservatives largely view that Japan should no longer have to continually bear responsibility for a war that is not waged by their generation. Further, Japan has made adequate apologies for contrition and that atoned for their wrongdoings by rendering help and aide to the countries that have been hurt by the misdeeds of the Japanese Imperial Army. This is a significant departure from those of their Conservative predecessors many who share a deferential attitude towards their neighbors, China and Korea because of the Pacific War. To that end, neo-Conservatives view that Japan's relations with either the Koreas and China are not special in any sense, particularly when their neighbors utilized "history" to put themselves on political and diplomatic moral high ground to extract political, economic and diplomatic concessions from Japan. A significant hallmark in neo-conservative is the way China is construed in their narratives. Their Conservative predecessors regard relations with China as friendly and hence do not constitute China as a security threat just as they regard South Korea's relations with Japan as a "special". Neo-conservatives in Japan, in their ideal form constitutes China as a security threat, and that even as the Republic of Korea is a common ally of the United States, Japan is not bound by any special relations with the Koreans. The neo-conservatives depart from their Conservative predecessors not only in terms of security outlook, relations with China and Korea and interpretations of war guilt, their also defer from their Conservative colleagues who have traditionally toed party-line factional politics.

Plate: A Black Van Outside Yasukini Shrine advocating for the downfall of the DPJ in 2010

The neo-Conservatives have called on the Japanese nation to imbue future generations with a sense of pride. The act of renouncing war and the use of force is self-reflexive and suggests an act of contrite and penance. Right now, the neo-conservatives are asking young people in Japan to reorient her historical understanding, particularly among young people to ensure that they are not being shackled by the historical narratives and social memories associated with the War for a few reasons.

First, the politics of the postwar period privileged and sympathize with left wing tendencies, particular in their attitudes towards China and Russia. This goes against the grain of LDP political philosophy and thinking since its founding in 1955. Second, Conservatives regard the postwar narratives erode the current young people's sense of nationalism and belonging, providing a self-defeatist attitude. In short, foreigners outside of Japan as less than desirable forces within Japan are fostering the national historical narratives of Japan, and this undesirable trend must be stopped. Third, unless this sense of self-defeatism and self-critical reproach is removed to Japanese society at large, it would affect Japanese society and nation's ability to compete in East Asia politics. Fourth, repeated acknowledgement of this history would only place Japan in a position of servitude—not only in relation to the United States, but also to China and South Korea in particular. This puts Japan in an untenable position of having to surrender the moral high ground and kowtow to her neighbors politically and diplomatically. Fifth, despite the subservience and apologetic attitude Japan has shown towards China and Korea, there is no sign that the political pressure to extract concessions using history would stop. Consequently, there is even more incentive to foster a correct sense of history as cordial relations with China and Korea remain a distant dream. Six and most importantly, advocating the correct sense of history would help shore up support for the normalization and rejuvenation of Japan, in particular for Constitution revisionism and the US-Japan Security Treaty.

The Prime Minister is a well-known conservative with historical revisionist tendencies. The most important document to understand the character of Abe's historical revisionism is Abe's book *Towards a Beautiful Country: My Vision for Japan* published in 2006. For personal and intellectual reasons, Prime Minister Abe has been at the forefront to free Japan from these perceived shackles, and in Abe's own words, he seeks a "departure from the postwar regime" by "bringing back Japan" (Abe 2006 cited in Takahashi 2014).

While the publication of this book certainly provided much fuel for the Conservative moment, the tone and tenure of the Prime Ministers' remarks certainly raised concerns for Japan's closest neighbors. Conservative politicians making revisionist remarks or visiting the Yasukuni shrines are a familiar theme in Japanese politics and diplomatic relations for China and Japan, but the problem is that Prime Minister Abe seems deeply convinced by his beliefs and committed to realizing them. The irony is that criticisms from outside, particularly from China or Korea only serves to enrage ordinary Japanese, rally political support and further embolden these politicians.

Unlike other politicians (such as Koizumi who had excellent public image advisors), this Prime Minister's deeply held revisionism stems from deeply held personal convictions. First, the Prime Minister is of the view that his grandfather's conviction as a War Criminal is unfair and questionable. Second, the unfairness of having the Tribunal imposed sentences is like the Victor's justice, as convictions were based on concepts determined by Allied courts after the War and this in turn raises question about the legitimacy of the Tribunal. Third, the Prime Minister also has difficulty with the blame apportionment, questioning the mass media, society at large and implicitly the institution of the Emperor. Is it fair to really just put all the responsibilities on the convicted War criminals? (Takahashi 2014).

Taken together, Prime Minister Abe's new Conservatism has served as a rallying cry for all conservative groups, from grassroots to the national level. Whilst there is a view that there is a rightward shift in Japanese politics, particularly since the election of Prime Abe in 2012, is the electorate seeking "stability" and driven by a desire to forestall economic problems of the inexperience of the DPJ—nonetheless the election of Shinzo Abe puts the rightwing of Japan's political spectrum in office—where they have a rightful platform to articulate their visions and formulate policy (Hoffman 2018). There are alternate views of course, and the dissenting opinion is that Abe's election can be distilled down to the lack of viable and appealing opposition (Takahashi 2013; Nakano 2017) which is a main contributing factor. Regardless of this, not counting the years prior to the Koizumi administration, Prime Minister Abe Shinzo and his associates (PM Taro Aso etc.) have been near or at the echelons of Japan's political system since 2003 (when he became Secretary-General of the LDP) during Koizumi's tenure. At the same time, there is increasing recognition that neo-Conservatives have been stealthily mobilizing political movements at the grassroots level to popularize their agenda through organizations like *Nippon Kaigi* that grew from the merger of two organizations in 1997—*Nihon Wo Mamoru Kokumin Kaigi* [National Conference to Protect Japan] and *Nihon wo Mamoru Kai* [Association to Protect Japan] (Tawara 2017). Its stated mission on its website (www.nipponkaigi.org) is to suggest that it is a "civic group that presents policy proposals and promotes a national movement for restoring a beautiful Japan and building a proud nation". The most important goal for this organization is to amend the Constitution, and counts among its ranks influential members of Japanese society. Tawara notes that as at November 2015, Nippon Kaigi accounted for 40% of the 717 Diet members in both houses of the Japanese parliament, and had help Abe mount the cabinets (Tawara 2017: 9).

The neo-conservatives had therefore tended to do two things through *Nippon Kaigi*. First, there is a movement to promote "patriotic education" within Japan from 1990s. This is achieved through the writing of revisionist history textbooks written with this aim in mind (Rose 2006). The activities of *Nippon Kaigi* include promoting the revision of Constitution, adopting the textbooks published by *Nihon Kyoiku Saisei Kiko* [Japan Education Rebuilding Organisation] as well as the Society for History Textbook Reform. There are other practical acts such as pressuring school boards to display the *Hinomaru* national flag and sing the *Kimiyago* anthem during assemblies, and to monitor against left wing content taught in Schools (Tawara 2017: 13). The second is build a grassroot movement by increasing membership of local politicians (such as governors, mayors, assembly heads and mayors) in different prefectures into *Nippon Kaigi*. This idea is to grow a grassroots right-wing movement aimed to cultivate the next generation of Japanese youths to rightwing ideas and to neutralize counter arguments as being presented by the "left". In short, the *Nippon Kaigi* aims to promote a narrative that has been suppressed but never eradicated since the 1950s, and to operationalize the ideas by inviting politicians and legislators into its ranks. The view that Japanese politics has shift "rightwards" in mainstream International Politics might actually not be quite accurate, as the Conservatives (alongside the nationalists) has never quit talking about Constitutional amendments or taking a "correct" view of history since the 1950s. They just "blended in" for most part with the Japanese population and many kept their convictions.

Even though there is belief among analysts that the history textbook issue emerged in the mid-1980s, Ienaga Saburo's battles with the Conservative and nationalist forces over the approval of his history textbook began as early as the 1952. The talk about overturning the Constitution began as soon as the Constitution was enacted, at least this is true in the LDP in the 1950s. Thus, the neo-Conservatives sought to bring to the fore an agenda that existed early on in the postwar period, suppressed and subsided because of the shame and stigma that pacifism brought to bear. This has however been reversed recently with domestic changes in Japan that generational change brought and in the shifting dynamics in international affairs in the post Cold War world.

Japanese politics is now characterized by two paradoxes (McCormack 2008). First, the word "conservative" applies to those who need to remake and remodel Japan's postwar institutions, undertaking radical changes.

Those who insist on "conserving" Japanese postwar democratic institutions are construed as "radicals" or "leftists". The second paradox is those who insist on subordination of Japanese interests to that of the United States describe themselves as "nationalists", while those who seek to prioritize Japanese over US interests are suspected of being "un-Japanese". McCormack argues this is nothing short of "Alice in Wonderland" confusion. Are we therefore to interpret that dominant ideology today in Japan is neo-conservatism with a nationalist twist in a democratic façade, and that pacifism is completely dead in the water? How do we reconcile with the success and longevity of nationalistic (Shintaro Ishihara or Hashimoto Toru) or Conservative leaders (Koizumi Junichiro or Abe Shinzo) as opposed to the politicians that truly advocate to listen to the people?

As in all fields that study human behavior, it is difficult to explain or predict Japanese politics here for certain. Yet, if there is one identity that most, if not all Japanese are proud of—it is the idea that Japan is a vibrant democracy. For all its imperfections, most Japanese people today are extremely proud of their democratic achievements.

Viewed from inside out, Japan's neo-conservatives calls for the nation to rally around the neoconservatives' idea of "values-based" foreign policy to defend against dictatorships (i.e. North Korea and the PRC) who are bent of asserting their will in the region both appeals to the democrat and the nationalist in the average Japanese. The neo-conservatives' articulation of a new Japan no longer troubled by issues concerned with the burden of history too resonates: why should successive generations of Japanese pay for their great-grandfathers' sins generations ago? As the neo-conservatism message resonated with those growing up during the postwar era, so did the nationalism and historical revisionism. At the same time, neo-Conservatives like Abe has never been shy to articulate that Japan is a democracy, and thus is "different" from China or Korea. The idea of "democracy" is therefore often used as a positive "value" that Japanese politicians sell their ideas (be it nationalism or neo-conservatism), but is also a reminiscent of the quest that Japanese people had across generations to seek out egalitarianism and excellence at the same time.

There are other possible explanations as well to the puzzle as to why nationalists and neo-conservatives are so popular in a democratic Japan. One convenient way is to view Japanese democracy in a new light: that Japan has never been truly a democratic country in the Western Liberal sense—particularly if democracy is defined in terms of party-turn over or the existence of a strong and well balanced civil society or the ability of citizens and local areas to change policy (think Okinawa) (McCormack and Norimatsu 2012).

There are some who might argue Japan's democracy is neither as well-established we often assume to be nor that democratic values are not as deeply ingrained in the electorate. In the words of one commentator, Japan became "democratic" in three months, soon after the Occupation Authorities system imposed the institutions on them. They never had to bleed for these democratic values, and certainly most figures that are enshrined as Yasukini *Jinja* did not die fighting for democracy (Leonard in Pyle 2007: viii–ix). The issue however is not whether they did or did not die fighting for democracy. The fact remains that for an entire generation, Japanese people have lived for pacifism and anti-militarism. As Japan never had much of a democratic tradition to begin with, the question as to why Japan became staunchly anti-militaristic in such a short time also deserves to be examined. For much of the postwar period, Japan's pacifist norm remained an important source of influence for much of the country's thinking. Since 1945, the Japanese nation made a conscious decision to disavow their right to use force. This disavowal of use of military force made the realization of Japan as a peace state entirely possible, and allowed Japan to build up not only her economic prowess, but also enable Japan to acquire an unprecedented amount of cultural capital, international respect and soft power (Vyas 2011). Thus today, many Japanese believe that pacifism and democracy are two sides of the same coin. Some believes that any attempt to erode pacifism is equivalent to eroding democracy, as Abe has learnt. The Japanese democracy is therefore facing unprecedented challenge. The best way to understand this is to view democracy as one of the competing ideological influences that is competing for the hearts and minds of the Japanese electorate.

Beyond ideas, the Japanese electorate prizes stability, pragmatism, traditionalism and cultural pride. In choosing their leaders, the Japanese people want these values, but on top of this they are often attracted to particular traits: strength and resistance—against great powers, against bullies against anything that Japanese feel that they do not stand for. They also value political brand names (hence the phenomenon of political dynasties in Japan). Thus, it is no surprise that the Japanese electorate would worship any politician who is able to articulate a romanticized notion of restoration and rejuvenation whilst using language that allude to tradition and democratic values at the same time (these two sets of values might not necessary match) as they address current concerns. Nakasone, Koizumi, Abe, Ishihara and Hashimoto are some who have projected the strongest and most appealing image in that sense (either through it is an image manipulation or pedigree) and who can persuasively convince the electorate that if elected, each (of them) will strongly articulate their interests, stimulate and preserve Japanese growth and restore Japanese tradition. These leaders are strongmen, not democrats, and ironically in a democratic Japan, they have the longest political longevity. These leaders will inevitably exhibit a strong leadership vis-à-vis other "strong" states in the international era (Satoh 2010), and guide Japan through the tempestuous waters of international politics and perilous economic times. In short, even if ordinary Japanese folks might be-pacifists and democrats at heart, their perspective view of international politics is informed by hardcore realpolitik ideals that they believe only hardcore realists such as the neo-Conservatives or nationalist politicians can rise to the challenge.

At the same time, the same people who elect these strong leaders often do so out of a sense of propriety and fear—in particular fear of economic collapse. Thus at a critical juncture, the electorate often reach out to the party that oversaw postwar growth. The LDP provides this, simply because of her non-democratic methods to remain as the dominant party throughout the War. To that extent, the electorate can support contradictory policies even at the expense of their democratic values. Like Prime Minister Abe, the Japanese nation largely did not see a problem in Abe's articulation of the values-based diplomacy against the authoritarian China, Prime Minister reaching out to Vietnamese government (a Communist regime), to current Philippines President Duterte (a strongman who has little regard for human rights given his extra-judicial campaign at home), and to the Southeast Asian states like Myanmar or Malaysia and to Russia. Realpolitik, as opposed to democratic values drives these policies. These contradictory views need not be surprising. It is entirely possible for a country to preach and practice liberalism and democracy within her borders and practice realpolitik in her foreign relations with little regard for democratic values. Whether it is in Taisho Japan or the United States under George Bush, democracies can implement imperialistic or neo-imperialistic foreign policy. In today's Japan, as much as the Japanese pride themselves as a democracy, domestically, the rights of Okinawa residents are being sacrificed in the name of national security (McCormack and Norimatsu 2012; McCormack and Aritza 2017) Therefore, just because a country espouses to be a democracy, one should not automatically assume that her foreign policy will be infused with democratic values. In all fairness however, there strong democratic voices of clarity emanating from Japanese civil society to challenge all that Abe and the neo-Conservatives stand for. As Koichii Nakano at Sophia University says about "Japan is Great" boom: "The economy of Japan continues to be in recession, its per capita GDP has been overtaken by Korea … The Abe government's repressive stance leading to repeated streamroller-voting in the Diet continues to undermine the dignity of the citizens. If we could become a nation that though about each and every person, we could put an end to the sobriquet 'Japan is great'" (Nakano cited in Shirana and Ikeda 2017: 5).

However, the Abe administration still faces a polity with deep seeded aversion to the State, the politicians and to the use of military force in general. As Oros notes (2017: 150), polling data has suggested that Japanese views of how to best provide for Japan's security has not been transformed by a more hostile environment. Even though the Japanese people recognize the challenges of a rising China and a belligerent DPRK (Hughes 2009; Landler 2018), they also recognize that the revision of the Constitution and the remilitarization of Japan [as encouraged by the United States (Shirana and Ikeda 2017: 1)] are detrimental to the values modern Japan holds dear. To that extent, even though reaffirming the US-Japan alliance might be the least offensive of the options they could take, the Japanese people have yet to figure out what is the best course of action to enhance their security both domestically and externally. This is to ensure that the achievements of postwar generation and the way of life of modern Japan are not sacrificed in the name of national security, and that Japan would continue its resurgence as a great nation and a responsible member of the international community in time to come. As Satoh (2010: 586) argues, we might now be seeing the clearest signs that democratic participation is replacing quiescent citizen obedience in Japan. At the same time, the desire for Japan to be a responsible member of the international community is providing resistance to the assertive state nationalist project that is currently underway. There is no question that Japan's democratic resilience will continue to moderate the excesses of the Japanese government for the foreseeable future.

References

Advisory Panel on the History of the 20th Century and on Japan's Role and the World Order in the 21st Century [APH20C], (Translated by Tara Cannon), Toward the Abe Statement on the 70th Anniversary of the End of World War II, (originally published as *Sengo 70 nen danwa no ronten* by Nikkei Publishing Inc, 2015), Tokyo: Japan Publishing Industry Foundation for Culture, 2017.

Bamba, N., & Howes, J.F. *Pacifism in Japan: The Christian and Socialist Tradition.* Vancouver: University of British Columbia Press, 1978.

Berger, T. *Cultures of Antimilitarism: National Security in Germany and Japan.* Baltimore, MD: Johns Hopkins University Press, 1998.

Berger, T. *War, Guilt and World Politics.* Cambridge: Cambridge University Press, 2012.

Blacker, C. *The Japanese Enlightenment: A Study of the Writings of Fukuzawa Yukichi.* Cambridge: University of Cambridge Press, 1964.

Brownlee, J.S. translated. "The Jeweled Comb-Box: Motoori Norinaga's Tamakushige." *Monumenta Nipponica* vol. 43, no.1, 1988, 45–61.

Catalinac A.L. "From Pork to Policy: The Rise of Programmatic Campaigning in Japanese Elections" The Journal of Politics. 2015;78 (1):1–18.

Chen-Weiss, Jessica. *Powerful Patriots: Nationalist Protest in China's Foreign Relations.* Oxford and New York: Oxford University Press, 2014.

Chien, S., & Fitzgerald, J. *The Dignity of Nations: Equality, Competition and Honor in East Asian Nationalism.* Hong Kong: The University of Hong Kong Press, 2006.

Dian, M. *The Evolution of the US-Japan Alliance: The Eagle and the Chrysanthemum.* Oxford: Chandos Publishing 2014.

Dower, J. *Empire and Aftermath: Yoshida Shigeru and the Japanese Experience, 1878–1954.* Cambridge: Harvard University Press, 1979 & 1988.

Faiola, A. "In Japan, the Lipstick Ninjas Get Out the Vote." *The Washington Post*, 3 September 2005.

Frankel, M. "Japan Inc." and "Nixon Shocks." *The New York Times*, Nov 25 1971.

Fukui, H. *Party in power: the Japanese Liberal-Democrats and policy-making.* Canberra: Australian National University Press, 1970, https://openresearch-repository.anu.edu.au/handle/1885/115041

Fukuzawa, Y. (1875). *An Outline of a Theory of Civilization,* (Retranslation based on the 1969 Keio Japanese version) David Dilworth & Cameron Hurst, New York: Columbia University Press, 2008.

Fukuzawa, Y. *Autobiography of Yukichi Fukuzawa,* (Revised Translation by Eiichi Kiyooka), New York: Columbia University Press, 2007 Edition.

Funabashi, Y. "New Centrist Conservatism", *The Japan Times*, 15 January 2016. https://www.japantimes.co.jp/opinion/2016/01/15/commentary/japan-commentary/new-centrist-conservatism/

Green, M. *Arming Japan: Defense Production, Alliance Politics, and the Postwar Search for Autonomy.* New York: Columbia University Press, 1995.

Hamano, S.B. "Incomplete Revolutions and Not so Alien Transplants: The Japanese Constitution and Human Rights." *Journal of Constitutional Law, University of Pennsylvania,* vol. 3, no. 1, pp 415–490.

Hastings, M. *The Korean War.* London, Simon and Schuster, 1988.

Hoey, F. *Sato, America and the Cold War: US-Japanese Relations 1964–1972.* New York and London, Palgrave Macmillan, 2015.

Hoffman, R. "Why Steve Bannon Admires Japan", *The Diplomat*, 22 June 2018.
Hoppens, R. *The China Problem in Postwar Japan: Japanese National Identity and Sino-Japanese Relations.* London: Bloomsbury, 2015.
Hoshino, T., & Satoh, H. Through the Looking Glass? China's Rise as Seen from Japan, *Journal of Asian Public Policy*, 2012, Vol. 5, No. 2: 181–198.
Hughes, C.W. *Japan's Remilitarisation.* London, Routledge for International Institute for Strategic Studies, 2009.
Hunter-Chester, David. *Creating Japan's Ground Self-Defense Force: A Sword Well Made, 1945–2015*, London: Rowman and Littlefield (Lexington Books), 2016.
Iokibe, M. "Fukuda Takeo: Winner in Policy, Loser in Politics" in Watanabe, A. (ed). *The Prime Ministers of Postwar Japan 1945–1995: Their Lives and Their Times*, (Translated by Robert D. Eldridge), London: Rowman and Littlefield (Lexington Books), 2016.
Johnson, C. "The 1955 System and the American Connection: A Bibliographic Introduction." JPRI Working Paper No. 11, July 1995, http://www.jpri.org/publications/workingpapers/wp11.html
Kantei Japan. "General Policy Speech by Prime Minister Junichiro Koizumi to the 156th Session of the Diet", 31 Jan 2003, https://japan.kantei.go.jp/koizumispeech/2003/01/31sisei_e.html
Katsube, Seigyi. *Sento zuihitsu* (ca 1785–88) In vol. 6 of *Zuihitsu hyakkaen*, ed. Mori Senzo et al. Chuo Koronsha, 1983.
Katzenstein, P. *Cultural Norms and National Security: Police and Military in Post War Japan.* Ithaca: 1998.
Katzenstein, P. *The Culture of National Security.* Columbia University Press, 1996.
Kissinger, H. *The White House Years.* Boston: Little, Brown and Co. Book Club, 1979.
Kissinger, H. *Years of Upheaval.* Boston: Little Brown and Co. 1982.
Kitaoka, S., "Kishi Nobusuke: Frustrated Ambition" in Watanabe, A. (ed). *The Prime Ministers of Postwar Japan 1945–1995: Their Lives and Their Times*, (Translated by Robert D. Eldridge), London: Rowman and Littlefield (Lexington Books), 2016.
Kitaoka, I. *Nihon Honshu Shugi.* Tokyo: Ocha Nomizu Shubo, 1992.
Koga, Y. *Inheritance of Loss: China, Japan, and the Political Economy of Redemption after Empire* (Studies of the Weatherhead East Asian Institute) University of Chicago Press; 1 edition (November 28, 2016).
Kosaka, M. "Sato Eisaku: The Truth about the Politics of Waiting" in Watanabe, A. (ed). *The Prime Ministers of Postwar Japan 1945–1995: Their Lives and Their Times*, (Translated by Robert D. Eldridge), London: Rowman and Littlefield (Lexington Books), 2016.
Kupchan, C. *How Enemies Become Friends: The Sources of Stable Peace.* Princeton and Oxford: CFR-Princeton University Press, 2010.

Kusano, A. "Nakasone Yasuhiro: The Appearance of a Presidential Prime Minister" in Watanabe, A. (ed). *The Prime Ministers of Postwar Japan 1945–1995: Their Lives and Their Times*, (Translated by Robert D. Eldridge), London: Rowman and Littlefield (Lexington Books), 2016.

Lai, Y.M. *Nationalism and Power Politics in Japan's Relations with China: A Neoclassical Realist Interpretation*, Oxford and New York: Routledge, 2014.

Landler, M. "North Korea Asks for Direct Nuclear Talks, and Trump Agrees." *The New York Times*, 8 March 2018.

Leung, P.E. *"China's Quasi-War with Japan: The Dispute Over the Ryukyu (Liu-Chiu) Islands"*, 1871, UC Santa Barbara, 1978 available at Proquest Dissertation database.

Mark, C. *The Abe Restoration*. Maryland: Rowan and Littlefield, 2016.

Maruyama, M. *Studies in the Intellectual History of Tokugawa Japan* (1975), New Jersey: Princeton University Press (Paper pack Reprint 2014).

Matsuzawa, Y. Dreams and Frustration of Liberal Democratic Movement, Tokyo: Iwanami Shoten, 2016 [松沢 裕作、自由民権運動〈デモクラシー〉の夢と挫折、岩波書店, 2016].

McCormack, G. *Client State: Japan in the American Embrace*. London and New York: Verso, 2007.

McCormack, G. "Conservatism" and "Nationalism". *The Asia-Pacific Journal: Japan Focus, in The Puzzle*, vol. 6, no. 6, 2008, https://apjjf.org/-Gavan-McCormack/2786/article.pdf

McCormack, G., & Aritza, S. The Japanese State Versus the People of Okinawa: Rolling Arrests and Prolonged and Punitive Detention, *The Asia-Pacific Journal: Japan Focus*, Vol. 15, Issue 2, No. 4, Jan 2017.

McCormack, G., & Norimatsu, S.O. *Resistant Islands: Okinawa Confronts Japan and the United States*. Maryland: Rowman and Littlefield Publishers, 2012.

Middlebrooks, W. *Beyond Pacifism: Why Japan must become a "Normal" Nation*. Praeger: Connecticut and London, 2008.

Morris, I. *Nationalism and the Right Wing in Japan: A Study of Post War Trends*. London and New York: Oxford University Press, 1960.

Mulgan, A.G. *Ozawa Ichiro and Japanese Politics: Old Versus New*. Oxford and New York: Routledge, 2015.

Nagai, K & Toshitani, N, eds. *Shiryo Nihonkoku Kenpo (Document: The Constitution of Japan)* Vol. 2 and 3 (Tokyo: Sanseido) 1986. 永井憲一、利谷信義編『資料日本国憲法2・3』(三省堂、1986).

Nakamura, M. *Shoburon* (1843), In Vol. 6 of *Bushido Zensho*, ed., Inoue Tetsujiro, Saeki Ariyoshi, Ueki Naoichiro, and Kokusho Kankokai, 1998.

Nakano, K. "The Death of Liberalism in Japan", *The New York Times*, 15 Oct 2017, https://www.nytimes.com/2017/10/15/opinion/liberalism-japan-election.html

O'Dwyer, E. *Significant Soil: Settler Colonialism and Japan's Urban Empire in Manchuria*, Harvard University Asia Center, 2015.

Onishi, N. "Why Japan Seems to be Content to Be Run by One Party", *The New York Times*, Sep 7, 2005, https://www.nytimes.com/2005/09/07/world/asia/why-japan-seems-content-to-be-run-by-one-party.html

Onishi, N. "Koizumi Exits Office as He Arrived: Defiant on War Shrine." *The New York Times* August 16, 2006, https://www.nytimes.com/2006/08/16/world/asia/16japan.html

Oros, A. *Japan's Security Renaissance: New Policies and Politics for the Twenty-First Century*. New York: Columbia University Press, 2017.

Overholt, W. Asia, *America and the Transformation of Geopolitics*, Cambridge: Cambridge University Press, 2007.

Ozawa, I & Gower, E. eds, *Blueprint for a New Japan: The Rethinking of a Nation*. Tokyo: Kodansha, 1994.

Paine, S.C.M. *The Japanese Empire: Grand Strategy from Meiji Restoration to the Pacific War*. Cambridge: Cambridge University Press, 2017.

Park, C.H. "Conservative Conceptions of Japan as a "Normal Country: Comparing Ozawa, Nakasone and Ishihara" in Soeya, Y., Tadakoro, M. & Welch, D.A., *Japan as "Normal Country"? A Nation in Search of its Place in the world*. Toronto: University of Toronto Press, 2011.

Pyle, K. *Japan Rising: The Resurgence of Japanese Power and Purpose*. New York: Public Affairs Perseus Books Group, 2007.

Richardson, B. *Political Culture of Japan*, Berkeley, UC Press, 1974.

Rousseau, D. *Identifying Threats and Threatening Identities: The Social Construction of Realism and Liberalism*. California: Stanford University Press, 2006.

Rose, C. "The Battle for Hearts and Minds: Patriotic Education in Japan in the 1990s and Beyond" in Shimazu, N., *Nationalisms in Japan*, Oxford and New York, 2006.

Pulsford, A., Bhattarai, N., & Shibuya, H. "March 11 disasters a turning point for Japanese civil Society." *The Japan Times*, Sep 15, 2011.

Sado, A. *The Self Defense Forces and Postwar Politics* (First published in 2006 and translated by Noda Makito), Tokyo: Japan Publishing Industry Foundation for Culture (JPIC), 2017.

Sakamoto, K. "Visits to Yasukuni Shrine by the Prime Minister and Japan-China Relations: What is Confusing about the Debate?", published in [阪大法学] The Law Association of Osaka University, Vol. 64, No. 3,4, 2014, https://www.jiia-jic.jp/en/resourcelibrary/pdf/Sakamoto_Visits_to_Yasukuni_Shrine_by_the_Prime_Minister_and_Japan-China_Relations_What_is_Confusing_the_Debate.pdf

Samuels, R. "Japan's Shifting Strategic Discourse, Sigur Center for Asian Studies Policy Brief", Jan 2013, pp 1–6, http://www.risingpowersinitiative.org/wp-content/uploads/policybrief_jan2013_japan.pdf

Samuels, R.J. *"Rich Nation, Strong Army": National Security and the Technological Transformation of Japan.* Ithaca, NY: Cornell University Press, 1994.

Satoh, H. Legitimacy Deficit in Japan: The Road to True Popular Sovereignty, *Politics and Policy*, Vol. 38, No. 3, 2010, pp 571–588.

Schaller, M. America's Favorite War Criminal: Kishi Nobusuke and the Transformation of U.S.-Japan Relations. JPRI Working Paper No. 11, July 1995, http://www.jpri.org/publications/workingpapers/wp11.html

Schaller, M. "The Nixon Shocks and US-Japan Strategy Relations (1969–74)", The University of Arizona, Working Paper No. 2, 1996 https://nsarchive2.gwu.edu/japan/schaller.htm

Schneider, E. *Democracy without Competition in Japan.* New York, Cambridge University Press, 2006.

Shimazu, N. *Nationalisms in Japan.* Oxford and New York, 2006.

Shinkawa, T., Miki Takeo: Politics of Conviction and Public Opinion in Watanabe, A. (ed). *The Prime Ministers of Postwar Japan 1945–1995: Their Lives and Their Times*, (Translated by Robert D. Eldridge), London: Rowman and Littlefield (Lexington Books), 2016.

Shirana, M., & Ikeda, T. (introduction by Nakano K.). "Japan is Great", *The Asia-Pacific Journal: Japan Focus*, Vol. 15, Issue 3, Feb 2017.

Smith, Sheila A. *Japan's New Politics and the U.S.-Japan Alliance.* Washington D.C.: Council for Foreign Relations, 2014.

Smith, S. *Intimate Rivals: Japanese Domestic Politics and a Rising China.* New York: CPR-Columbia University Press Book, 2015.

Soeya, Y. "A Normal Middle Power: Interpreting Changes in Japanese Security Policy in the 1990s and After" in Soeya, Y., Tadakoro, M. & Welch, D.A., *Japan as "Normal Country"? A Nation in Search of its Place in the world.* Toronto: University of Toronto Press, 2011.

Soeya, Y., Tadakoro, M., & Welch, D.A., *Japan as "Normal Country"? A Nation in Search of its Place in the world.* Toronto: University of Toronto Press, 2011.

Strom, Stephanie. "Japan's Ultimate Insider: The Premier's Secretary." *The New York Times*, 26 June 2001, https://www.nytimes.com/2001/06/26/world/japan-s-ultimate-insider-the-premier-s-secretary.html

Tamanoi, M.A. 2009 *Memory Maps: The State and Manchuria in Postwar Japan.* Honolulu: University of Hawaii Press.

Tanaka, A. (translated by Hoff, J.C.). *Japan in Asia: Post Cold War Diplomacy*, (first published 2007 in Japanese), Tokyo: Japan Publishing Industry Foundation for Culture (JPIC), 2017.

Tanaka, A. "Why has the LDP Stayed in Power so Long in Post-War Japan?: Democratic System Support and Electoral Behavior." UC Irvine Centre for the Study of Democracy Working Paper, 2007, https://escholarship.org/uc/item/5gm0f2jf

Takahashi, T. "Abe's Campaign to revise Japan's Constitution", East Asia Forum, 15 June 2013, http://www.eastasiaforum.org/2013/06/15/abes-campaign-to-revise-japans-constitution/

Takahashi, T. "Japanese Neo-Conservatism: Coping with China and North Korea", *Security Challenges*. Vol. 6, No.3 (Spring 2010) pp 21–40.

Takahashi, T. "The National Politics of Yasukuni Shrine in Shimazu, N., *Nationalisms in Japan*, Oxford and New York, 2006.

Takahashi, T. "Why Abe is pushing for the right to collective self-defence", East Asia Forum, 20 June 2014, http://www.eastasiaforum.org/2014/06/20/why-abe-is-pushing-for-the-right-to-collective-self-defence/#more-42220

Tawara, Y. What is the Aim of Nippon Kaigi, the Ultra-Right Organization that Supports Japan's Abe Administration ?", The Asia-Pacific Journal: Japan Focus, Vol. 15, No.1 1st Nov 2017.

Taylor, A. "Japan in the 1950s." *The Atlantic*, 12 March 2014, https://www.theatlantic.com/photo/2014/03/japan-in-the-1950s/100697/

Tominomori, E. *Nihongata Minshuhugi no Kozu*. Tokyo: ND Books, 1993.

Vosse, W., Drifte, R., & Blechinger-Talcott, V. *Governing Insecurity in Japan: The Domestic Discourse and Policy Response*. Oxford and New York: Routledge, 2017.

Vyas, U. *Soft Power in Japan-China Relations: State, sub-state and non-state relations*. Oxford and New York: Routledge, 2011.

Watanabe, H. *A History of Japanese Political Thought, 1600–1901*. Translated by David Noble. LTCB International Library Trust, International House of Japan, 2012.

Watanabe, A. (ed). *The Prime Ministers of Postwar Japan 1945–1995: Their Lives and Their Times*, (Translated by Robert D. Eldridge), London: Rowman and Littlefield (Lexington Books), 2016.

Will, G.F. "The Legacy of Japan's Lion Heart." *The Washington Post*, 24 August 2006, https://www.washingtonpost.com/archive/opinions/2006/08/24/the-legacy-of-japans-lion-heart/5562dba3-04ee-47e9-bba8-7caa8402a393/?utm_term=.30e665c9206d

Winter, M. Abe and the Bureaucracy: Tightening the Reins, *The Diplomat*, 16 June 2016, https://thediplomat.com/2016/06/abe-and-the-bureacracy-tightening-the-reins/

Winkler, C. *The Quest for Japan's New Constitution: An Analysis of Visions and Constitutional Reform Proposals*. 1980–2009, Oxford and New York: Routledge, 2011.

Yomiuri Shimbun Political News Department. (Translated by John Rossman). *Perspectives on Sino-Japanese Diplomatic Relations*, Tokyo: Japan Publishing Industry Foundation for Culture (JPIC), 2017.

Yuasa, Jozan. *Bunkai zakki* (n.d.) In *Nihon zuihitsu taisei, (ed) Nihon Zuihitsu Taisei Henshubu*, first series, vol. 14, Yoshikawa Kokunkan, 1993.

Yoshida, S. (Ed by Hiroshi Nara). *Yoshida Shigeru: Last Meiji Man* (Translated from Japanese Edition in 1961). Plymouth: Roman and Littlefield, 2007.

Yamamoto, M. *Grassroots Pacifism in Post-War Japan*. Oxford and New York: Routledge Curzon, 2004.

孫崎 享, 戦後史の正体 (「戦後再発見」双書1) 単行本, 東京,創元社, 2012.

Open Access This chapter is licensed under the terms of the Creative Commons Attribution 4.0 International License (http://creativecommons.org/licenses/by/4.0/), which permits use, sharing, adaptation, distribution and reproduction in any medium or format, as long as you give appropriate credit to the original author(s) and the source, provide a link to the Creative Commons licence and indicate if changes were made.

The images or other third party material in this chapter are included in the chapter's Creative Commons licence, unless indicated otherwise in a credit line to the material. If material is not included in the chapter's Creative Commons licence and your intended use is not permitted by statutory regulation or exceeds the permitted use, you will need to obtain permission directly from the copyright holder.

CHAPTER 3

Japan's Rejuvenation and the US-China Divide

> The main focus of Japanese foreign affairs in Meiji, Taisho and even Showa eras concerned China … but what was interesting is that the elite course for career advancement in the Ministry was not curiously, "China service" or looking after Japan's interest in China, and definitely not holding posts in Japanese Consulates in China. The sunniest road to success in the ministry had traditionally been assignments in capitals and large cities in Europe and the United States, such as London; Paris; Berlin; Washington D.C.
>
> Prime Minister Yoshida Shigeru, 1961

> If you consider the case of aggression carried out against Japan, will the UN protect us? Of course not. Japan cannot maintain peace and security for the nation all by itself, so we have signed the US-Japan Treaty … I do not think the UN would form a UN force to protect Japan from invasion.
>
> Prime Minister Junichiro Koizumi, 2004

> It is necessary for the United States to take a fresh look at the relative value of Japan to the U.S. and the world, as well as what Japan has to offer to the U.S. and to the world … Japan is not a dependent state, it's not a Puerto Rico to the U.S. and this is something both nations must recognize … I think that the U.S. should be

seriously questioning whether there is real value in defending Japan. The U.S. must be explicitly clear in its answer to this question. If the answer is no, then Japan will make up its own mind to defend itself, and our efforts to defend ourselves may lead to the nuclear armament that everyone is concerned about.

Tokyo Governor Ishihara Shintaro, 2012

Japan's Asia Strategy and the US-China Challenge

The onset of the Cold War and the subsequent implementation of the San Francisco system witnessed the birth of one of the most successful about-turns in the bilateral relationship between the US and Japan. In a short span of six decades, it has moved from enmity to friendship. Over half a century, Japan steered clear of foreign military adventurism as it focused its efforts to grow its economy to become one of the largest in the world. Japan's relationship with China has taken on a very different trajectory. Like the US, the Chinese fought a bitter war with Japan. The conflict between China and Japan began about 44 years before the bombing of Pearl Harbor, in 1898, when the first Sino-Japanese war was fought. By the time the Japanese surrendered, China was deeply embroiled in a civil war between nationalist and communist forces. With the defeat of the nationalists, and the founding of the People's Republic, Japan's relations with China bifurcated into an official relationship with the nationalist Republic of China (at the behest of Washington) and an unofficial relationship with communist China that was constrained and low key. By 1972, with the realignment between the US and China, Japan followed suit and switched recognition between Beijing and Taipei. By the 1980s, relations between China and Japan reached new heights, last seen during the Tang dynasty. The end of the Cold War brought a diametrically opposite implication for Japan's relations with the US and its relations with China.

The US-Japan partnership was called into question in the early 1990s as the principal nemesis and the fundamental reason for the US-Japan alliance, the USSR, disintegrated. As Japan struggled to debate on the future of the alliance and the direction of its diplomacy, a parallel process was happening in China. Deng's reforms had taken off remarkably and in the 1990s, analysts from Washington to Singapore to Tokyo were debating the implications of the rapid rise of China economically and consequently politically and strategically. By the mid-1990s, differences between China and Japan began to surface. The rise of China has been particularly problematic over the last two decades for Japan. First, from Japan's vantage point, China is seen to be more aggressive as it grows its economy. Second, Sino-Japanese relations took a dip from the mid-1990s onwards over a range of issues: China's nuclear test, the Taiwan Straits Crisis, democratization issues in Hong Kong and Taiwan, confrontations over gas deposits in the East China Sea, and the issues over the Senkaku Islands. Domestically within Japan, generational change meant that the special place China held in the hearts of the wartime generation no longer was dominant in public narratives and worldviews. This shift in attitude was accompanied by a hardened nationalistic discourse. Mutual demonization in both China and Japan is now the norm, not the exception. The challenges are real, but their magnification by international and domestic media has created a real sense of urgency and crisis in Japan. This has generated a national consensus that the US-Japan alliance is to be reaffirmed to meet the challenges facing Japan, prompting a measured support to rally behind the neo-conservatives' agenda, even though it is against the grain of Japanese pacifist and democratic culture. Over the course of the next two decades, Japan's relations with China deteriorated drastically to the point that Beijing and Tokyo have become major strategic competitors in the truest sense of the world, locked in what analysts would term as the Thucydides' Trap, driven by insecurity, competing interests and a nationalistic struggle for honor.

Japan's relations with the US took on a very different trajectory. By the early 1990s, Washington and Tokyo came to a consensus that the alliance was needed to provide continued support to the peace and security that Asia has enjoyed since the end of the Vietnam War. First, international reactions to Japan's checkbook diplomacy in the aftermath of the Gulf War led to both shock and dismay within Japan. This prompted a rethinking and reorientation of Japanese diplomacy better to meet its international challenges, and also a deep hard introspective look at Japanese demands and needs from this bilateral relationship. Japan realizes that it cannot be as "disengaged" from the world as it was during the Cold War, and Japanese diplomacy has to match the aspirations of the new era. Second, Tokyo decided that the best strategy Japan could undertake was to engage or confront a rising China and a belligerent North Korea. China-Japan relations were for most part cordial from the 1970s till the mid-1990s, with the exception being the brief period that China came under sanctions for the Tiananmen Square incident. Until the late 1990s, China was never construed as a national security threat. By the mid-1990s, the "China threat" was discussed in moderate tones, but by the turn of the millennium, the hysteria over the North Korean missiles overflying Japan led to the framing of the rising China and a belligerent North Korea being discussed openly in Japan's security narratives. The US-Japan alliance was always portrayed by the US and its allies as the anchor of stability in the region (Armitage and Nye 2012).

The strategic threats and the election of Prime Minister Koizumi (April 2001–September 2006) provided the opportunity and basis for a conservative resurgence to emerge in Japan. Koizumi's priorities were never about China in the first place. His primary concerns were domestic and economic, and his political strategy relatively unorthodox. Until the September 11 attacks, he believed in adjusting Japan's foreign policy posture to ensure that Japan would continue fulfilling its international commitments. Koizumi's popularity was unprecedented largely because of two attributes. He had an excellent media team, which was very able in cultivating the tabloids as opposed to the traditional mainstream broadsheets, and generating public support independent of the traditional factional support system within the LDP. Thus, he was able to turn the tables on the powerful bureaucracy (such as the all-important Ministry of Finance and Ministry of Industry and Trade) and had the *Kantei* issue policies to the bureaucrats as opposed to being told what to do by the bureaucrats, as in the past. His popularity enabled him to challenge the traditional patronage system and pork-barrel politics and challenge powerful constituents—the bureaucracy, big business and the LDP itself. His resolve to tackle the woefully inefficient postal savings system and to change the nature of politics led his era to be known as "The Koizumi Restoration"—an attempt to compare him to the Meiji elites (*The Economist*, September 14, 2006). *The Economist* also wistfully notes that he did not achieve the constitutional amendment, which is something he should have focused on, as was the disastrous China policy his successor inherited. Koizumi's popularity rested on the image that he projected to the electorate—his resistance to the LDP Party *genros* and their corrupt ways of doing things, and his preservation of traditional Japanese values and cultures, in particular his appreciation of all those who sacrificed themselves for their country. This is exemplified by his repeated annual visits to the Yasukuni Shrine, despite Chinese pressure. By the end of Koizumi's tenure in 2006, there was a popular joke between Chinese and Japanese analysts that the greatest achievement of Prime Minister Koizumi was that he had caused bilateral relations to deteriorate to the extent that they could not get any worse—apart from outright declaration of war between China and Japan.

The next several years (2006–2012) saw the rapid rise and descent of several prime ministers on a revolving door basis. Prime Minister Koizumi was succeeded by Prime Minister Abe (Sept. 2006–Sept. 2007), then Prime Minister Yasuo Fukuda (Sept. 2007–Sept. 2008) and then Prime Minister Taro Aso (Sept. 2008–Sept. 2009) and finally, before the LDP was defeated at the polls, by Yukio Hatoyama (Sept. 2009–June 2010) of the DPJ. The DPJ's tenure did not last very long as Hatoyama was successively replaced by Naoto Kan (June 2010–Sept. 2011) and Yoshihiko Noda (Sept. 2011–Dec. 2012). Prime Minister Abe won the second election and became the second longest-serving prime minister in postwar Japan.

There are two reasons why Sino-Japanese relations deteriorated during Koizumi's era. The first concerned the latitude that the prime minister had in foreign affairs, particular in his dealings with China. Distracted by the Wars on Terror, the Bush administration neither had the time, expertise nor attention to keep track of what was going on between China and Japan. Both were important allies in the War on Terror, and US foreign policy played a relatively neutral role in their contestation over interpretations of history and other issues. Despite this, the US emerged out of this period as the clear winner in its Asian strategy, simply because Japan had embraced the US-Japan alliance tighter as Sino-Japanese relations spiraled downwards, and the Chinese in turn felt helpless over the maverick politicians in Tokyo they had little sway over. Many in Beijing felt that only the US could reason with the Japanese, and if the US-Japan alliance was tightened, then this might be a good thing as Beijing could rely on the US to sway or tame Tokyo. Consequently, by the time Koizumi's era ended, both Tokyo and Beijing were reaching out to the US as a mediator of sorts to calm issues between them. The Bush administration's hands-off policy had paid off surreptitiously.

Prime Minister Koizumi's immediate successor was his chief cabinet secretary Shinzo Abe. In his first term as prime minister, Abe started by making constitutional amendment a priority, but this did not go down well with the electorate, as many of the Japanese voters had voted LDP because of their desire for economic growth and stability. Prime Minister Yasuo Fukuda largely helped heal Sino-Japanese relations by signaling Japan's desire to work with China and signed the fourth political instrument that contemporary Sino-Japanese relations is predicated upon, with both China and Japan agreeing to premise their relations upon "mutually beneficial strategic interests."

This period of brief respite did not last very long, as by 2010 the Chinese and Japanese were at loggerheads over the detention of a Chinese boat crew that had been fishing off the vicinity of the Senkaku Islands. It involved a high-speed chase in which the boat crew is alleged to have rammed one of the Japanese Coast Guard ships. Japan released the video of the chase and the incident inflamed nationalistic sentiments on both sides. The episode only ended when the Chinese arrested four Japanese nationals for espionage (with the prospects of a capital sentence) and only then did Japan release the Chinese nationals.

To date, most of the efforts in "normalizing" Japan focused on chipping away at the constraints imposed by Japan's constitution so that the US-Japan alliance could function more effectively (Martin 2016). Hence from the mid-1990s onwards, Japan has instituted frequent bilateral meetings with the US to work out measures to tighten the alliance through more frequent working consultations, passing primary and secondary legislation to facilitate the alliance. This started in earnest after the Japan-US Joint Declaration on Security Alliance for the twenty-first century (The Clinton–Hashimoto agreement) in 1996, and has continued largely unabated to this day. This primary and secondary legislation, as well as discussions and dialogs, allowed for JSDF operations to be harmonized with the missions of the US missions, and legitimized the deployments of JSDF units beyond traditional geographical and functional constraints.

From Japan's point of view, these series of steps to "normalize" Japan would not only enhance the operational capability of the US-Japan alliance, but more effectively politically legitimize and legalize the role of Japan in regional and international security. This development also restored a certain "balance" to Japan's foreign policy as it removed one of the main criticisms levied at Japan as a "free-rider" in the alliance, enabling Japan to mature into a more "responsible" partner in terms of burden and risk sharing.

With the re-election of Prime Minister Abe in 2012, there was no question that the neo-conservative element's agenda of bringing incremental reforms to Japan's political institutions took on an added momentum (Soeya 2012; Martin 2016; McCormack 2016). Prime Minister Abe enacted a "proactive pacifism" doctrine, promising to transform Japan's security policy and enable Japan to exercise the right of "collective self-defense," which was actually unconstitutional until the prime minister changed its interpretation (Akimoto 2018). Even though this was somewhat controversial, it must be remembered that it was Prime Minister Yoshida (and subsequently all other prime ministers) who had used a very conservative interpretation of Article 9 to fend off US pressure to rearm. Prime Minister Abe went against the grain and did the exact opposite of his Cold War predecessors: He remilitarized and increased Japan's global engagement (Kingston 2016).

One of the most important documents is the 1979 Guidelines for US-Japan Defense Cooperation, which was revised in 1997 and 2013. Under the new guidelines, the US and Japan recognized and planned for a greater and more flexible response to the possible threats surrounding Japan. On October 8, 2014, Japan and the US announced the publication of an interim review report on the six-decade US-Japan alliance.[1] This review effectively removed the geographical constraints on the US-Japan alliance that previously limited it to the "situations in areas surrounding Japan" established by a similar review in 1997.[2] This report also complements Japan's decision to change its interpretation of its constitution and lift the ban on collective self-defense in July 2014 that effectively allowed Japan to use military force to assist its principal ally, the US, should it come under attack. The October report further indicated that the US-Japan alliance would remain a cornerstone of US policy in Asia's and Japan's foreign policy for the next quarter of the century, cementing the cooperation between the US in marine safety, intelligence gathering and missile defense, from "peacetime to contingencies." This development not only broke from Japan's pacifist tradition, but enabled Japan basically to intervene in an operation, should the US go to war in the name of self-defense, or enter a conflict that extended well beyond its backyard. This of course has raised concerns, not only from China but also from other US allies such as South Korea.[3] Many Japanese mistakenly believe that the Chinese or Korean governments are not convinced that they have been rehabilitated—this is not strictly true. Most Chinese and Koreans think the world of Japanese people and culture—it's the Japanese politicians that they have trouble trusting.

Prime Minister Abe also lifted the ban on weapons exports in the same year in the same creative manner that Japan had used when defending the Senkaku Islands. Tokyo had skirted the constitutional constraints on

---

[1] See media release by the US Department of State, October 8, 2014, http://www.state.gov/r/pa/prs/ps/2014/10/232694.htm

[2] See The Guidelines for Japan-US Defense Co-operation, http://www.mofa.go.jp/region/n-america/us/security/guideline2.html

[3] "U.S. official reassures South Korea over revision of defense guidelines with Japan," Kyodo News Agency, http://www.japantimes.co.jp/news/2014/10/06/national/politics-diplomacy/u-s-official-reassures-south-korea-over-revision-of-defense-guidelines-with-japan/#.VDwgxL5UhT8

increasing the armament of the maritime self-defense forces by transferring Japan's bigger warships to the Coast Guard. Deployments against Chinese vessels in the territorial waters around Senkaku actually constitute police enforcement action. In lifting this weapons ban, the prime minister has mandated that the weapons exports and transfers are made under the "overseas development assistance" packages. This allows for direct military ties to Southeast and South Asian countries, as the ODA rules allow for capacity and infrastructure building. The same weapons ban lift also applies to military technology transfer between allies (Jain 2017). Currently, Japan has only been successful in selling arms to three countries of significance to the South China Sea—the Philippines, Vietnam and India (Pejsova and Stanley-Lockman 2016). The Philippines (2013) and Vietnam received "donations" or "loans"—these are the two countries with the most antagonistic relations with China. The Philippines Coast Guard (PCG) received five patrol aircrafts as part of the bilateral Maritime Safety Capability Improvement Project, and a ten vessel donation in 2016, while the Vietnamese received in 2014, six secondhand vessels and also P-3C anti-submarine aircrafts. Japan is also in talks to sell 12 amphibious U2 Aircraft to India to allow it to beef up its maritime patrols in the Indian Ocean (Pejsova and Stanley-Lockman 2016). Japan has also tried its very best to rope India into the US-Japan alliance, but the effectiveness of India as an alliance partner remains to be seen.

Hideaki Watanabe, head of Japan's Defense Agency's Acquisition, Technology and Logistics Agency said that Japan's attempt to share weapons technology with ASEAN states is in direct response to "aggressive" attempts to change the status quo by some nations (*Straits Times*, June 12, 2017). Even though Prime Minister Abe is linking ODA with defense capability development and has built up the defense capacity of these states, there are limitations. First, much depends on the personal politics of the leaders. Then, the Philippines President Benigno Aquino III was staunchly pro-US and hence very anti-China, but his successor, President Rodrigo Duterte is pro-China. The latter, however, maintains good relations with both President Xi and Prime Minister Abe, accepting loans and aid from both sides. Thus, the attempt to rally Southeast Asian states against China is an on-going tussle, with no clear winners because ASEAN states usually remain neutral. On top of this, weapons donations alone are hardly adequate. Even if their capabilities are beefed up, these countries are still no match for China's military, nor have they been able to stop China from reclaiming and building artificial reefs in the region.

Photo: Japan lifted the ban on military exports and hardware in 2014. Japan is now exporting aircraft and vessels to countries such as the Philippines and Vietnam as a feature of its ODA, to "strengthen capacity." Japan is also negotiating with India about selling military aircraft. (Photo of a JSDF amphibious aircraft. The work is licensed under the Government of Japan Standard Terms of Use (Ver.2.0). The Terms of Use are compatible with the Creative Common Attribution License 4.0 International; image available: https://commons.wikimedia.org/wiki/File:Japan_Maritime_Self-Defense_Force_butai01_-_01.jpg)

Cautioning America's Unilateralism

There are of course politicians and segments of Japanese society who have imperatives to seek some sort of rebalance in Japan's relationship with the US, particularly with the election of Donald Trump. There are two reasons. The first of course has to do with Japan's indigenous development. The Cold War is over and Japan is no longer the weak, defeated nation it was after the Pacific War. The US-Japan alliance was conceived for a very different purpose and under very different circumstances. There is a recognition that even though the Yoshida Doctrine has served Japan well, it was also a shrewd neo-realist realpolitik maneuver on the part of Japan to make the best use of its circumstances at that time. The Yoshida Doctrine provided a shield used by successive Japanese prime ministers to resist US pressure for Japan to rearm or commit politically and militarily to fight the Cold War. Even though pacifism and the Yoshida Doctrine is being sold as a liability of the past and a legacy of the San Francisco system, the truth is that it was a question of judgment and interpretation of the *Kantei* (prime minister's office) as to which strategic direction to lean toward. Over the past two decades, the neo-conservatives have successfully managed to direct the political and strategic narratives to cast China as the dominant threat, and the US as the dominant savior and friend that can help Japan enhance its own security and protect its freedom. At another level, it might be even possible that the Japanese elites believe that only through the tightening of its embrace of the US, would it be bestowed with the trust and the latitude to rejuvenate as a global power. This is not something new.

Back in the 1970s, it was abundantly clear that Japan then was already keen to use its new-found economic strength in order to increase its power and leverage over the countries it provided assistance to. By the late 1980s, Japan was no longer the "weak" war-torn nation in the aftermath of the Second World War.[4] In military terms, Japan possesses the most formidable hardware in the whole of East Asia. It is only natural that Japan would seek to achieve political status commensurate with its level of economic development. However, by the 1980s, there were increased strains in the US-Japan relations, as politicians and scholars in the US debate the strength of their ally. The incessant Japanese purchase of prime real estate in Manhattan and Los Angeles, the rise of Japan's technological and manufacturing prowess and the dominance of the Japanese yen all but suggest that, in its economic ascent, Japan would threaten to overshadow the US. Japan's rise during the 1980s foreshadowed a similar path that China would take about three decades later. Yet, by the 1990s, Japan's rise was stymied by a variety of political and economic factors, but many Japanese commentators privately groused that US containment was at least part of the reason for Japan's failed rejuvenation.

---

[4] By almost all measures, Japan is an extremely wealthy and powerful nation. Until 2010, Japan was the world's second largest economy. World Bank data showed that in 2017, Japan's GDP was USD 4872 trillion, and on a per capita basis, USD 38,428. Even though China's economy overtook Japan's as the second largest economy in the last quarter of 2010 (China GDP for 2013 was USD 9.24 trillion), Japan's GDP per capita basis is still over six times that of China's (USD 6807). Therefore, at the height of its supposed stagnation, the average Japanese person was not feeling the effects of the so-called "depression."

However, this did not quell Japan's ambition to normalize or its desire for rejuvenation as a global power. The end of the Gulf War and the rise of China provided further impetuses. The lessons learned during the 1980s have not been forgotten, even though they are not articulated too loudly in Japan today lest it prematurely depletes one's political capital. With the new generation coming to the fore, and the dominance of the media in framing the nation's challenges, the concerns of pacifism have been completely overwhelmed by the seemingly difficult political and strategic circumstances Japan faces externally. For that reason, traditional concerns with the US are articulated in private discourse, not public narratives. Any politician who dared to question the role of the US or question the sacrosanctity of the US-Japan alliance would have his political career end prematurely. One need not look far. Prime Minister Hatoyama came to power promising he would seek to restore a balance in Japan's relations with the US and seek better relations with its Asian neighbors—he only lasted nine months. There were widespread criticisms against the DPJ—both domestically and internationally.

Hatoyama's successors, Prime Minister Naoto Kan and Prime Minister Yoshihiko Noda, did not fare better from the challenges posed by great power contestations. Prime Minister Kan first faced his challenge in the form of the trawler boat collision incident near the Senkaku Islands in 2010, as mentioned earlier. The simmering tensions from this incident did not subside, and by 2012 an even bigger incident occurred.

The DPJ faced its most severe crisis yet in 2012. Ishihara Shintaro and Hashimoto Toru, who were then planning to set up an independent party in Tokyo and Osaka respectively, hatched a plan for the Tokyo metropolitan area to "purchase" the Senkaku Islands. On April 16, 2012, the Tokyo governor announced that the Tokyo municipality government would purchase the islands from their private owners (*Straits Times*, April 16, 2012). This immediately provoked reactions from the people and governments of China and Taiwan. During the summer of 2012, Hong Kong activists and Japanese activists both visited the islands to plant their respective flags to claim sovereignty. In September 2012, widespread protests broke out in approximately 125 cities across China, with widespread damage caused to Japanese businesses and interests that belonged not just to the Japanese but also to the Chinese.

This crisis provided Shinzo Abe with an opportunity to actively bring forth a series of measures (as discussed in Chap. 2) to effect changes across the three central pillars of Japan's rejuvenation at policy administration, legislative and political level (Ichiyo 2016; Tawara 2017). It is not known to what extent Ishihara and Abe acted in concert but again, as discussed previously, even though nationalists and neo-conservatives are technically very different, there is consensus when it comes to the harkening of traditional culture and values as mobilizing vehicles for their platforms. By the end of the crisis, Ishihara had launched his new party with Hashimoto Toru, which devastated DPJ's foreign policy platform, helped Shinzo Abe win the elections and drove all factions and political parties further rightwards with regards to China. This heightened and in the process reignited and mobilized both Japanese and Chinese nationalism. This episode effectively finished the DPJ politically. Even Beijing preferred the incoming LDP to the DPJ, simply because they could at least find the person who was in charge of Japan to talk to (even if he was a neo-conservative).

Photo: Protestors in Hong Kong on September 12, 2012, brandishing a Taiwanese flag and a Hong Kong flag. (Public domain photo, Photo source: https://www.voacantonese.com/a/hk-activists-to-hold-march-on-defending-diaoyu-islands-live-qa/1508949.html)

The handling of the nationalization of the Senkaku Islands was regarded as rightful in some quarters in Japan, while there were contrarian views that Japan was risking war to save the US-Japan alliance, as most constituents in Japan's political entity did not expect this kind of response from China—even though the country's ambassador to China, Uichiro Niwa, had warned in June 2011, after communications with the Chinese, that a move to "nationalize" the islands would trigger an "extremely grave crisis" and "decades of past efforts would be brought to nothing" (*Financial Times*, June 6, 2012; *Straits Times*, January 28, 2018). There is a view that Japan's almost "reckless" behavior in attempting to "purchase" the islands was not an administrative blunder caused by the DPJ's inexperience in foreign policy in general or with China in particular, but rather an all-out attempt by conservative elements within Japan to forestall the realization of a greater threat—that the US and China might have been moving toward a new East Asian shared paradigm by which they would adopt a shared security architecture (Harner 2012; White 2013). This is the classic "abandonment" dilemma of alliance theory.

Shinzo Abe's victory came on the heels of the US "pivot" to Asia after Secretary Clinton announced President Obama's new initiative to focus on Asia. While Japan was contesting China in the East China Sea, the Philippines and Vietnam confronted China in the South China Sea. The US pivot rested nicely on these fulcrum points. What was happening in the East China Sea must be contextualized against a larger hegemonic struggle that was going on in the South China Sea. This happy coincidence of the rise of the Abe 2.0 administration, coupled with the refocusing of US policy, meant that the alliance became even more important in taking down China, by now widely perceived as an irredentist systemic challenger.

The argument against overreliance on the US-Japan security alliance is well rehearsed and often heard: is it too much for Japan to trust the US to go to war for them against China in order to defend Japanese interests? Apart from its military strength, today's China is stronger in almost every way than the USSR was. China believes that time is on its side; if anything, the aggressive diplomatic maneuvers on the part of the US in response to China's emerging Ocean strategy is a reaffirmation of this view. As the quote from former Tokyo Governor Ishihara shows, a real but unspoken thought in Japanese minds is how far would the US go to defend Japanese interests *against* China. Despite the promises of senior US officials and successive presidents, Japanese officials wonder privately if Washington's actions would match up to its rhetoric, especially if the conflict was over something that Washington considered non-essential. Beyond that, being chain-ganged into a conflict with China is something that Tokyo should not take lightly, given the Trump presidency. The treaty binds Japan to US military action that is decided primarily in Washington D.C. Not all issues that crop up in a US-China confrontation would necessarily involve Japan, and even if they did, Japanese domestic circumstances or national consensus might not allow Tokyo to intervene. In order to enhance the military aspects of Japan's normalization, the Japanese government has over the course of the last 15 years striven to beef up its military strength, even though it is confined by the US-Japan alliance. Regardless of what the official position is, from a theoretical perspective, tightening the alliance under the guise of "normalization," even though convenient, is likely to make Japan more dependent rather than less.

It is this overt dependency that should be reconsidered. The inhibiting constraints of the US-Japan security alliance is well known and well understood by most Japanese commentators and US officials. One need not look far—the literature on technological cooperation between the US and Japan in the field of high-tech defense, such as in space cooperation or the Joint Strike fighter, is replete with these references. Officially, the treaty puts the US and Japan on equal footing as allies. Unofficially, even though the treaty has appeared from different angles to treat the US and Japan on unfair terms, what is surprising is how officials in both countries have consistently managed and interpreted the alliance to their advantage, and persuaded domestic audiences and third parties of its worth.

From the Japanese perspective, there are three important reasons for doing so. First, Japanese officials are of the view that this partnership, despite its imperfections and issues, provides Japan with the easiest, best and cheapest security insurance for them to hedge militarily against China. This is a neighborhood security concern, and backyard fires triumph security concerns elsewhere. The second reason is tactical. Given Japan's penchant for a political low profile and relative inexperience in global affairs, partnering with the US might offer them relatively low barriers of entry into the affairs of regions afar. With decades of experience under their belt, riding alongside the superpower through the alliance is a great way to sell the alliance both at home and reassure Japanese neighbors abroad. Third, it socializes China to the fact that Japan can and will act in concert with the US to defend itself, and that China has little or no chance of prying this alliance apart. Most importantly, the tightening of embrace prevents China from usurping Japan's role in the alliance. This fear of abandonment is as real as the fear of entrapment into a war caused by excessive American adventurism.

From a distant viewpoint, Tokyo has largely ignored the constraints imposed upon Japan by the US. As long as Japan is unable to fully speak for its own defense requirements, conceptualize its own strategic ambitions or stipulate its national interests abroad, Japan will always be a "subnormal" country. Thus, one of the most important but unspoken subtexts of normalization that needs to be considered is its relationship with the US, not just China. Even though the US-Japan alliance appears more robust than in any previous period, there is always an element of tension between Tokyo and Washington to define and redefine the terms of their relationship.[5]

Photo: Prime Minister Shinzo Abe and Chinese Xi Jinping at an APEC Meeting in November 2017. (This work is licensed under the Government of Japan Standard Terms of Use (Ver.2.0). The Terms of Use are compatible with the Creative Commons Attribution License 4.0 International; image available: http://www.kantei.go.jp/jp/98_abe/actions/201711/11apec.html)

---

[5] There has always been a contestation between the US and Japan in terms of research and development, particularly in high-tech industries such as the aerospace sector and defense industries (Green 1995; Samuels, 1994, 2007).

Is the "Anti-China" Position Necessarily Conducive to Japanese Interests?

A prominent retired foreign ministry official and former ambassador, Ukeru Magosaki, has argued that the primary goal of US policy has always been to advance US interests, not Japan's interests (mainly). Therefore, US policy determined the kind of sacrifices that Japan needed to make that were not in Japan's interests. As the former ambassador to Iran, Magosaki frequently cited the example of the development of an oil field in Iran where the concession had already been won by Japan but which it was forced to give up to China instead. A Japanese diplomat told the author that Ambassador Magosaki's thinking is an exception and "un-Japanese"— a code for not following the direction of the majority. This is interesting because it speaks to the extent to which most of the diplomatic corps, bureaucrats and scholars in Japan are willing to explain away the problematic aspects of US-Japan cooperation unconditionally. Another example of an important sacrifice is the issue of Okinawa. After almost three decades of post-Cold War years, Japan (in particular Okinawa) continues to host over 35,000 troops, and 5000 military related personnel in bases across Japan, even though Tokyo builds on its indigenous capability. In short, the democratic rights of those who oppose these bases have been ignored and violated (McCormack 2010; Araki 2012). Again, scholars outside Japan who articulate these views are not given the attention and time they deserve.

Magosaki argues that this is problematic as from the long term perspective the US has changed its policy at different junctures, and demanded that Tokyo should adhere to these policies even when it violated its constitution or ran contrary to its interests. Recent history is replete with these examples: asking Japan to rearm almost immediately after imposing the constitution on it as the Cold War set in; keeping nuclear weapons on its naval vessels, despite Japan's Three Non-Nuclear Principles; curbing the rise of Japan in the 1980s (e.g. preventing Japan from acquiring indigenous capability in many sensitive high-tech fields); reversing its policy on China (1972) and North Korea (2018) and not notifying Japan.

The China factor has therefore always loomed large. For the initial part of the Cold War, Sino-US relations were under strain, and therefore the US always blocked the prospects of Sino-Japanese reconciliation and bridge building between the Japanese and Chinese people. Like Hugh White, Magosaki suggests that Japan should not be too comfortable with the US approach with China as there is a tendency on the part of the US to negotiate with China to find a modus vivendi and sacrifice Japan's interests. In other words, Japan would be like a "pawn" or a "rook" in a chess game.

The question facing Japanese elites is therefore this: By treating the Chinese as a military threat, will this vision change into a reality? Yet for China to cause disruption to its neighbors or pose a threat, China need not use force. In the past, Chinese leaders have always maintained that all they had to do was to let their border guards go on leave and Southeast Asia would be flooded with Chinese migrants. Humanitarian concerns such as infectious diseases, poisonous food stuff, and fake goods such as medicines and other consumables would continue to flow from China. These are probably the real dangers to China's neighbors as opposed to a military invasion. Even though the various island disputes in the East and South China Seas have existed since the 1970s, they have never had the kind of contestation and contention we have seen in the last decade. The entry of the US and Japan into the South China Sea dispute had internationalized and politicized what was essentially a bilateral dispute into a multilateral one. During the 1990s, there was hardly any mention of the Spratly dispute, even though all the claimants had dug into the same position as they had today.

Also, beyond the Asia-Pacific, there are regions that have been more amicable to a Chinese presence than they have been to the US, simply because of historical dynamics. Today, most Arab countries prefer strong political relations with China (regardless of their relationships with the US), simply because they all believe China to be capable of being a counterweight to the US. China also has had a long experience with the developing world, given its status and role in countries that many G7 shunned, such as Sudan, Angola and others in Africa. The US and the rest of the G7 might have limited ability to engage in these areas, whereas Beijing might have better luck. If China and Japan are able to have a sustained and more in-depth dialog on the possibilities of joint engagement with these countries to improve their conditions, then Japan might increase its political role in these areas much quicker. This would also certainly help improve confidence in their bilateral relations.[6]

---

[6] There is a sign that this is already happening as China and Japan already reached an agreement to consider joint building of infrastructure in third countries during Prime Minister

Furthermore, a tight embrace of the US will prevent the US from leaving the alliance, and this is not something that China will oppose fundamentally. However, the rhetoric cannot be sharply anti-China, simply because public opinion would drive the Chinese to take a harder stance. In short, reducing the anti-China hysteria would improve relations with China and increase security, not reduce it. Maintaining a hardline posture would only invite escalation. Many Japanese analysts have cited privately that Beijing "understands" the nature of competitive electoral politics, but they underestimate the emotive and nationalistic response it might build in China. The lack of high level contact between China and Japan between 2011 and 2018 is certainly a case in point.

The Contestation in Southeast Asia: Winning Hearts and Minds

Southeast Asia has always been a traditional backyard for both China and Japan. Since the 1990s, Sino-Southeast Asia has been relatively warm. China sought to calm the Southeast nation fears in the mid-1990s when it displayed willingness to abide by a code of conduct for the South China Sea (Catley and Keliat 1997; Lo 2007), and subscribed to ASEAN's preference for multilateral as opposed to bilateral negotiations with regards to the South China Sea disputes (Chin 2003). For the last two decades, China has provided much of the momentum for the economic development of the region, averaging 9–12% of growth each year. Overall trade with ASEAN has increased. In 1997, with the onset of the Asian financial crisis, China's role left an indelible impression upon the Southeast Asian countries, and most if not all were to an extent grateful to China for its steadfast position in not devaluing the RMB and driving the region into another round of speculative devaluation (Gurtner 1999). This is accentuated by the fact that the US, the principal power in Asia, suffered a relative (if somewhat temporary) decline in its stature when viewed from the eyes of its allies and enemies alike.

With the onset of the War of Terrorism, the US myopic focus on terrorism meant that it was slow to react to the series of issues affecting East

Shinzo Abe's visit to China in October 2018 to celebrate the fortieth anniversary of the Treaty of Peace and Friendship between China and Japan.

and Southeast Asia. From the Sino-Japanese spat that escalated during Prime Minister Koizumi's reign (2000–2005) to the outbreak of the SARS (2003) and bird flu (2005) epidemics, to the Korean nuclear crisis and the dispute over the Spratly Islands, Southeast Asians came to realize two things. First, the power of the US as the global and region hegemon is limited when it comes to these issues and second, that the role China plays in these events (and subsequent repeats of these events) is critical and can have a decisive outcome on the region. It is therefore in the region's interest to encourage and socialize China into playing a constructive if not leading role in these events. Rightly or wrongly, China's role in the events conveys the impression that China's ascendance is inevitable, and its Asian neighbors had better jump on the bandwagon to welcome its rise. Even Vietnam and the Philippines were looking to further their relations with China.

Yet, by the mid-2000s, as China's economy grew from strength to strength, Southeast Asians watched anxiously the direct tensions of the bilateral Sino-Japanese issues on one hand, and increased China-Japan spillover competition in Southeast Asia on the other. Beyond trying to outdo each other in development projects, technology transfer or expanding their influence and market share, Tokyo and Beijing lobbied for influence among the ASEAN countries. As a group, the ASEAN region was blessed as both China and Japan slugged it out to pour money into the regional economies as investment for influence. Even though the countries accepted assistance and money from both, some members of ASEAN were effectively lobbying the US to try and play a mediating role between the two. ASEAN members too held a consensus that the region should try and limit great power competition to prevent another "Vietnam" from happening.

The Spratly Islands dispute has been dormant for the most part of its existence. There are six claimants in the dispute, each claiming in part or whole the sovereignty of the islands concerned: China, Malaysia, the Philippines, Taiwan and Vietnam, with Brunei laying claims to the waterways but not the islands. Each of the claimants (Brunei excepted) has militarily occupied some of the islands and reefs concerned.

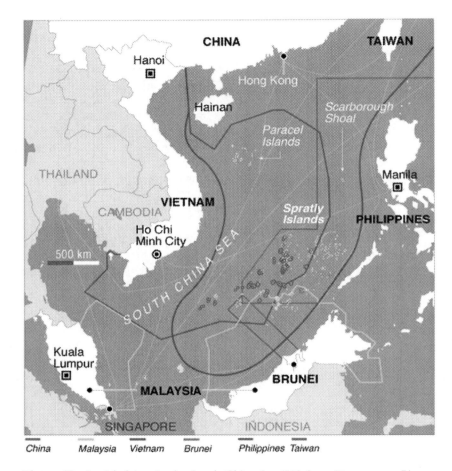

Plate: Territorial claims in the South China Sea (US State Department Picture 2012. Public Domain Picture by Voice of America, US Department of State, https://en.wikipedia.org/wiki/Territorial_disputes_in_the_South_China_Sea#/media/File:South_China_Sea_claims_map.jpg)

In the meantime, China fought naval skirmishes with the Vietnamese in 1984 and 1988 over the Paracel Islands, but like the Spratly Islands, the Paracel dispute was largely dormant until the turn of the century. Since the mid-2000s, the claimants have been filing reports over the presence of

Chinese (or other claimants') fishing and naval vessels in their territorial waters.

There are three issues that offend the Southeast Asian states. First, the 1947 9-dash line drawn up by the Chinese government laid claim to almost all of the South China Sea. Theoretically, Chinese vessels could anchor anywhere near the coast of Brunei or Indonesia and still call it territorial waters if this holds. Second, China, in reaction to attempts by the US and Japan to insert themselves into the dispute with ASEAN, began to dredge a couple of the reefs into islands. The Philippines has been protesting against Chinese actions over Mischief Reef since the 1990s, and the Chinese too were working on Tree Island and North Island, as well as Woody Islands in the Paracel Islands group. Third, the US and Japan began to act in concert with regards to aerial and naval sorties to challenge the Chinese military presence in the region, backed by an extensive media campaign against each other. In de facto terms, the US, China and Japan have militarized the South China Sea—something that ASEAN states are uncomfortable with.

This dispute enabled the US to "pivot" back into the region (Kubo 2013), as some ASEAN states such as Singapore, the Philippines and Vietnam have called on the US and other members of the international community to balance Chinese actions in the South China Sea. However, as we have seen, the South China Sea dispute(s) comprising the Spratly Islands and Paracel Islands has had a long history, and for most years of its existence, the disputes have been dormant (Catley and Keliat 1997; Chin 2003; Lo 2007; Torode and Scarr 2018). Hillary Clinton, as Secretary of State, stated in Hanoi that the South China Sea was of "core interest" to the US, much to the annoyance of the Chinese. From Beijing's perspective, all the problems, resistance and tensions in the South China Sea is a smear campaign created by Washington and Tokyo to stoke ASEAN neighbors into rallying against the rise of China. In particular, Beijing perceives that for much of the time after 2012, Prime Minister Abe's government has been instrumental in pushing for various states to help contain China, particularly in ASEAN and South Asia. In a manner characteristic of an aggrieved party, China reacted badly to the Philippines' attempt to lodge a protest with the International Tribunal for the Law of the Sea (2011) and subsequently with the Permanent Court of Arbitration (2013–2016). In response, China began to build up different reef islands— at the Subi Reef (2014), located 1200 km from China's coast; at Mischief Reef near to the Philippines; at Johnson South Reef (2014); and Fiery

Cross Reef (2015). China's building exercise signaled the pyrrhic victory the Philippines had won at the international tribune. Unless the Philippines, the US and Japan are willing to attack, destroy and take control of the reefs China has occupied, little can be done to eject the Chinese from these islands. To make matters worse, reports indicated that the Chinese installations contained airstrips, air defense artillery and short-range missile encasements to strengthen its claim to sovereignty. If anything, Chinese inspiration for reclaiming the islands comes from Japan, who had largely been using similar methods to build up the islet of Okinotorishima in the Pacific since 1987.

Today, even though the Chinese staunchly defend their actions in the Spratly Islands, they are still engaging the ASEAN states and reassuring them that dialog is important, to the extent that they have agreed on an ASEAN Code of Conduct in the South China Sea. China's diplomatic moves are aimed at countering the campaign by the US and Japan to stoke up fears of a rising China in the region. Each and every member of ASEAN knows the stakes involved, the importance of keeping the sea-lanes open and free, and the importance of balancing the powers in the region. The nightmare scenario for the ASEAN states is for the US and China to ask them to choose between them. To that end, the ASEAN states will try and persuade each other to resist the division of the region collectively.

Japan's political instinct on the other hand has been to try and lobby for greater involvement of the US-Japan alliance in the region to "balance" the rising China. Today, by all indicators, Japan is doing better in terms of soft power and economic influence than China in Southeast Asia. From Tokyo's perspective, it appears imperative that Japan works with the US to balance China in the region.

As demonstrated in previous chapters, there are major challenges facing US-Japan relations too (Walsh 2007; Yabuki 2012; Mizokami 2012; Harner 2012). The US alliance with Japan and Korea also faces inherent limits (Taylor 2012). Even though Prime Minister Abe implements with zeal (Akimoto 2018), Japan itself faces a great dilemma in implementing its proactive activism (Weston 2014). As counter-intuitive as it may sound, the biggest challenge for Japanese diplomacy is to rise above this hegemonic contention between China and the US and to balance, if not moderate, the excessiveness of their confrontation. Therefore, even though Japan works with the US to prevent China from dominating the region, Japan should also try and work with China and ASEAN to moderate the excesses of the US and ensure that regional harmony is preserved.

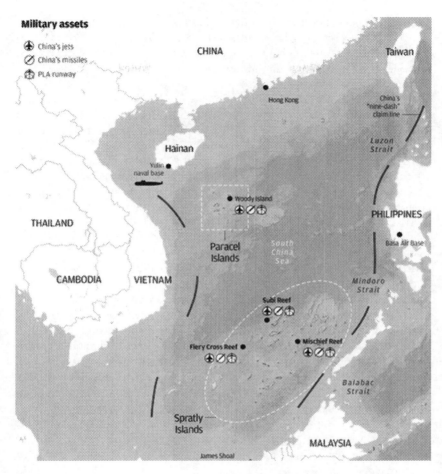

China's militarization of the South China Sea. (Reproduced with kind permission from the *South China Morning Post*, June 2, 2018)

Japan should be aware that ASEAN also holds reservations about Japan acting as a major military power in the region, as memories of the Second World War are still fresh in the social memories of these countries. For Japan to rise and lead as a rejuvenated power, its developmental assistance is more needed than anything else. For Japan to become respected, it must transcend the US-China divide in the region, and act as a mechanism for regional stability. For the most part, China's economy, like Japan's, has grown to be deeply integrated with ASEAN's economy. ASEAN states no longer believe that the US has the capacity to unilaterally drive world events. For one, the US is very much in debt and the continued projection of its power, in the Asia-Pacific and elsewhere, is heavily contingent on its debtors (in East Asia and Europe) to continually fund it by buying US Treasury bonds and using the US dollar as a reserve currency. To that extent, Japan is one of the debtors, and so is China. Admiral Mike Mullen, then chairman of the joint chief of staff, noted that China holds about USD 2 trillion in US Treasury debt, and in any confrontation China would naturally sell or ask for the demand repayment of its debt holdings (Yabuki 2012).

There is no question that the trade war today is about addressing the economic, trade and fiscal imbalance. Japan has also found itself at the receiving end of Trump's unreasonable demands. Thus, it is imperative that Japan allies itself with the ASEAN states to transcend the hegemonic struggle between China and the US as a way forward. Maneuvering ASEAN states to choose between Japan (alongside the US) or China is one of the worst ways forward for engaging Southeast Asian states. It is therefore most important for Japan to calibrate a relationship with China, because Sino-Japanese relations are historically rooted and geographically fixed, and these conditions are bound to inform the future course and relations of Sino-Japanese relations, and as such these bilateral relations must match in degree the complexity and sophistication of Japan's relations with the US (Hoshino and Satoh 2012: 181). A possible way forward is for Japan to work with ASEAN to realize the developmental potential in the region. Bread and butter, not guns, will make Southeast Asia stronger than ever before. Rather than inducing a great power competition in the region, enhancing regionalization and the integration of Southeast Asia with East Asia might be the best way for Japan to engage Southeast Asia.

References

Akimoto, D. *The Abe Doctrine: Japan's Proactive Pacifism and Security Strategy*. London: Palgrave Macmillan, 2018.

Armitage, R. L., Nye, J. S., & Center for Strategic and International Studies. *The U.S.-Japan Alliance: Anchoring Stability in Asia: report of the CSIS Japan chair*. Washington, D.C.: Center for Strategic and International Studies, 2012. Available: https://csis-prod.s3.amazonaws.com/s3fs-public/legacy_files/files/publication/120810_Armitage_USJapanAlliance_Web.pdf

Araki, L. *Interview with Jennifer Lind: Okinawa and the Future of the U.S.-Japan Security Alliance*, The National Bureau of Asian Research, 11 May 2012, https://www.nbr.org/publication/okinawa-and-the-future-of-the-u-s-japan-security-alliance/

Catley, R., & Keliat, M. *Spratlys: The Dispute in the South China Sea*. London: Ashgate Publishing, 1997.

Chin C.Y. *Potential For Conflict in the Spratly Islands*, California: Naval Postgraduate School 2003, https://calhoun.nps.edu/bitstream/handle/10945/6221/03Dec_Chin.pdf?sequence=1

Green, M. *Arming Japan: Defense Production, Alliance Politics, and the Postwar Search for Autonomy*. New York: Columbia University Press, 1995.

Gurtner, F. "The Stability of the Renminbi in the Wake of the Asian financial crisis," *Intereconomics* 34, no. 3 (May/Jun 1999): 135–143, https://archive.intereconomics.eu/downloads/getfile.php?id=65

Harner, S. Is Japan Risking War to Save the U.S.-Japan Alliance? *Forbes Online*, 11 July 2012, https://www.forbes.com/sites/stephenharner/2012/11/07/is-japan-risking-war-to-save-the-u-s-japan-alliance/

Hoshino, T., & Satoh, H. (2012). Through the Looking Glass? China's Rise as Seen from Japan. *Journal of Asian Public Policy*, Vol. 5, No. 2: 181–198.

Ichiyo, M. Retaking Japan: The Abe Administration's Campaign to Overturn the Postwar Constitution. *The Asia-Pacific Journal: Japan Focus*. Vol. 14, Issue 13, No. 3, July 2016, https://apjjf.org/-Muto-Ichiyo/4917/article.pdf

Jain, P. Japan: The World's Next Big Arms Dealer? *The National Interest*, 17 Feb 2017, https://nationalinterest.org/blog/the-buzz/japan-the-worlds-next-big-arms-dealer-19477?page=0%2C1

Kingston, J., Nationalism in the Abe Era. *The Asia-Pacific Journal: Japan Focus*, Vol. 14, Issue 20, No. 3, Oct 2016, https://apjjf.org/2016/20/Kingston.html

Kubo, F. The Second-Term Obama Administration and Japan. *Asia-Pacific Review*, 20(1), 24–34, 2013, https://doi.org/10.1080/13439006.2013.788339

Lo, C.K. *China's Policy Towards Territorial Disputes*. London: Taylor & Francis, 2007.

Martin, C. Jus ad Bellum Implications of Japan's New National Security Laws, *Opiniojuris*, 2016, http://opiniojuris.org/2016/04/21/jus-ad-bellum-implicationsof-japans-new-national-security-laws/

McCormack, G. Ampo's Troubled 50th: Hatoyama's Abortive Rebellion, Okinawa's Mounting Resistance and the US-Japan Relationship, *The Asia-Pacific Journal: Japan Focus*, Vol. 8, Issue 22, No. 3, 2010, https://apjjf.org/-Gavan-McCormack/3365/article.html

McCormack, G. (2016). Japan: Prime Minister Abe Shinzo's Agenda, *The Asia-Pacific Journal: Japan Focus*, Vol. 14, Issue 24, No. 1, 2016, https://apjjf.org/2016/24/McCormack.html

Mizokami, K. Japan and the U.S.: It's Time to Rethink Your Relationship, *The Atlantic*, 27 Sep 2012, https://www.theatlantic.com/international/

archive/2012/09/japan-and-the-us-its-time-to-rethink-your-relationship/262916/

Pejsova, E. & Stanley, Z., *Japan's Policy Shift: Arms and Transfers, Zurich*: ETH Center for Security Studies, 2016, http://www.css.ethz.ch/en/services/digital-library/articles/article.html/269f638b-c376-41d4-a804-da71dc78475f/pdf

Samuels, J. S. *Securing Japan*. Ithaca and London: Cornell University Press, 2007.

Samuels, R.J. *"Rich Nation, Strong Army": National Security and the Technological Transformation of Japan*. Ithaca, NY: Cornell University Press, 1994.

Soeya, Y. China, and Japan's foreign policy posture, *East Asia Forum*, 8 April 2012, http://www.eastasiaforum.org/2012/04/08/china-and-japans-foreign-policy-posture/

Tawara, Y. (Translated by Brooks, W., Lu, P., Asia Policy Point) What is the Aim of Nippon Kaigi, the Ultra-Right Organization that Supports Japan's Abe Administration?, *The Asia-Pacific Journal: Japan Focus*, 1st Nov 2017, Vol. 15, Issue 21, No. 1, https://apjjf.org/2017/21/Tawara.html

Taylor, B. Japan and South Korea: The Limits of Alliance. *Survival*, 54(5), 93–100, 2012, https://doi.org/10.1080/00396338.2012.728346

Torode, G., & Scarr, S. Concrete and Coral: Beijing's South China Sea Building Boom fuels concerns, *Reuters*, 24 May 2018.

Walsh, B. Why Japan Is Unhappy with the U.S., *Times Magazine*, 21 Feb 2007, http://content.time.com/time/world/article/0,8599,1592181,00.html

Weston, S. A. The Dilemma of Japan's Proactive Pacifism in Asia, *Fukuoka University Review of Law*, Vol. 59, No. 2, pp 169–212, Sep 2014.

White, H., *The China Choice: Why We Should Share Power*, Oxford and New York: Oxford University Press, 2013.

Yabuki, S. US-China-Collusion-and-the-Way-Forward-for-Japan, *East Asia Forum*, 30 June 2012, http://www.eastasiaforum.org/2012/06/30/us-chinacollusion-and-the-way-forward-for-japan/

Open Access This chapter is licensed under the terms of the Creative Commons Attribution 4.0 International License (http://creativecommons.org/licenses/by/4.0/), which permits use, sharing, adaptation, distribution and reproduction in any medium or format, as long as you give appropriate credit to the original author(s) and the source, provide a link to the Creative Commons licence and indicate if changes were made.

The images or other third party material in this chapter are included in the chapter's Creative Commons licence, unless indicated otherwise in a credit line to the material. If material is not included in the chapter's Creative Commons licence and your intended use is not permitted by statutory regulation or exceeds the permitted use, you will need to obtain permission directly from the copyright holder.

CHAPTER 4

Peacekeepers But Not Quite Peacebuilders: Japan's Evolving Role in the Middle East Peace Process

> For an independent Japan, which is among the first rank of countries in economics, technology and learning to continue to be dependent on another country is a deformity (*katawa*) of the state ... For Japan, a member of the United Nations and expecting its benefits, to avoid support of its peacekeeping mechanisms is selfish behavior. This is unacceptable in international society. I myself cannot escape responsibility for the use of Constitution as a pretext (tatemae) for this way of conducting national policy.
>
> Yoshida Shigeru in *Sekai to Nippon*, 1963

> Since wars begin in the minds of men, it is in the minds of men that the defences of peace must be constructed.
>
> UNESCO Charter

The author gratefully acknowledges the support of funding of this chapter by the Hong Kong Research Council General Research Fund, HKU Project number 753310H.

© The Author(s) 2019
V. Teo, *Japan's Arduous Rejuvenation as a Global Power*,
https://doi.org/10.1007/978-981-13-6190-6_4

Japan's Foray into the Middle East

Japan's foray into the Middle East pre-dates the end of the Cold War. Even though Japan has largely kept a non-intervention posture as enshrined by its pacifist position throughout the Cold War, a critical indication of its normalization and rejuvenation is its ability to play a greater role in global affairs. There cannot be a better test for assessing the extent of Tokyo's normalization and rejuvenation drive than observing its behavior in the Middle East. This is particularly important as Japan has interests in the Middle East, putting Tokyo's position at odds with the official position that her principal ally, the United States, holds on the same issues, such as policy over Iran and military intervention in the Middle East. To that extent, the Middle East has become an area of critical importance to Tokyo.

Over the course of the last two decades, the dominant narrative on Japan's involvement in the Middle East has focused principally on the notion of "peacekeeping" (Suzuki 2013; Ishizuka 2005; Takahara 1996; Harrison and Nishihara 1995; Kozai 2001; Yamanaka 2003; Togo 2010: chapter 12; Dobson 2003; Leitenberg 1996). Most descriptions of Japan's "peace" activities focus on its dispatching of troops to support the US in Iraq; its deployment of minesweepers and refueling vessels to support the US in its War on Terror; and its participation in the anti-piracy efforts in the Gulf of Aden. All these activities are usually conducted under the auspices of the US-Japan alliance or under the UN mandate. Domestically, the narrative is framed within the twin objectives of supporting the alliance as well as fulfilling Japan's international obligations. Externally, the deployment of Japanese forces under the US or UN umbrella might make this more palatable for other Asian nations.

These activities complement a far more important and understated aspect of Japan's peacebuilding activities pursued through agencies such as the Japan International Cooperation Agency (JICA) and through Japan's foreign ministry since the institution of the Fukuda Doctrine in 1979. As part of Japan's global efforts, JICA has been very successful in integrating itself into the local activities of the regions it has targeted to help. Due to the JSDF's own constraints abroad, it has always participated in two categories of activities: disaster relief and domestic reconstruction. Japan has therefore always relied on this route to promote its soft power through humanitarian activities (Yoshizaki 2008: 107–120).[1] Any narrative justified

---

[1] Tomonori Yoshizaki argues that even though the JSDF has been dispatched to Iraq, their deployment is still severely circumscribed as the Japanese contingent could only serve in "non-combat" zones, and more importantly refrained from participating in "stabilization"

based on humanitarian grounds rather than premises of normalization or rejuvenation is always more palatable to the Japanese public.

After the collapse of the USSR, the Middle East has therefore taken on a new "instrumental" meaning for Tokyo. Deployment to the Middle East extends far beyond Japan's backyard of the Asia-Pacific. Such a move therefore severely tests Japan's constitutional limitations and both its long held, cherished notion of pacifism and its self-imposed restraints on Japan's defense forces. Such deployments will also increasingly socialize the Japanese people to Japan undertaking missions of global and regional significance.

Japan has been actively supporting the US in the region (Shelter-Jones 2012), but the extent of its involvement has been circumscribed due to domestic constraints, policy inertia and an understated deference to the US. In short, Japan's political stature and influence in regions outside of the Asia-Pacific cannot be regarded as commensurate with its credentials, financial contributions and resources devoted to developmental assistance.

A rejuvenated Japan must therefore first take into account its own interests and the sensitivities of others second, and must be able to partake actively in the region's important affairs, offering fresh ideas and perspectives on age-old problems. Despite the difficulties, Japan has made important strides in achieving this, particularly under Prime Minister Abe. Nonetheless, Japan's determination to increase its efforts is still carefully choreographed to ensure that there is some parity between increasing Japan's profile and preserving the unity of the US-Japan alliance.

Since the 1990s, Japan has decided to incrementally deviate from its traditional behavior in the region. Tokyo has decided to double down and extend support to US/UN operations in the region, ensuring the globalization of the US-Japan alliance. This directly assists Japan's aspirations to achieve rejuvenation as a global power on the back of a US global presence. Thus, over the last two decades, much of the focus of the Japanese polity has been centered on whether or not Japan should dispatch its military to the Middle East. Be it naval minesweepers and refueling tankers to support US missions in the Gulf, reconstruction brigades to Iraq, or naval ships to help fight piracy, the debate has always revolved around (i) the constitutionality of such deployments, (ii) the reasons for and against such missions, (iii) whether Japan should undertake such missions. The overall result is that the narrative involving Japan's activities in the Middle East revolves around Japan's incremental inroads in chipping away at the constraints of the constitution through such deployments.

operations that involved the use of force, but this form of participation can only rely on the goodwill of other militaries to provide the force projection needed.

This chapter argues, however, that when viewed from the perspective of Japan's rejuvenation, this focus on military deployment and peacekeeping is lopsided. If the neo-conservative's agenda is to transform Japan into a substantial power in all senses of the word, then Japan should also focus on its role as a peacebuilder rather than just within the frame of a peacekeeping role and a secondary combat support role. While not attempting to replace the role of the US in the peace process, Tokyo is attempting to mount complementary platforms that support Washington's efforts, particularly in an era where US foreign policy seems to have lost its balance. To that end, Japan has the requisite credentials to play a greater role than it has done in the past, given its historic status as a pacifist economic power, a US ally and a relatively neutral party in the Arab-Israeli dispute. This is not to suggest that Japan can replace any country in the peace process or even think from the get-go it can resolve the dispute all at once, but rather that Japan should aspire to have a greater political role in the region.

Japan has had a long history of undertaking work and activities that can be considered to be the core of peacebuilding activities. Between JICA, the foreign ministry and other related agencies, the Japanese government collectively dispatches billions of yen as loans, technical assistance and grassroots programs. This is done through the official overseas developmental assistance program and also bilateral programs administered by the foreign ministry. It would appear that JICA is far ahead of the Japanese foreign ministry when it comes to work done to help Japan reach out to places traditionally neglected by Japanese foreign policy.

The section below provides a brief overview of the Arab-Israeli conflict, and a discussion of Japan's evolving role. It then takes a step back and discusses these developments against the notions of normalization and rejuvenation.

A Brief Synopsis of the Arab-Israeli Conflict

The genesis of the problem began toward the end of the seventeenth century with the migration of Jewish people into the Ottoman Empire territory of Palestine, which had a sizable Muslim population. The impetus behind the migration was the significant historical and religious value of the sites located in Jerusalem for both Islam and Judaism. The Dome of the Rock (otherwise known as the Rock of Abraham) and the Al-Aqsa Mosque in the Old City of Jerusalem are among the most important Muslim sacred sites in the world (alongside Mecca and Medina in Saudi Arabia). Jerusalem is also home to the Wailing Wall (otherwise known as the Western Wall or Buraq Wall to

Muslims), which is now the only surviving structure of the Herodian Temple, and thus the holiest site in Judaism. At the end of the seventeenth century, the Muslim population was significantly higher than the incoming Jewish migrants, but the demographics changed radically after Imperial Britain moved to fill the vacuum left behind by the Ottoman Empire.

In 1903, the British offered the territory to the Jewish people as a homeland and refuge from persecution; this was known as the "Uganda Scheme" but was rejected by the Zionist Congress. (The Balfour Project 2016: 1). This sympathy for the Jewish nation was aided by the presence of substantial Jewish communities in Russia and the US, swinging international public opinion toward the cause supported by the US (The Balfour Project 2016: 8). With the outbreak of war between Great Britain and Turkey, the idea of a Jewish nation became entirely plausible. The British passed the "Balfour Declaration," mandating the creation of a Jewish homeland in Palestine. By 1914, there were 60,000 Jews in the area, in comparison to the 683,000 resident Arabs, with increased immigration from Europe (Beinin and Hajjar 2014: 2). The idea behind this was to provide Jews with a refuge from persecution, as well as a place for homeless Jewish people that would prevent their assimilation into other cultures (Balfour Project 2016: 3). Naturally, this support empowered the Jews, but it also enraged the Arabs and resulted in major armed conflict between the two groups in the period between 1920 and 1921. Due to immigration, land purchases and land settlement, the growth of Jewish settlements threatened the Arabs to the extent that violence became common place. By 1928, the communities began to clash over the religious sites in Jerusalem, specifically the Western Wall and the plaza about the Wall known as the Temple Mount, home to two Israelite temples. This place is sacred to Muslims, who call it the Noble Sanctuary, and it hosts the Al-Aqsa Mosque, believed to mark the spot of Prophet Muhammad's ascension to Heaven on a winged-horse (Beinin and Hajjar 2014: 3). By this time, what started out as an issue of immigration had morphed into a protracted conflict with ethnic, religious and territorial dimensions. Hitler's rise in 1933 brought immigration to great heights, with a corresponding increase in resistance resulting in the Arab Revolt (1936–1939), suppressed by Britain with the help of Zionist military. By 1945, Britain had referred the problem to the UN, with 1.26 million Arabs and 608,000 Jews settled in the area and the latter owning about 20% of arable land (Beinin and Hajjar 2014: 4).

Much to the annoyance of the Arab-speaking world, the UN proposed and voted in a plan that sought to divide Palestine into two states in 1947, with the larger portion (56%) going to the Jewish nation, and the smaller portion (43%) allocated to the Palestinians. The Arab states and the Palestinian Arabs rejected this plan, and in their eyes, Jewish statehood had no legitimacy at all. By May 15, 1948, the British evacuated Palestine, and the State of Israel was proclaimed, sparking the First Arab-Israel War (1948–1949) with Israel expanding beyond its borders. This created an exodus of refugees from Palestine—owing to both the conflict and more so to the expulsive actions of the Jewish military (Beinin and Hajjar 2014: 5). Only about 150,000 Palestinians remained in the area that became the State of Israel, and they effectively became second-class citizens in a state defined by both religious and ethnic identity. By 1949, the end of the Arab-Israeli War saw the Israelis capture about 60% of the land initially allocated to the Arabs under the Partition plan, Jordan ruled the West Bank, and Egypt occupied the Gaza Strip. The conflict between Israel and the Arab states from without and within Palestine escalated throughout the 1950s and 1960s. In 1956, Egypt closed the Straits of Tiran to Israeli shipping and nationalized the Suez Canal, effectively blockading Israel. The Israelis captured the Sinai Peninsula and Gaza Strip and were pressured by the US and UN into accepting a ceasefire, with the USSR threatening to intervene on behalf of the Egyptians (BBC July 26, 1956). This episode saw the rise of Nasser as the president of Egypt and the hero of the Arab world when he resisted the French and British then assisting Israel. It also saw the rise of Yitzhak Rabin, a young military prodigy who eventually became the Israeli prime minister. The Six-Day War in 1967 occurred after Egypt expelled UN peacekeepers and moved troops into the Sinai, instating a blockade of the Israelis, who were simultaneously subject to constant harassment via the guerilla warfare waged for years by the Palestinians from Syria territory. Israel launched a surprised attack, destroying most segments of the Egyptian, Jordanian and Syrian air forces. By the end of the Six-Day War, the landscape of the Middle East had changed. Israel had captured the Sinai Desert from Egypt, the Golan Heights from Syria and the West Bank and Jerusalem from Jordan (Bowen 2017). This war hardened Palestinian resolve to revolt against Israel, as the latter had become a de facto occupying state in what was previously Palestinian territory, continuing its "resettlement building policy" in contravention of UN Resolution 242.

The 1973 Yom Kippur War, led by Egypt's Sadat, was waged to recover all territories taken by Israel after the 1967 War and to prompt Israel to achieve a just, peaceful solution to the Arab-Israeli conflict (Bean and Girard 2001: 4–6). Assad, however, wanted to reclaim the Golan Heights, particularly as Syria was armed with Soviet weapons. Despite this, Israel's military performed exceptionally well and was able to push the Arabs back.

Hitting back with the Oil Embargo led to US intervention to ensure oil supplies. This led to a mutual ceasefire, and the beginning of peace talks. By this time, the role of the US and USSR in the conflict had become clear—they were both stoking regional actors to confront each other, thereby becoming two of the largest geopolitical sponsors in the Middle East. The UN passed Resolution 242 and it was adopted in the aftermath of the Six-Day War, attesting to the "inadmissibility of the acquisition of territory by war and the need to work for a just and lasting peace in the Middle East" and calling for the "withdrawal of Israeli armed forces from territories occupied by recent conflict." Palestinians had always been outraged by Israel's violation of the initial Partition plan, taking 78% of historic Palestine when only allocated 55% of the land.

Thus, the question of the Palestinian identity and statehood has been defined by a series of escalating conflicts and uprisings (most significantly the 1967 Six-Day War, the 1973 Yom Kippur War, the First Intifada of 1987, the Second Intifada of 2000, and the rise of Hamas). The relationship between the Israelis, the Palestinians and the Arabs has become intricately linked to the question of territory and security for all nations involved. The governments of Jordan, Syria and Egypt, however, have had differing positions on Palestine and policy toward Israel. Suffice to say that after the wars, Jordan and Egypt were amenable to reaching an agreement of coexistence with Israel, more so than the Syrians, and thus their policies toward the Palestinians weren't particularly consistent or united. By 1964, the Palestine Liberal Organization (PLO) was founded. It was recognized as the sole legitimate representative of the Palestinian people, with observer status at the UN beginning in 1974. Since its inception, the PLO has dedicated its existence to the liberation of Palestine through armed struggle. Consequently, both the State of Israel and the US (since 1987) ruled the PLO to be a "terrorist organization" until the Madrid Conference of 1991. By 1993, even though the PLO reached a consensus with Israel to recognize the two-state solution, mutual violence has continued unabated until today.

US intervention in the Middle East began in earnest with the end of the Second World War. The Truman administration's Middle East policy was defined principally by US concern for continued access to petroleum, the overarching danger of the Soviet threat and concern for the nascent State of Israel. Even though the US stayed neutral in the 1950s, by 1962, Washington was beginning to supply Tel Aviv with air defense systems, such as the Hawk anti-aircraft missiles, via West Germany, as it suspected that the Soviets were arming the United Arab Emirates and Iraq. In order to entice Jordan away from the Soviets, the US began arms sales to both Jordan and Israel as "balance" (US State Department Memo, March 11, 1965). By the end of the 1967 War, US restraint on weapons sales eroded as Washington firmly believed that the USSR was arming the Arab states, inciting the Palestinians against the State of Israel. Even though the US continued to supply both sides in order to prevent development of the Arab-Soviet relationship, this became untenable by the early 1970s. US interests in supplying Israel escalated exponentially from just fighter jets to all sorts of armaments (codename Nickel Glass) when the Soviets supplied the Arab states in a large-scale manner at the start of the Yom Kippur War (Dunstan 2003: 67). The state of tensions abated with the disengagement agreement signed in 1975. Throughout the Carter and Reagan administrations, the US-Israel relationship improved overall. The relationship was formalized through the signing of the 1981 Strategic Cooperation Agreement between Israel and the US, the conduct of joint military exercises in 1984, and the granting to Israel of the status of NATO ally in 1987. Such an unprecedented assurance allowed the US to establish a dialog with the PLO in 1988, continuing the work of the Carter administration's pledge to establish the Palestinian homeland. The first Bush administration encouraged the Israelis to continue dialog with Palestinians, urging both parties to accept the territory for peace principle and the fulfillment of the Palestinian people's rights. The Bush administration was finally able to bring the parties to the table at the Madrid peace conference, laying the basis for subsequent engagement. President Clinton was able to bring about what looked like permanent peace with the signing of the Oslo Accords by Yitzhak Rabin and Yasser Arafat. However, with the assassination of Rabin, and the beginning of the resettlement policy by Israel, the agreement quickly fell apart. From the events of September 11 to this day, peace in the Middle East looks increasingly fragile, as religious and ethnic religious tensions increase on a daily basis to the extent that Haass has suggested we are witnessing a new Thirty Year's War in the region.

Japan's Involvement in the Arab-Israeli Conflict

Japan's engagement with the Arab-Israeli conflict had its genesis in the immediate aftermath of the 1973 war (Halloran 1973). Japan was at the height of its postwar economic recovery efforts. In order to secure a constant access line to Middle Eastern energy and to provide for stable and long-term growth, Japan was keen to facilitate some kind of peace talks between the two sides. This caused Japanese policy to align with public sentiments sympathetic to the Arabs, and reassured the Japanese business community concerned with the 1973 Oil Embargo. Officially, the Japanese government's position broke ranks with that of the US and stipulated principles that spelled out Tokyo's position (Kuroda 2001: 106–110) on the issue as the basis of conflict. Named after Chief Cabinet Secretary Susumu Nikaido, the principles outlined in support of UN Resolution 242 were:

1. Inadmissibility of the acquisition and occupation of territory by force
2. Withdrawal of Israeli forces from all the territories of all countries occupied in the 1967 War
3. Respect for the integrity and security of the territories of all countries in the region and the need for guarantees to that end
4. The recognition of and respect for the legitimate rights of the Palestinian people in accordance with the Charter of the United Nations in bringing about a just and lasting peace in the Middle East

Tokyo expressed that it would observe the situation and reconsider its relations with Israel should the need arise, against which Tel Aviv strongly protested. This is somewhat at odds with the position of the US, particularly with regards to the characterization of the PLO's explicit methodology of armed struggle against Israel as terrorism, and only something that was eventually accepted during the Carter and Reagan administrations.

Prime Minister Masayoshi Ohira remarked that "Japan understands that the right of self-determination of the Palestinian people includes the right to establish an independent state," with Chair Yasser Arafat being invited to Tokyo by a Diet group in October 1981 (Naramoto 1991: 80). However, this was adjusted in the 1980s when Japan decided to strengthen its ties with Israel, given that there was an oil glut and that its relationship with the Arab states had been established by then. Arafat was officially invited by the Japanese government in 1989 and met with Prime Minister Toshiki Kaifu. Tokyo, however, stopped short of establishing direct economic exchanges or sending supplies because the PLO was not considered a state (Naramoto 1991: 81).

Nevertheless, Japan also reached out to the Israelis during this period, with an invitation to Israel after Arafat's visit in February 1990. This occurred two years after Foreign Minister Souseke Uno's visit to Israel, being the first cabinet level official to visit the country since the establishment of bilateral relations in 1952 (*Deseret News*, July 4, 1988). The PLO then requested that Japan lobby the US to compel the Israelis to be brought to the negotiating table. Arafat's visit was ostensibly held at ministerial level and represented a change to previous positions in which Japan deemed that no change would occur in bilateral relations unless there was an improvement in the peace process (Naramoto 1991: 81). Tokyo believed that it was important to have a "positive balanced relationship" with both the Palestinians and the Israelis. Like the US, Tokyo sought to build a "balanced" relationship with both. From a Palestinian perspective, this meant that Tokyo began to adopt a more pro-Israel (or a more pro-US) policy, even though government policy was premised on UN Resolution 242 and the principles outlined in the 1973 Nikaido statement. By and large, the public interest in the Middle East waned over the 1980s. According to a survey conducted in the 1980s by the prime minister's office, 30% of the respondents noted the Middle East as a region that concerned them, but by 1986 this number had dropped to 9.5%, only to rebound after the Gulf War (Naramoto 1991: 84). Most pertinent was the finding that public opinion was against the disbursement of USD 9 billion to fund the war effort.

The demise of the USSR ushered in an era where local political dynamics were less politicized by the dynamics of the Cold War, but at the same time, it also meant that the US was less prone to behaving in a multilateralist manner than the Europeans, Japanese and Russians. This, however, is somewhat mitigated by the fact that both the Arabs and Israelis grew increasingly vulnerable and reliant on the US, enhancing the ability of the US to serve as the "honest broker" (Miller 1997: 103–142). Through the careful cultivation of Jordan's King Hussein and Egyptian President Mubarak, President Bill Clinton was able to successfully bring Yasser Arafat and Yitzhak Rabin to conclude the peace agreement. Even though the US had been in the main driving seat of the peace process for decades, the Oslo Accords signed in Washington (1993) and Taba in Egypt were one of the most fundamental achievements to date. The Accords are a result of the Oslo process by which both the Israelis and the Palestinians agreed to a peace treaty in the spirit of UN Resolutions 242 and 338, aiming to realize the vision of the "right of the Palestinian people to self-determination" (Gadzo 2017). Up to this point, the US had been principally responsible for most of the direct peace initiatives in the Middle

East, investing huge amounts of money, effort and prestige into the peace process (Touval 1982). The Oslo Accords were a culmination of five decades of diplomatic efforts. Despite the awarding of the Nobel Peace Prize to Yasser Arafat, Yitzhak Rabin and Shimon Peres in 1994, the peace did not last. With the assassination of Yitzhak Rabin and the changes of domestic political leadership in Israel, the peace process was scuppered. The US has not been able to prevent the increased populating and settlement of East Jerusalem, the forcible removal of Palestinian families (*Russian Times*, Feb 8, 2014), or the securitization of critical cultural sites in Jerusalem,[2] accentuating and reflecting the emotional conflict between the Arabs and the Jewish nation. The Mount is considered to be the third holiest site in the world, after Masjid al-Haram, (the Grand Mosque in Mecca); Al-Masjid an-Nabawi (the Mosque of the Prophet), and Al-Aqsa Mosque (the furthest mosque) which includes al-Aqsa congregation mosque and the Dome of the Rock. Collectively, until these "final status" items are resolved,[3] the gulf between the two nations remains insurmountable. In particular, the continued settlement in the West Bank, with a good portion of Jewish settlers in East Jerusalem (the future capital of the supposed Palestinian state), undermines any discussion of a two-state solution of the question.

Japan's contribution has been relatively insignificant compared with that of the US at this point, as it has focused on supporting US efforts principally through the disbursement of aid and developmental assistance. Even though Japan and other countries have tried to play a more active role (Lam 2009), they are unable to sidestep the US as it has shown little interest in allowing any other countries to intervene in the peace process, even in the case of Europe or Japan. This pivotal position allows the US to have exceptional access and influence over all actors and allows Washington to continually exploit its positional power in the region.

---

[2] For example, the Temple Mount is the primary site which is at the core of Judaism, Christianity and Islam. The site is known as: Haram al-Sharif in Arabic and Har haBayit in Jewish (Dumper 2014).

[3] The items are (1) security, (2) borders, (3) refugees, (4) Jerusalem and (5) mutual recognition and end of conflict and claims. For a succinct explanations of these concerns, please see "The Final Status Items for Israeli-Palestinian Negotiations: Challenges and Complexities", February 7, 2014, available at: http://www.aipac.org/~/media/Publications/Policy%20and%20Politics/AIPAC%20Analyses/Issue%20Memos/2014/IssueBriefPeaceProcess.pdf

Washington has always shown exceptional support for Israel for a variety of reasons: sympathies for the Jewish nation stemming from the Holocaust; the power of the Jewish lobby in the US (Bard 1991); maintaining a central strategic position in Middle Eastern affairs; securing one of the largest arms sales markets; and most importantly, a genuine belief that it alone can secure peace in the region. Despite this, US support for the Israelis has always been challenged by other equally exigent priorities that are competing for funding and strategic attention in both the administration and in Congress—from Iraq to Yemen, from Afghanistan to Iran. The War on Terror might have made things worse, as the rise of Al-Qaeda and ISIS subsequently has led to conflict that has radically polarized the already divided Middle East.

The Need to Revamp Japan's Peacebuilding Strategy

Since the end of the Cold War, Japan's more pro-Arab policy has shifted to more pro-US positions over time. This can be explained by international structural change and powershift, in part due to a decline in Arab unity and in part because of US hegemony (Miyagi 2011: 9–32). Notwithstanding this, it is erroneous to assume that Japan's national interests and US national interests coincide completely. While the US and Japan share an interest in securing access to oil (hence the propensity to support the Arabs at some level), and at the same time ensuring that the Jewish people are protected (hence the pro-Israel sentiments), Tokyo is not involved in arms sales and has a genuine interest is advocating an agenda of peace between the warring nations because of its pacifist culture.

Japan has increased its participation in the peace process since its inauguration in Madrid in 1991 and has worked alongside the major powers of the US and the EU to create frameworks for regional cooperation. Tokyo's strategy is to co-sponsor developmental projects, engage in dialog and administer aid to support US efforts. The aim of this is to create and foster economic conditions that can enable improvement of basic services and population recognition of the importance of building long-term peace. Japan in particular believes that without peace and economic vitality in these countries, it will be quite difficult to achieve peace in the Middle East on a larger scale. Beyond bilateral arrangements, Japan is also an active supporter of the Middle East and North African Economic Conferences (1994), Amman (1995) and Cairo (1996).

Fostering Better Socio-Economic Conditions

Japan has co-organized multilateral negotiations and working groups since the January 1992 Moscow Conference, including: (1) the Upper Gulf of Aqaba Oil Spill Contingency Project (2) Project to Combat Desertification (EWG) (3) Tourism Workshop (4) support for the establishment of the Middle East Desalination Research Center. Additionally, Japan has also provided a substantial amount of economic assistance to the Palestinian Authority (Inbari 2011) and also to the countries involved in the peace process—namely Egypt, Jordan, Syria,[4] and Lebanon.

According to Japan's Egyptian Embassy, Tokyo, in utilizing the Japanese Grant Scheme, has implemented important projects such as the Cairo University Pediatric Hospital, the Cairo Opera House, Suez Canal Bridge, and the Water Supply and Sewage Upgrading Project. Up until fiscal year 2013, Japan had provided a total of JPY 13 billion (USD 1200 million) to Egypt under this grant scheme. Funds provided in these schemes are not under any refunding or returning obligations. There is also grant assistance for grassroots projects (waste treatment systems, provision of medical services and projects aimed to improve employment rates in the country). Other forms of aid include cultural grant aid, technical cooperation and soft loans.[5]

In the case of Jordan, Japan has been at the forefront of aid efforts since 1974. As of 2004, Japan had provided a cumulative amount of USD 3 billion. In particular, Japan supports projects in the areas of water provision, environment, and health and medicine.

For Syria, prior to the War on the Islamic State, Japan focused its aid on five fields: (1) modernization of industries; (2) water resource use and management; (3) improvement of social services; (4) environmental protection and (5) promotion of regional stability in the Middle East. Like Egypt and Jordan, Japan's assistance to Syria includes a grant component: yen loans, grant assistance, grassroots human security projects and grants for cultural projects. Between 2001 and 2009, Japan provided JPY 7919 million to Syria for various projects. In 2010, Japan funded projects aimed at improving Japanese language learning, ensuring the provision of a

---

[4] For more details, see: http://www.sy.emb-japan.go.jp/econcoop.htm#grant

[5] See detailed write-up on Economic Assistance to Egypt by the Embassy of Japan to Egypt: http://www.eg.emb-japan.go.jp/e/assistance/grass_roots/20121018.htm

mobile library, building orphanages and deaf-mute schools, and improving medical equipment and handicap transportation in Syria (Japanese Embassy in Syria 2018).

The approach taken by Japan toward peace has been a comprehensive one. It fuses the regular elements of an overseas development assistance program with civilian components of peacekeeping. Along with the US and the EU, Japan is one of the largest donors to the Palestinians today. Tokyo has provided the Palestinians with generous assistance through a wide variety of programs.[6] It has invested and tried to promote a structure for a viable future Palestine state; aimed to improve financial conditions; pushed for the strengthening of the private sector in Palestinian territories; provided assistance to refugees in Lebanon, Syria and Jordan; and disbursed food aid throughout the territories. Since 1993, Japan has provided USD 1.47 billion in aid to the Palestinians.[7] After the peace process initiated by the Clinton administration, Japan pledged a total of USD 2 million, making it the third largest donor to the Palestine cause after the US and the EU. Admittedly, Japan first made the donation under pressure from the US, but nonetheless, it appears that Japan has actively lobbied on behalf of the Palestinians whenever it has been able to. Through its humanitarian and developmental assistance, Japan hopes to facilitate the governance aims (institution-building; improving the lives of Palestinians; building infrastructure) of the Palestinian Authority in order to give it legitimacy and viability and enhance the peace process.

By 2004, under the "Roadmap for Japanese Assistance to the Palestinians," Japan had given the Palestinians a sum that amounted to USD 760 million. With the election of US-backed candidate Mahmood Abbas as the head of the Palestinian Authority, Japan provided an additional USD 60 million. Even with the success of Hamas in January 2006 in Palestine's parliamentary elections, and a Hamas dominated legislature hostile to the US, Japan pushed through with the promised assistance.

While this might be interpreted as a "move" independent of the US, this might not necessarily be the case for several reasons. First, if Japan rescinds the aid, Japan would lose all its credibility in any work done with the Palestinians.

---

[6] See Japan's foreign ministry factsheet on Japan's aid to the Palestinians, November 2010, http://www.mofa.go.jp/announce/announce/2010/11/pdfs/112402.pdf

[7] Press release, Representative Office to Palestine Authority of Japan, October 28, 2014; available http://www.ps.emb-japan.go.jp/PressRelease/PressRelease2014/n28October.pdf

Second, it would only embolden the hardliners among the Palestinians and improve the prospects of Hamas politically because it would show that any US allied country would only back US-endorsed regimes, but never Hamas. Third, it would damage Japan's reputation irreparably as it would be perceived as a US lackey in the region. Lastly, if Japan pulled back its funding from the Palestinians, it might bring about greater problems in the Middle East peace process. It is not only therefore in Japan's interests but also in the interest of the US for Japan to keep funding the Palestinian Authority (Miyagi 2008, 2014).

One of the main pillars of Japan's approach to the Arab-Israeli conflict is Japan's concept of the "corridor for Peace and Prosperity." Japan has indeed exhibited an interest in playing a greater role in the region, hosting confidence-building conferences in 2003 and 2004, and once again in 2007. As reported by Gallup, during the May 2003 conference, Japan wanted to "explore ways in which Japan can contribute to peace," and in 2005, Prime Minister Junichiro Koizumi told *Kyodo News* that "Japan can provide support and cooperation in a different way from the US and Europe" by operating from a more "independent" position than the current players.[8] In 2007, Japan attempted to rope in key players in a peace process, getting them started on a "non-political" ground-level project with low stakes but important functionalism. Japan proposed its "Corridor for Peace and Prosperity"', comprised of an agro-industrial park in the West Bank meant to help build the Palestinian economy (Reuters, March 15, 2017).

Tokyo has cooperated with local and international governments to design and build the Jericho Agro Industrial Park. The facility draws its workers from the Palestinians living in the region, and engages in agriculture or industrial activities to help drive the region's economic growth. For example, local entrepreneurs grow and process vegetables and fruits (tomatoes and oranges) on a commercial scale. These are distributed locally and exported to Jordan. The park also has helped local entrepreneurs to establish various small scale manufacturing operations, such as a factory producing wipes (tissues) for the region, or health supplements made from olive tree leaves. Other Japan-financed business includes Al Masra and Dates Kingdom, with the former producing soft fruit-flavored beverages, and the latter processed date products (EUEA 2018). Japan has supported the financing of the park (via ODA and JICA),

---

[8] Ibid.

ensured park security and shared technical expertise in training the workers. Japan also helps with infrastructure improvements such as roads being built to facilitate trade and transfers over the Jordanian border, which is located a few kilometers away. The park will provide access to electricity and water, which is difficult for the Palestinian entrepreneurs to source. A video released by the Japanese Prime Minister's Office in July 2018, showed that approximately 200 people have found employment in the park, with an estimated 3500 people potentially to benefit from work opportunities in a few years' time (JPMO 2018). This park, conceived during the Koizumi era, has now materialized under Prime Minister Abe's tenure. Japan hopes that this "Corridor for Peace and Prosperity" initiative with the Palestinian Authority, Israel and Jordan will invite investment, create employment and facilitate exports to international markets. As Takeshi Okubo, Japanese Ambassador for Palestinian Affairs has said, this project symbolizes hope, peace and a better future for the people in the region (JPMO 2018).[9] Deeply embedded behind this thinking is Japan's subscription to the idea that Palestinians should be able to take steps to build a viable economy in order to materialize Palestinian statehood (Bryen 2000). To this end, Japan has also supported the main regional players directly affected by the peace process (Egypt, Jordan and Syria) through grant aid, loan aid, technical assistance and infrastructure projects, which shows the influence Japan could have, not just with Palestinians but with Arab countries as a whole.[10] Japan has also contributed enormously to supporting women and children throughout the conflict. For example, in August 2014, the Japanese government committed USD 1 million toward providing fresh water and sanitation for the relief of 285,000 Palestinians, over 50% of them children staying at 90 camps and 19 schools. This number was dramatically revised in 2018, as the Japanese government increased funding to help Palestinian children to USD 4.5 million (UNICEF March 4, 2018).[11]

---

[9] "Japan's stance in the Middle East," Japan foreign ministry website, http://www.mofa.go.jp/region/middle_e/stance.html

[10] Reuters, March 15, 2007, cited in "Israel, PA, Jordan agree to build joint agro-industrial park in West Bank," http://www.haaretz.com/news/israel-pa-jordan-agree-to-build-joint-agro-industrial-park-in-west-bank-1.215610

[11] "UNICEF Welcomes Japan's US$4.5m in support of Palestinian Children," https://www.un.org/unispal/document/unicef-welcomes-japans-us-4-5m-in-support-of-palestinian-children-press-release/

Japan's Undisputable Credentials as a Peacemaker

Japan's efforts seem to be capped at playing supporting role to the US. The most important aspects of enforcing peacebuilding, beyond placing peacekeepers in the Golan Heights, are not high on Tokyo's priority list. Efforts aimed at improving interactions between the Israelis and Palestinians appear to be elusive to Japanese diplomatic efforts. Does Japan's inability to play a greater role in the Middle East peace process stem from the fact that it lacks both the experience and capacity to do so? At first glance, many analysts do attribute it to a lack of experience.[12]

Traditionally, aside from the US, there have been three candidates that are most suited to play an enhanced role in the mediation of the Arab-Israeli conflict. They are the EU, the Scandinavian countries and Japan (Saad and Crabtree 2007). For historical reasons, including colonial history, both the Arabs and Israelis do not have a high preference for intervention by the EU. Additionally, the members of the EU have different interests and positions on many issues of foreign policy, which often complicates rather than facilitates the peace process (Nye 2014). Beyond this, as the democratic allies of the US, it is striking that they are excluded from the peace process (Miller 1997: 131). Not many other countries have actually tried to play an important role in the mediation of the problems between the Arabs and the Palestinians. Tokyo, however, has shown itself to be remarkably adept at peacebuilding efforts in other regions, such as Southeast Asia. Interviews with Middle Eastern academics concerned with the peace process revealed that Japan's weakness comes from the fact that Tokyo is being perceived as "lacking experience." It is, however, not difficult to understand why Japan does not have the requisite "experience" in the region, as peacebuilding efforts have largely been spear-headed by the US. Having said this, experience is not entirely necessary as there are other candidate countries who have played a relatively successful role in peacemaking with little experience, such as Norway.

The second factor is perhaps Japan's capacity. Even a country as strong as the US often finds itself as impotent as anyone else when it comes to influencing the Jewish state. According to Israel's famous defense minister Golda Meir, "Our American friends offer us money, arms and advice. We

---

[12] Personal communication with three academics from Israel who study Japan or the Middle East peace process, who gave the author this impression on three different occasions.

take the money, we take the arms and we decline the advice" (Quoted in Shlaim 2001: 316; 401–402). The US, despite its profound ties with Israel, has on more than one occasion found itself ostracized from Israel's decision-making process. If a power such as the US has not made headway, then surely one would assume that Japan might not be able to do so. The issue, however, hinges on the question of the impartiality of the country in question. As the largest arms supplier to the State of Israel, the US also sells arms to select Arab countries. In this pivotal position, the military-industrial complex located within the US actually stands to gain from conflict. Japan, on the other hand, has no such vested interest.

Due to the history of two oil shocks and the hostility that Japan has faced previously from the Arab states over its professed neutrality, Japan has sought to cultivate closer ties with the Arab-speaking world by becoming one of the few industrialized nations to follow Arab demands to boycott Israel (Bakshi 2014). The harsh actions of the Israeli military have somewhat galvanized public support for the Arab states and have swayed Japan to the side of the Arabs. This still holds true today, as the use of force against the Palestinians generally does not go down well with the Japanese public. Conversely, because of its somewhat lackluster economic relations with Israel, Japan does not have the same sort of economic clout it has with other countries necessary to be able to influence the internal politics (Waage 2007: 157–156).[13] However, because Japan has been perceived as pro-Arab, many Israeli officials tend not to view the country as neutral. Just as the EU would have to establish political goodwill with the Palestinian state, Japan would have to do the same with the Israeli government.

The fact that Japan does not carry a large stick around like Uncle Sam might be advantageous to this situation. Even though it has donated generously to the Palestinian cause and played an invaluable developmental role in the Arab world, the Arabs have been accustomed to Japan's

---

[13] However, this is not necessarily a deal breaker for Japan's future as a facilitator or mediator in the Arab-Israeli conflict, it just puts Japan at a disadvantage as Israel rather than the Palestinians have greater power in this relationship. One of the main reasons that the Norwegians were able to successfully broker the 1993 Oslo Accords was because the Norway-Israeli relationship was and still is extremely close, and Norway recognized then that goodwill from the Israelis was essential for the talks to move forward. Likewise, partly because of this relationship, the Israelis were persuaded to move forward with the concessions to the Palestinians. This was done independently of the 1991 Madrid framework the US had set up for the peace process.

relatively inexperienced and unforceful role in the Arab-Israeli peace process. At the same time, the intricacies of the peace process not only require a genuine and altruistic player but also one with exceptional clout, who is savvy in international politics. The confidence-building conference is an attempt by Japan, which relies heavily on Middle Eastern oil, to play a mediating role in the regional peace process. Japan has always appeared to defer to the US on the question of the Arab-Israeli conflict. This is unfortunate as Japan has the necessary credentials and is equipped to mediate in the dispute.

Japan possesses unique credentials to promote peace in the Middle East for several reasons. Japan's track record of embracing pacifism (drawn from the constitution) is an extremely important source of inspiration envied by many Arabs and Israeli intellectuals. Even though the domestic narrative today focuses on the normalization or rejuvenation of Japan through the rewriting or modification of its constitution, by and large, the impression in the region is that Japan is a country where pacifism still reigns. Second, Japan has little to do with the origins of the region's problems and does not have a direct interest in the politics of the region except in the search for a lasting solution toward peace. Even though Japan has a tendency to favor the Arab nations in order to secure its energy supplies, Japanese diplomats understand that Israel has the upper hand in the conflict, and that no amount of pressure on Israel can move them to compromise on their positions should the Israelis not want to. With that starting point, whether Japan is more sympathetic to the Palestinian cause is immaterial, since no peacemaker can ignore Israel's upper hand in the conflict. Third, Japan has very few ties to Judaism and Islam and is not intimately tied to either of the ethnic groups in this dispute. Unlike the US, Japan does not have a strong Jewish lobby in Tokyo. The majority of Muslims in Japan are of Turkic and Central Asian origins. Fourth, Japan's official position supports a two-state solution in which Israel and a future independent Palestinian state would live side by side, all the while encouraging dialog and negotiation for the solutions to be materialized in the near future.[14] Fifth, Japan is perceived to be an economic superpower with ambition for a permanent seat on the UN Security Council. Serving as the peacemaker might augment the building of a track record in this aim. Sixth, some commentators feel that Japan has earned a right to go its own

---

[14] Japan's Stance on the Middle East, Nov 24, 2010, Japan foreign ministry website: http://www.mofa.go.jp/region/middle_e/stance.html

way from the US in its Middle East policy, particularly when it comes to the Middle East peace process (McGlyn 2008). Japan has been a loyal ally in the US War on Terror, sending MSDF ships to provide logistical support, as well as joint patrols in the Gulf. It funds a huge portion of the US presence in East Asia, and has for years provided financial resources, political backing and strategic support. Japan just needs to refocus its attention and clarify its role in the Middle East (Curtin 2004). Seventh, Japan has put in the time and resources to extensively cultivate ties on both sides; it holds the prerequisite patience and tact. As Nye (2014) argues, if you take the Palestinian and Israeli representatives from their native surroundings and put them in a "pleasant, remote Japanese hotel with a view of the Sea," they might find some common ground.

Photo: UN International Media Seminar on Peace in the Middle East in Tokyo. (2014 International Media Seminar on Peace in the Middle East, Sophia University, Tokyo, June 9–10, 2014, organized by the United Nations Department of Public Information in cooperation with the Ministry of Foreign Affairs, Japan. Photo: United Nations/John Gillespie, Attribution-share alike 2.0 Generic License (CC By-SA 2.0) https://www.flickr.com/photos/johnji/14415948003)

To that end, Japan has been doing some important work in this regard. It is uniquely placed to ensure that the cultural and socio-psychological work needed for reconciliation takes effect. Cultural exchanges reduce prejudice and demonization, encourage the idea that friendship across nations can take place during conflict, allow for the healing of political wounds, and enable the restoration of pride in traditional cultural heritage. Once this happens, it can be mobilized for national reconstruction and peacebuilding (Ogoura 2009). Ambassador Ogoura gives the example of a Japanese NGO that invited Palestinian and Israeli high school students to Hiroshima and enabled them to interact through football matches. It made this younger generation realize that it is possible for them to become friends and interact, and that their future interactions need not be tied to the fate of preceding generations (Ogoura 2009).

Losing Sight of the Forest for the Trees

So why is Japan not playing a larger role in the peace process? There are two aspects to this answer. First, Japan's domestic support for greater intervention in the Middle East is not strong. For the last two decades, Japan's strategic attention has been fixated on the rise of China and the implications this has for Japan. Much narrative is focused on the dispatching of military units (minesweepers, refueling vessels, troops in support roles) to various hotspots. Such deployments lend support to the US, provide good training opportunities for the JSDF, and socialize the Japanese people and Japan's neighbors to the idea of Tokyo "normalizing" its political and military status. Even though there is a certain measure of support among the Japanese people for Japan's fulfillment of international responsibilities, the support tends to dwindle when the question touches on whether precious resources such as money should be used, and the lives of Japanese troops put at risk. The inertia created by Japan's pacifist culture is strong because it is deeply embedded in the Japanese national identity. For many Japanese, pacifism is linked with democracy, or even seen as one and the same, even though they are conceptually different things. The resistance that the neo-conservatives embarking on constitutional amendment face today at the grassroots level stems from the fact that many Japanese citizens feel that what the Abe government is doing erodes their democratic rights and innately Japanese identity and culture. Even though the "rational" narratives about China and North Korea are put forth to assuage the electorate, it is still an uphill battle.

Second, and most importantly, is Japan's own conceptualization of its relationship with the US. The crux is that Japan's Middle East strategy is premised on the Yoshida Doctrine, which indicates that Japan should follow the lead of the US in strategic and foreign affairs. Tokyo took this to heart for most of the Cold War, particularly in the Middle East. For the most part, the "positive balance" policy that Japan has undertaken in the Middle East peace process is circumscribed by three important elements that the US has allowed Japan to partake in: political dialogs, confidence building, and the extension of economic assistance to the Palestinians (Curtin 2004; Inbari 2014). Japanese diplomats often have to work under US sponsored events, and Japanese aid or developmental projects are designated to complement US plans. In privileging the US-Japan alliance, Japan is forgoing the opportunity to carve out a more independent role for itself in the peace process.

Despite diplomatic rhetoric, the US has worked hard to ensure that no other power is able to become dominant in the peace process, including Japan. The Clinton administration was said to have been furious at Japan's attempt to play a more central role in the Arab-Israeli peace process, and every effort was made to ensure the US maintenance of a position of centrality in the peace process (Soetendorp 2002: 283–295). The US would have hated losing control of an issue as central to Middle Eastern politics as the Arab-Israeli peace negotiations. Beyond that it, it would not have tolerated the rise of another nation with potential to surpass US influence in Middle Eastern affairs. This, however, should not come as a surprise. Every country will strive to maximize its own interests in the region, even in the case of Japan. It therefore comes as no surprise that Japan's overtures to play a greater role in the Arab-Israeli negotiations, as well as in the Iranian nuclear issue, were rejected by none other than its close ally, the US (Schulze 2015).[15]

The onus for Japan to play a greater role rests on Japan's prioritization of its interests above its relationship with the US. This would include spelling out a greater role for itself as a "peace" state in the region, rather than seeing its role as being one of deference to and unconditional support of US policies. There are four main immediate impediments to improving

---

[15] This point is also reiterated by the various interlocutors whom the author has spoken to over the years. Most Japanese colleagues who articulated this view do not want to be identified, because there is a real fear that their careers will be affected. There seems to be a consensus that even with on-the-ground activities, Japanese groups are often given "guidance" as to what is permissible and what is not.

Japan's position in the Middle East, and all these stem in part from the imperfect conceptualization of Japan's normalization and rejuvenation.

The first principal impediment is Japan's inability to foster an independent vision for Japan in the region and beyond. Despite the rhetoric and the official narratives, Japan has yet to reach a clear and well-defined goal for Japan's normalization and rejuvenation with regards to its policy outside the Asia-Pacific. The direction and tone of Japan's recent diplomacy certainly reflects a hint of desire to seek a foreign policy that maintains a streak of independence from the US, but a Japan that could possibly survive and thrive on its own is beyond the imaginary reach of most Japanese strategic thinkers. Certainly, the author is not the only one to feel strongly that Japan should conceptualize and articulate a clearer vision of its role to date, particularly in the Middle East. As one editorial argues, even though since 1993, Japan has contributed USD 1.7 billion to the Palestinians via programs that aid socio-economic development, there is a marked difference between official government policy and Japan's prime ministerial outreach (Cooper and Gover 2018).

Second, Japan has developed a culture of deference to the US alliance, and this has inhibited it from developing an independent and forward-looking agenda with regards to its global strategy. This has consequently led Japan to allow its goals to be subsumed into US foreign policy goals and sensitivities rather than trying to harmonize their interests where possible and pursue its own interests when not. Cooperation with the US has therefore become a goal in itself rather than a means to spring-board to something greater. If Japan seeks rejuvenation as a global power, then it has to consider that there might be times when it has to speak beyond the confines of the US-Japan alliance. Prioritizing the preservation of the US-Japan security alliance and US goals in the region might not be in the best interest of the region. Most observers agree that deep down, at the protracted root of the conflict, is the fact that Israel illegally apportioned and annexed territories that belonged to Palestine at the onset of the conflict. The very fact that Japan supports UN Resolution 242 is indicative of this. Yet, no one has called upon the US not to support Israel or requested that the US enforce the requisite law on the State of Israel. Failure to act in the first place is the very reason why the conflict has grown to be so protracted.

Third, this essentially meant that even though one of the principal goals Japan has articulated in recent years is the promotion of peace in the international community, its ability to realize its potential as a peacemaker has been thwarted by its image as a country subservient to US foreign policy goals. While the idea of becoming a global power by relying on the "globalizing" US-Japan alliance might seem desirable to the neo-conservatives in Tokyo, the question of whether or not it serves Japanese interests directly is something that needs to be considered. Take for instance how third parties might view this relationship. Today, the Israelis view Japan as extremely polite but utterly powerless over the Palestinians in terms of curbing the violence and improving Israel's homeland security situation, and in turn, the Palestinians may feel that as much as Japan might want to assist them, it has neither the influence to affect the settlements nor clout to enforce the peace.

Fourth, the lack of autonomy insofar as the peace talks are concerned is a facet that is remarkably absent from Japanese public narratives about its intervention in the Middle East. Instead, Japan's focus has been solely on peacekeeping and humanitarian assistance. In particular, these narratives relate to the "normalization" of Japan's security forces by enhancing their operational readiness and deployment capabilities. Unless the Japanese government decides to make this a priority and shift the debate from military to political rejuvenation, then Japan is unlikely to ever garner public support for this. A healthy discussion on the desired role of Japan in the peacebuilding process in the Middle East would be welcome. Japan has failed to do what it perhaps might be in the best position to do—become a genuine peacemaker in the region. Achieving this requires Japan to adopt a higher profile and a more independent position from the US, something it may be reluctant to do. Japan's 2007 Peace Corridor initiative for common economic development is an interesting diversion for both the Arabs and the Israelis to come on board and jointly engage in an economic partnership, but it is unfortunately insufficient to promote peace between them. The strategy is a good one, shifting the focus from land deals, but it stops short of pushing the two sides to come together for some sort of more permanent peace.

In his second term, it is clear that Prime Minister Abe had also learned something important from his first stint as prime minister and from his predecessors' experience—from providing financial resources for the first Gulf War and JSDF deployments for anti-piracy deployments, to the Persian Gulf, Japan has been providing political, logistical and military assistance to the US. For Prime Minister Abe, it would therefore be wise for Japan, rather than US, to earn the recognition it deserves when it makes contributions. Consequently, in 2014, Prime Minister Abe offered

Japan's support of USD 200 million in the War against the Islamic State of Iraq and Syria (ISIS), just days before the hostage crisis (which incidentally is the amount demanded by the hostage takers) (Schulze 2015). Translated to the neo-conservative's language, this means that in order to have the rejuvenation that Japan seeks, it might be necessary for Japan to refrain from seeking approval from the US, instead contributing to substantial direction and narratives as an independent nation seeking a greater role and status in the region.

The Neo-Conservatives' Peacebuilding Efforts in the Trump Era

It is of no surprise that between 1993 and 2017, Japan provided USD 1.77 billion to Palestinian causes (Kabilo 2017). By the early 2000s, Japan had shifted its policy in the Middle East to take a more independent and proactive stance. Even though the Middle East, particularly Saudi Arabia (Cafiero et al. 2016), is critical to Japan's interests, the domestic media and political narratives have often underestimated the region's importance to Japan. But since this period of neo-conservative power acquisition, the region has become a "target" for Japan's reinvigorated foreign policy. In 2002, the Japan Institute for International Affairs (JIIA) released a white paper recommending several courses of action. One notable suggestion was that Japan should strengthen cooperation and build coalitions with regional partners beyond Jordan and Egypt, but also Saudi Arabia; that Japan should endeavor to expand the "Quartet" (US, EU, Russia and UN) in conjunction with Egypt, Jordan and Saudi Arabia. Other recommendations included the intensification of dialog and discussion on both sides at the Track 2 level, along with a strengthening of consultation. Most interestingly, the JIIA asked to develop a bilateral youth initiative to ensure future generations can co-exist, with JIIA indicating that they would help to develop history textbooks for both sides (JIIA 2002: 4–5).

Most of Japan's prime ministers have run under the motto of peace, pride and internationalism, and of the most commonly articulated policy platforms, "international contribution" was most routinely called upon (Le 2012: 21). This reflects the general socialization of Japanese prime ministers who grew up in a pacifist Japan that was content to do its part in the postwar San Francisco system, with seemingly little appetite for participation in global affairs or great power status. Yet, even when Prime

Minister Koizumi first came to power, his immediate concern was Japan's economic progress, not foreign policy. In June 2004, when he decided to send JSDF forces to help in Iraq, there was a sharp drop in the cabinet approval rating from 54% to 40% (Shinoda 2007: 152–153).

One of the stimuli is undeniably China. Unlike Japan, which has historically been firmly entrenched in the Western Cold War bloc, China has long had historical interactions with the Middle East. During the Cold War, China maintained most if not all of its ties with the Middle Eastern countries. Today, China is now viewed as a major independent political power. All Middle Eastern powers are keen to cultivate relations with China as a major political power. This is as true for traditional US allies such as Israel and Saudi Arabia, as it is for rivals such as Iran or Egypt. The need to increase Japan's political weight (i.e. vis-à-vis China and the US) exists. This is particularly true as the US currently holds all the cards in bilateral dealings. From the perspective of countries such as Iran, Yemen or Palestine, China's role as a potential honest broker in regional problems is a particularly critical one, as many states do not see the US (or Japan) as ever having played an even-handed role. This is particularly important in an era where over the last 30 years, civil and proxy wars have become impossible to distinguish (Haass 2014). Eradicating Saddam Hussein's regime has led to a certain imbalance which Saudi Arabia, Iran and Turkey are eager to address. For China, the contentious Middle East represents a new opportunity for her to realize its One Belt One Road (OBOR) initiative by involving countries in the region. Beijing argues that as opposed to the US's desire to control the developments in the region via proxies and managed low-intensity conflict, China's OBOR vision promises developmentalism without control and connectivity without dominance.

China's grand vision has been met with skepticism and disdain from the US-led bloc. Since his first administration, Japan's Prime Minister Abe has appeared determined to meet the China challenge globally, and to that end Abe's vision of Japan offering these regions an alternative economic network ensures that nation-states are not enticed into, or entrapped in, a "China centric" economic network, ending up with an asymmetrical relationship with Beijing. In denying China an extended hinterland for a Beijing-style Marshall Plan, Japan, along with the US, is also preventing these countries from becoming economically (and somewhere down the line) politically connected with (and reliant on) Beijing. China's determination to promote the connectivity of the ancient Silk Road that runs overland from China through Central Asia to the Middle East has led to a series of "strategic partnerships" in eight countries, six of which are founding members of the Beijing-backed Asian Infrastructure Investment Bank (AIIB) (Zhao 2016). The Chinese factor is therefore an important motivating reason for Japan's keenness to take on a greater role in its Middle East strategy, particularly since Xi's proposal at the China-Arab States Cooperation Forum, where he emphasized that China will collaborate with the Middle Eastern states on a "1+2+3" formula (Industrialization, Commercial Capacity and Concessional loans).

Prime Minister Abe's "proactive pacifism" strategy, put in place after the 2014 election, is precisely geared in this direction. By seeking to reinvigorate Japan's presence in the region, Prime Minister Abe is hoping that Japan will be able to counter China's grand plan and instead raise Japan's own profile in the region. Although there is no clear indication that China and Japan see each other's presence as a threat, it is clear that Tokyo does see the Chinese presence as something that needs to be watched very carefully.

On September 12, 2017, Japan's foreign minister met the Arab League and articulated the "Kono Principles," where the foreign minister promised that Japan will (i) drastically expand the intellectual and human contribution to peace and prosperity in the Middle East; (ii) invest in human resource development geared toward the promotion of peace and development in the region; (iii) put in enduring efforts to cultivate peace; and (iv) enhance political efforts in the Middle East. In sum, Japan continued to reiterate its commitment to the "Corridor for Peace and Prosperity," where Tokyo encourages and supports the independence of the Palestinian economy through regional cooperation with Palestine, Jordan and Israel. Japan also committed to help enhance the fruit harvesting economy and other agriculture in the region, also as well as the IT, AI and tourism in the region. Tokyo will continue to help realize comprehensive peace in the Middle East and expand cooperation on education and human resources development in the Arab League. Japan also promised to enhance political dialog in the region, not only on a bilateral basis, but also on a multilateral one, including strategic dialogs, promotion of reconciliation (e.g. between Qatar and Arab countries) and more facilitate open discussions on the incorporation of the Middle East into the "Free and Open Indo-Pacific Strategy." Lastly, Japan committed USD 25 million to new humanitarian assistance for Syria, Iraq and other countries (MOFA Japan, September 12, 2017).

By December 2017, Japan was still under criticism for being as helpless as ever after it joined 128 countries in support of a UN General Assembly resolution condemning the US decision to recognize Jerusalem as the political capital of Israel (Kabilo 2017). The criticism is leveled at Japan from both sides. The Arabs feel that even though Japan is a generous donor, it is unable to rein in Israel, particularly when the US maintains its protection of Israel.

Ironically, Jewish intellectuals and officials grouse about Tokyo being "unfriendly" toward Israel. Prime Minister Abe, while being tremendously generous and friendly toward both the Palestinians and Israel (Taylor 2015), is behaving in such a manner that is at odds with Japan's official policy thinking. From the perspective of some observers, particularly those from the Israeli camp, this resembles cognitive dissonance. In an editorial, two Jewish intellectuals complain about this:

> The marked difference between Abe's positive engagement of Israel and the Japanese Ministry of Foreign Affairs' shortsighted and at times hostile political positions towards the Jewish state is confounding. One would be forgiven for thinking that the Foreign Ministry didn't get the memo from the Prime Minister's Office on Abe's new forward-thinking engagement with the Jewish state While the Japanese government is to be commended for decades of generous international aid, its March 2018 $23.5 million aid package to the United Nations Relief and Works Agency for Palestine Refugees in the Near East (UNRWA) has been transferred to an entity whose Hamas-controlled teachers have allegedly been teaching Palestinian children with curricula that praise 'martyrdom' (read terrorism) and do not even show the State of Israel on a single map in any of the books. (Cooper and Gover 2018)

Despite these difficulties, there is a proverbial pot of gold waiting for Japan if it keeps plugging away with the peace process. As argued earlier, Japan's strategy to collectively engage the future generations of Israelis and Arabs is a wonderful exercise, particularly if these youths are transported out to various parts of Japan. Japan's relative neutrality, economic prowess, and proximity to the US have certainly helped with Washington's "tolerance" of its involvement in these matters. As Japan increases its engagement, it will provide a measure of balance to the peace process that the US perhaps cannot offer (Nikkei Asian Review 2017). Tokyo's attempt to invite Israel's leader to Tokyo for a 4-way summit in 2018 is a good example (JTA 2018). Japan, however, has to decide what kind of peacemaker it wants to be. While this is not a suggestion to encourage Tokyo to revolt against the US, it is important that Japan aims to become a fair, moderate voice that can call out its longtime ally when there are genuine grievances and wrong doings. There is certainly support for the fact that Tokyo could become a fair, impartial and effective peacemaker. There are three possible things Japan could do. First, Japan should try and transcend the "allowed" perimeters the US has set for it (encouraging reconciliation, enabling political dialog and enhancing socio-economic conditions for the Palestinians), to become an independent and moderate influence. One example is to rally for sanctions against Israel for breaking international laws such as the UN resolutions, or when it violates the human rights of Palestinians. Perhaps Japan does not have the power to accomplish this, but given the recent moves by the Trump administration to support Jewish settlements in Palestinian areas and recognize the embassy in Jerusalem, more can be done by Japan. As Japan builds coalitions to balance the excesses of its close ally, a possible and imaginative way forward is to work with China to build a different coalition and pursue an alternative peace process. There are few people in the world that are not aware of the tensions in the Sino-Japanese relationship, but a political partnership between the Asian giants might provide a sorely needed balance in the region. In the past, the Arabs could rely on the Soviets to moderate US adventurism in the region, but since the end of the Cold War, the US has had the main positional power and exploited it, exacerbating difficulties in the region. Working with China has the added bonus of boosting bilateral cooperation and building confidence currently lacking in Sino-Japanese relations. As the next chapter on anti-piracy missions outlines, it is not entirely impossible for China and Japan to collaborate. This gesture would certainly be appreciated by the Chinese and signal to both Israel and the Arab nations that Japan could transcend its traditional role as the ally and play the part of a peacemaker for the twenty-first century. Whether Japan succeeds or fails is another matter but having the legitimacy and credentials to be endorsed as an important political power in its own right certainly speaks to the prospects of achieving rejuvenation and attaining the goal of a "Beautiful Japan" through achieving peace in the Middle East.

REFERENCES

Bakshi, G. "Israel-Palestine Conflict – Need for a New Third Party Negotiator." *Middle East Monitor*, 30 Jan 2014, https://www.middleeastmonitor.com/tag/israel-palestine-conflict/
Balfour Project. "The Balfour Declaration, November 1917", http://www.balfourproject.org/wp-content/uploads/2016/11/The-Balfour-Declaration.pdf

Bard, M.G. *The Water's Edge and Beyond: defining the limits to domestic influence on U.S. Middle East policy.* Transaction Publishers, 1991.

BBC News. "1956: Egypt Seizes Suez Canal", 26 July 1956, http://news.bbc.co.uk/onthisday/hi/dates/stories/july/26/newsid_2701000/2701603.stm

Bean, James W., & Girard, Craig S. "Anwar Al-Sadat's Grand Strategy in the Yom Kippur War." National War College Report, 2001, http://www.dtic.mil/dtic/tr/fulltext/u2/a442407.pdf

Beinin, J., & Hajjar, L. "Palestine, Israel and the Arab-Israeli Conflict: A Primer." Middle East Research and Information Project Paper, Feb 2014, https://www.merip.org/sites/default/files/Primer_on_Palestine-Israel(MERIP_February2014)final.pdf

Bellamy, A., Williams, P.D., & Griffin, S. *Understanding Peacekeeping.* Cambridge & Malden: Polity Press, 2010.

Bowen, Jeremy. "1967 War: Six Days that Changed the Middle East." *BBC*, 5 June 2017, https://www.bbc.com/news/world-middle-east-39960461

Bryen, R. *A Very Political Economy: Peacebuilding and Foreign Aid in the West Bank and Gaza.* Washington D.C.: United States Institute of Peace Press, 2000.

Cafiero, G., Karasikm, T., Miotto, C., & Wagner, D. "Japan's Important Role in Saudi's Vision 2030." *Huffington Post*, 29 November 2016, https://www.huffingtonpost.com/giorgio-cafiero/japans-important-role-in-_b_13334900.html

Cooper, A., & Gover, T. "Japan has important role in Middle East buy must clarify it." *Asia Times*, 29 July 2018, http://www.atimes.com/article/japan-has-important-role-in-middle-east-but-must-clarify-it/

Curtin, J.S. "Japan seeks bigger Middle East Role: Economic Diplomacy." *The Asia-Pacific Journal: Japan Focus*, vol. 2, no. 12, 2004, https://apjjf.org/-J.-Sean-Curtin/1984/article.html

Deseret News. "Role for Japan as Peacemaker?" 4 July 1988, https://www.deseretnews.com/article/9455/ROLE-FOR-JAPAN-AS-PEACEMAKER.html

Dobson, H. *Japan and UN Peacekeeping: New Pressures and New Responses.* London and New York, Routledge, 2003.

Dumper, M. *Jerusalem Unbound: Geography, History, and the Future of the Holy City.* New York: Columbia University Press, 2014.

Dunstan, S. *The Yom Kippur War 1973: The Sinai*, p. 67. Osprey Publishing, 2003.

EUEA (European Union External Agency), "Japan provides two new contributions to the Jericho Agro Industrial Park incentives programme implemented by the EU", Press Release, 12 June 2018, https://eeas.europa.eu/headquarters/headquarters-homepage/46344/japan-provides-two-new-contributionsjericho-agro-industrial-park-incentives-programme_en

Gadzo, M. "Palestinians speak out on Anniversary of Resolution 242." *Aljazeera*, 19 November 2017, https://www.aljazeera.com/news/2017/11/palestinians-speak-anniversary-resolution-242-171117092925628.html

Haass, Richard. "A New Thirty Years' War" Council for Foreign Relations, Commentary published on *Project Syndicate*, 21 July 2014, https://www.project-syndicate.org/commentary/richard-n%2D%2Dhaass-argues-that-the-middle-east-is-less-a-problem-to-be-solved-than-a-condition-to-be-managed

Halloran, R. "Japanese Caution Israelis on Ties." *The New York Times*, 22 Nov 1973, https://www.nytimes.com/1973/11/22/archives/japanese-caution-israelis-on-ties-tokyo-hints-break-possible-if.html

Harrison, S., & Nishihara, M. *UN Peacekeeping: Japanese and American Perspectives*. Carnegie Endowment for International Peace, 1995, https://carnegieendowment.org/1995/10/01/u.n.-peacekeeping-japanese-and-american-perspectives-pub-203

Inbari, P. "Japan and the Palestinian Authority: Foreign Policy and Economic Interest." Jerusalem Center for Public Affairs, 4 March 2014.

Inbari, M. "Japan, the Middle East and the Palestinian Authority." Jerusalem Institute of Public Affairs, 2011, http://jcpa.org/japan-the-middle-east-and-the-palestinian-authority/

Ishizuka, K. "Japan's Policy Towards UN Peacekeeping Operations." In Mely Cabellero-Anthony & Amitav Acharya, *UN Peace Operations and Asian Security*. Routledge, Oxford and New York, 2005, pp 56–72.

Japan Institute of International Affairs Middle East Peace Policy Study Group (JIIA MEPPSG). "Japan's Future Politics Towards the Middle East Process: Recommendations." Tokyo: JIIA, 26 July 2002.

Japanese Embassy in Syria. "Summary of Assistance to Syria," http://www.sy.emb-japan.go.jp/econcoop.htm#summary

JTA. "Japan invites Netanyahu to four-way peace summit in Tokyo." *The Jerusalem Post*, 25 August 2018, https://www.jpost.com/Arab-Israeli-Conflict/Japan-invites-Netanyahu-to-four-way-peace-summit-in-Tokyo-520085

JPMO - Japan Prime Minister's Office, Video on "Japan's cooperation with the Jericho Agro-Industrial Park in Palestine", 18 July 2018, https://www.youtube.com/watch?v=HP8KPijCEFE

Kabilo, G. "Risk-Adverse and Dependent on Oil, Japan tiptoes through the Middle East." *Calcalist Opinion*, 27 Dec 2017, https://www.calcalistech.com/ctech/articles/0,7340,L-3728311,00.html

Kozai, S. "Japan and PKO; Japanese Experiences and its Policy." *Journal for International Studies*, Osaka Gakuin University, vol. 12, no. 2, 2001.

Kuroda, Y. "Japan's Middle East Policy: Fuzzy Nonbinary Process Model" in Miyashita, A. & Sato, Y., *Japanese Foreign Policy in Asia and the Pacific: Domestic Interests, American Pressure and Regional Integration*, New York & Basingstoke: Palgrave, 2001, pp 101–119.

Lam, P. *Japan's Peace-Building Diplomacy in Asia: Seeking a More Active Political Role*. Oxford and New York, Routledge, 2009.

Le, T. "Assertive Peacemaking: Japan's Evolving International Role." Western Political Science Association 2012 Annual Meeting Paper (WPSA Paper), Portland, Oregon, 22–24 March, 2012.

Leitenberg, M. *The Participation of Japanese Military Forces in UN Peace Keeping Operations*. Maryland: Center For International and Security Studies, University of Mary Land, 1996.

Maeda, T. *The Hidden Army: The Untold Story of Japan's Military Forces*. Chicago: Edition Q, 1995.

McGlyn, J. "With One Sentence Japan Cold Set the Stage for an Israeli-Palestinian Peace." *The Asia-Pacific Journal: Japan Focus*, vol. 6, no. 10, 2008.

Miller, B. "Greater Powers and Regional Peacemaking: Patterns in the Middle East and Beyond." *Journal of Strategic Studies*, vol. 1, no. 20, 1997, pp 103–142.

Ministry of Foreign Affairs, Japan, (MOFA Japan). Speech by Foreign Minister Kono at the first ever Japan Arab Political Dialogue, 12 September 2017, https://www.mofa.go.jp/files/000288921.pdf

Miyagi, Y. "Japan's Middle East Security Policy: Rethinking Roles and Norms." *Ortadogu Etuleri*, vol. 3, no. 1, 2011.

Miyagi, Y. *Japan's Middle East Security Policy: Theory and Cases*. Oxon, OX; Routledge, 2008.

Miyagi, Y. "Japan and the Middle East After the Arab Spring." *IDE ME Review*, vol. 1, 2014, pp 28–45, http://www.ide.go.jp/library/Japanese/Publish/Periodicals/Me_review/pdf/201402_02.pdf

Naramoto, E. "Perceptions on the Arab-Israeli Conflict." *Journal of Palestine Studies*, vol. 20, no. 3, 1991, pp 79–88.

Nikkei Asian Review. "Japan seeks more active role in bring peace to the Middle East." 24 August 2017, https://asia.nikkei.com/Politics/Japan-seeks-more-active-role-in-bringing-peace-to-Middle-East2

Nye, D. "After the American century: Might Japan be the Broker to Negotiate Peace between Israel and Palestine ?" *After the American Century*, 18 August 2014, http://aftertheamericancentury.blogspot.com/2014/08/might-japan-be-broker-to-negotiate.html

Ogoura, K. "The Peacemaking Process has a cultural dimension." *The Japan Times*, 11 April 2009.

Russian Times Editorial. "Israel's destruction of Palestinian homes at five-year high – aid orgs" *Russian Times*, 8 Feb 2014, http://rt.com/news/israel-palestinian-destruction-aid-134/

Saad, L., & Crabtree, Steve. "Israel/Palestine: Support for Potential Peace Brokers: EU, Japan appear more acceptable to both populations." *Gallup News Service*, 26 Jan 2007, https://news.gallup.com/poll/26290/IsraelPalestine-Support-Potential-Peace-Brokers.aspx

Samuel, H. "The Future of Palestine." Memorandum to the Cabinet, January 1915, The National Archives of the UK, hereafter TNA, CAB 37/123/43.

Schulze, K. "Shinzo Abe's Middle East Ambition." *Emerging Equity*, 12 Feb 2015, https://emergingequity.wordpress.com/2015/02/12/shinzo-abes-middle-east-ambition/

Shelter-Jones, P. "Peacebuilding as a Field of Joint Endeavor in the Japan-U.S. Alliance: The View from an International Organisations' Perspective", in Hoshino Toshiya and Weston S. Konishi, *US-Japan Peacebuilding Cooperation: Roles and Recommendations toward a Whole-of-Alliance Approach*, Joint Compendium Report published by Institute of Foreign Policy Analysis (IFPA) and Osaka School of International Public Policy (OSIPP), Osaka and Washington D.C., CreateSpace Independent Publishing Platform, 2012, pp 29–43, http://www.ifpa.org/pdf/peaceBuildingCompendium.pdf

Shinoda, T., *Koizumi Diplomacy: Japan's Kantei Approach to Foreign and Defense Affairs*. Washington: University of Washington Press, 2007.

Shlaim, A. *The Iron Wall: Israel and the Arab World*. New York, W.W. Norton & Company, 2001.

Soetendorp, B. "The EU's Involvement in the Israeli-Palestinian Peace Process: The Building of a Visible International Identity." *European Foreign Affairs Review*, vol. 7, no. 3, 2002, pp 283–295.

Soeya, Y. "Japanese Security Policy in Transition: The Rise of International and Human Security." *Asia-Pacific Review*, vol. 12, no. 1, 2005.

Spiegel, S.L. *The Other Arab-Israeli Conflict: Making America's Middle East Policy from Truman to Reagan*. Chicago: Chicago University Press, 1985.

Suzuki, H., editor. *The Middle East Turmoil and Japanese Response – For a Sustainable Regional Peacekeeping System*. Tokyo, JETRO, 2013, http://www.ide.go.jp/Japanese/Publish/Download/Seisaku/201307_mide.html

Swisher, Clayton E. *The Truth About Camp David: The Untold Story About the Collapse of the Middle East Peace Process*. New York, Nation Books, 2004.

Takahara, T. "Japan." In Findlay, T., (ed.) *Challenges for New Peacekeepers*. Oxford: Oxford University Press, 1996.

Taylor, P. Warming Relations Between Israel and Japan Result in Trade Agreement, Jan 2015 US State Department, National Archives and Records Administration, RG 59, Central Files 1964–66, DEF 12–5 JORDAN. Secret; Immediate; Exdis. Received on March 10 at 8:38 p.m. and passed to the White House and DOD., outlining Johnson Administration plans to sell to Israel that balances sale to Jordan. This memo is reproduced and housed by the Jewish Virtual Library, https://www.jewishvirtuallibrary.org/u-s-promises-arms-sale-to-israel-that-balances-sale-to-jordan-march-1965

Togo, K. *Japan's Foreign Policy, 1945–2009: The Quest for a Proactive Policy*. Leiden: Brill Academic, 2010.

Touval, S. *Mediators in the Arab-Israeli Conflict, 1948–1979.* New Jersey: Princeton University Press, 1982.

Waage, H.H. "'The 'Minnow' and the 'Whale'" Norway and the United States in the Peace Process in the Middle East." *British Journal of Middle Eastern Studies*, vol. 34, no. 2, 2007, pp 157–176.

Yamanaka, A. "Why Japan Needs to Contribute to International Peace Now." *Gunshuku Mondai Shiryou* [Journal for Disarmament Issues], March 2003.

Yoshizaki, T. "The Role of the Military in Peace-Building: A Japanese Perspective." Proceeding of NIDS International Symposium on Security Affairs 2008–2009, Tokyo: NIDS, 2008, http://www.nids.mod.go.jp/english/event/symposium/pdf/2008/e_12.pdf

Zhao, Minghao. "China's New role as a Middle East Peacemaker", The *Japan Times*, 4 February 2016, https://www.japantimes.co.jp/opinion/2016/02/04/commentary/world-commentary/chinas-new-role-middle-east-peacemaker/

Open Access This chapter is licensed under the terms of the Creative Commons Attribution 4.0 International License (http://creativecommons.org/licenses/by/4.0/), which permits use, sharing, adaptation, distribution and reproduction in any medium or format, as long as you give appropriate credit to the original author(s) and the source, provide a link to the Creative Commons licence and indicate if changes were made.

The images or other third party material in this chapter are included in the chapter's Creative Commons licence, unless indicated otherwise in a credit line to the material. If material is not included in the chapter's Creative Commons licence and your intended use is not permitted by statutory regulation or exceeds the permitted use, you will need to obtain permission directly from the copyright holder.

CHAPTER 5

The Provision of International Public Goods: Japan's Anti-Piracy Operations in the Gulf of Aden

> I will carry forward a diplomacy which contributes to world peace, so that Japan will realize its responsibilities commensurate with its national strength in the international community, and become a country which is relied upon internationally.
>
> Policy Speech by Prime Minister Yasuo Fukuda to the 169th Session of the Diet, January 18 2008

Piracy as a Security Challenge

As discussed in Chap. 4, the Middle East is one of the most important regions in the world to Japan, considering that a huge bulk of Japan's energy supplies come from the area. According to Japan's Ministry of Economy, Trade and Industry's Agency for Natural Resources and Energy, in 2015, Middle Eastern countries supplied about 78% of Japan's 1.23 billion barrels of crude oil. The most important countries that provide for Japan's energy needs are as follows: Saudi Arabia (33%), UAE (25%), Qatar (8%), Kuwait (8%), Iran (5%) and Iraq (2%). Since the oil crisis in the 1970s, Japan's relationship with the Middle Eastern world, particularly the Arab states, has moved beyond a "buyer–seller" relationship, with Japan building political relations with much of the Arab world. Japan has also undertaken steps to source energy products from alternative markets such as Venezuela, Mexico and Indonesia, as well as diversify on the types

© The Author(s) 2019
V. Teo, *Japan's Arduous Rejuvenation as a Global Power*,
https://doi.org/10.1007/978-981-13-6190-6_5

of energy it uses. Needless to say, Tokyo has always been extremely concerned about the freedom and security of the shipping lanes from the Middle East to East Asia. By 2014, due to the Great East Japan Earthquake in 2011, Japan was forced to increase reliance on energy imports (oil/gas/coal) up to 88%. Thus, undertaking measures to secure its energy imports became more important than ever. This is why Japan has quietly been struggling to maintain a common position with the US over Iran and has assiduously cultivated the various Gulf states by increasing its engagement with the Arab states.

Beyond the issue of securing energy imports, Japan has also been undertaking other activities in the region. First, the JSDF has engaged in humanitarian and peacekeeping missions. In the aftermath of the Gulf War, Japan deployed four wooden-hull naval vessels to help in minesweeping operations (Woolley 1996). Japanese troops have been deployed on UN peacekeeping missions to Angola (1992), the Golan Heights (1996–2012), Sudan (2012–present). Japan participated in international humanitarian relief operations in such countries as Rwanda (1994), Afghanistan (2001) and Iraq (2003). In their deployment to Iraq, Prime Minister Koizumi forced legislation through the Diet that paved the way for 1000 Japanese troops to be deployed in a US-led occupying army trying to quell a guerilla war, even though they were supposed to undertake "non-combat" duties in "safe-areas." In short, Japan's intervention in the Middle East has therefore increasingly taken on a military nature (Wagner and Cafiero 2014). From the deployment of minesweepers to the dispatching of troops piggybacking on the US or UN missions, Japan has shown an increasing propensity to deploy military force to achieve its goals.

This chapter highlights this important aspect of Japan's normalization and rejuvenation vis-à-vis its deployment of its naval assets to fight piracy. Remilitarization remains one of the obvious hallmarks of Japan's normalization and rejuvenation. In dispatching military forces, Japan's neoconservatives continually erode or sidestep its constitutional constraints. The deployment of Japanese forces to the Gulf of Aden to fight piracy is marketed under the auspices of assisting the US in their military operations. The importance of this "assistance" is presented to domestic audiences in Japan as one of fulfilling Japan's treaty responsibilities, participating in the provision of an international public good, thus fulfilling Japan's international obligations. It allows Japan to stifle accusations of a free-riding Japan and enables the US to justify and continue its alliance in face of the difficulties both at home and in Japan. More importantly, it provides an opportunity for Japan's MSDF to gain more experience of blue-water naval operations, and allows for an opportunity for the international community to be socialized into seeing a Japan that can operate far from its shores. The same act of deployment essentially carries a coded message to all actors in and outside the region that Japan is indeed a rejuvenated global power.

Japan's foray to provide the international good of keeping piracy at bay also stimulated developments on the Chinese side. As elaborated in Chap. 2, Japan's identity and ambition is not just anchored by the US-Japan security alliance, it is also heavily referenced by China. Prime Minister Abe has clearly and unequivocally stated that Japan's foreign policy is not *all* about China. If this is the case, there should not be the need to mention this at all. The fact of the matter is that one of Japan's main concerns in foreign relations over the last two centuries, not decades, has been about China, whose ascendance has buoyed and worried Asian states, Japan included, in numerous ways. As a colleague commented to the author recently, "it's like living next to an elephant—what it does affects and worries you in so many ways—even when it snores." When it comes to Japan, this is doubly true, given Japan's antagonism with China over so many issues, ranging from the arguments over the ideational, for example, whether Japanese politicians have a right to worship at Yasukuni, to the contestation of the Senkaku Islands, to gas deposits in the East China Sea—one of the prime reasons, or perhaps the excuse, that drives Japan's normalization efforts. This understandably so, as throughout the Cold War, the US and its allies have been accustomed to a huge strategic capability gap between themselves and China, and that chasm is now closing and closing fast.

Japan's attempt at rejuvenating itself politically is not without cost. The first cost is apparent—the alliance is not cheap to maintain, much less enhance. Japan is now showing signs of recovery from years of economic stagnation. Both the US and Japan face opposition at home from time to time, throwing into question the veracity and usefulness of this alliance. General Tamogami, one of Japan's retired generals, favored Japan's alliance with the US, but questioned openly whether the US could be counted on to defend Japan in a conflict against China (Halloran 2011). In Japan, the opposition in Okinawa is particularly jarring, and raises the extent of Japan's democratic credentials (McCormack and Norimatsu 2012). Justified on the grounds of national security, most Japanese living outside of Okinawa are of the view that it is even more necessary, given the rough neighborhood they live in. Facing a belligerent North Korea, an equally nationalistic South Korea and worst of all, a resurgent irredentist China, the Japanese public is almost persuaded that it is necessary to "confront" China. The US in fact has to do very little these days to persuade Japan of the merits of the US-Japan security alliance. Likewise, it would be sacrilegious in Japan to suggest that all this chest thumping has gone slightly overboard, but it would be prudent to put forth this reminder for the Japanese politicians: The US makes foreign policy to enhance US national interests first and foremost, and Japanese interests never take precedence. In truth, Japan's interests cannot be guaranteed by the US-Japan alliance alone, and many Japanese policymakers know this.

Japan's rejuvenation as a global power largely began in the 1980s as its economic clout grew. Despite this, Tokyo has been extremely circumscribed in its foreign policy arsenal—as certainly by the country's very narrow interpretation of Article 9 of its constitution, the constraints of pacifist culture and anti-militaristic norms that had so engrained in the country's strategic culture.

This chapter argues that one small step forward in this relationship is perhaps for China and Japan to show that it is not implausible that they could work together. In this case, Japan and China working in the Gulf of Aden should be lauded as one of the more successful multilateral collaborations, in particular to domestic audiences in both China and Japan, so that the public sentiments necessary for building better relations could be established. There must be political will to do this very successfully of course in the domestic media, but unfortunately to date there have been few reports on this. However, this does not preclude scholarly endeavors to identify and explore this as a possible front or opening for Sino-Japanese cooperation.

The provision of international public goods—for example, helping bring pipe water to isolated parts of Africa and Latin America or co-sponsoring poverty alleviation or health projects—might be options for China and Japan to build more confidence in their partnerships and at the same time enable them to achieve their great power aspirations. Instead of focusing their energy on competitive endeavors to fight for territorial possessions or resources in the East China Sea, these projects could actually be good for Sino-Japanese relations in the long run. East Asia can only become harmonious if, and only if, China and Japan consider the stakes more carefully. This chapter shows that Japan's cooperation with China in combating piracy in the Gulf of Aden is a small but important development, holding much significance for both theoretical and empirical studies on Japan's foreign relations.

Genesis of Japan's Anti-Piracy Efforts

According to current international law, the act of piracy as defined in Article 101 of the 1982 United Nations Convention on the Law of the Sea (UNCLOS) consists of the following acts:

1) any illegal acts of violence or detention, or any act of depredation, committed for private ends by the crew or the passengers of a private ship or a private aircraft, and directed -
   (a) on the high seas, against another ship or aircraft, or against persons or property of any State;
   (b) against a ship, aircraft, persons or property in a place outside the jurisdiction of any State;
2) any act of voluntary participation in the operation of a ship or of an aircraft with knowledge of facts making it a pirate ship or aircraft;
3) any act of inciting or of intentionally facilitating an act described in subparagraph (1) or (2).

The UNCLOS definition constrains the acts of piracy to the "high seas" and "outside the jurisdiction of any state," essentially stating that the acts of piracy cannot take place within the sovereign boundaries of any nation-state. The International Maritime Bureau (IMB) has, in turn, adopted a more liberal definition, defining piracy as "an act of boarding or attempting to board any ship with the intent to commit theft or any other crime and with the intent or capability to use force in the furtherance of that act" (Ece 2012: 12). This definition includes acts occurring in territorial waters of states, but it separates conceptually cases whereby the hijacking of crafts might not be for private ends (i.e. not for profit or monetary reasons, but say for politically motivated goals). Terrorism would, therefore, be included in this definition. The IMB definition, however, is used more for reporting, and technically, the UNCLOS definition is still for all intents and purposes the primary definition adopted for piracy.

Historically, all countries in Asia, including Japan, have had to grapple with this issue within the region. The root of the "modern" piracy problem began in the 1990s with a series of hijackings in the Straits of Malacca and the South China Sea (Beckman et al. 1994). Japan saw a series of attacks on its shipping, which prompted a reconsideration of its maritime policies and its general security policies concerning piracy as some of the incidents were particularly troubling. In 1992, the hijacking of the Nagasaki Spirit, which collided with another vessel, caused an oil spill of over 100,000 tons of oil, which in turn started a massive fire that ultimately killed 44 sailors (Fort 2006: 34–36; Burnett 2003). There were other ships that were hijacked or attacked: the Tenyu (1998), the Odyssey Rainbow (1999), the Global Mars (2000) and the Arbey Jaya (2001).

These attacks occurred primarily (Beckman et al. 1994) in the vicinity of the Straits of Malacca, prompting Tokyo to focus its initial anti-piracy efforts in Southeast Asia. Until then, piracy had never been construed as a fundamental problem for Japan and Japanese security.

Due to the direct threat to its shipping, piracy was, for the first time in the postwar era, construed as a threat to Japan's comprehensive national security in the postwar period. Japan imports almost all its petroleum needs, over 70% of its food sources, and in turn ships over 90% of its exports globally. The series of incidents in the South China Sea sparked off a debate within Japan and propelled this to become one of the most important items on the government's agenda. Beyond the question of crafting a response to the perceived threat to its comprehensive national security, there have been calls for Tokyo to build up a more coherent global strategy (Watanabe 2007: 160–167). Within Japan, domestic actors also had a vested interest in urging the government to formulate a more coherent response. In particular, both the Japan Defense Agency and the Japan Coast Guard (Takeda 2004: 47–50) were keen to play a greater institutional role in helping enhance sea-lane safety and preventing ships from being hijacked. The singular focus of attention from the Japanese government, legislators, Defense Agency, Coast Guard and other interest groups pushed Japan to overcome decades of inertia.[1]

The impetus to "normalize" Japan became stronger from the mid-1990s onwards. This stemmed from a series of external "jolts": the loss of the USSR as a strategic threat, the international reactions to Japan's perceived checkbook diplomacy (especially in the wake of the Gulf War that liberated Kuwait); and more importantly, the evolution of a new generation of Japanese who perceived the constraints imposed by the legacies of the Pacific War as an unnecessary burden on Japan's gaining of its rightful

---

[1] It has been argued that a constructivist approach should be used to view Japan's intervention in the Gulf of Aden, in particular the debate on the responsibilities between the Japanese Coast Guard and the MSDF demonstrates the continuing resilience of the normative force of Japan's pacifist identity (see Black 2012: 259–285).

status and respect in the international community. Since the mid-1990s, a series of Japanese prime ministers with relatively conservative views—the likes of Ryutaro Hashimoto, Junichiro Koizumi, Shinzo Abe and Taro Aso—have been steering the country on a right-of-center political agenda. As a vehicle of the normalization agenda, Japan has been keen to dispatch naval vessels to areas outside the Japanese navy's traditional zone of operations. Consequently, Japan strove to reach out to Southeast Asian states to cooperate on this problem. Japan's overtures were a mixed bag of successes, with countries such as Singapore, Malaysia and Indonesia reacting differently (Bradford 2004: 480–505). By the early 2000s, with the rise of domestic voices calling for a rethinking of the role Japan was playing in global affairs, the Japanese government was extremely keen to demonstrate its "normality" by dispatching troops to the Middle East.

Japan supported the Regional Maritime Security Initiative (RMSI) proposed by the US in 2004. However, some ASEAN states such as Malaysia and Indonesia—littoral states adjacent to the Straits of Malacca—were apprehensive about US-led efforts here. There was of course resistance from China, which was eager to avoid discussing a possible US-led presence in the area known as the Hong Kong-Luzon-Hainan triangle, and at the same time, regional cooperation had been and continued to be, hindered by territorial disputes between China, the Philippines and Vietnam (Chan et al. 2012: 170). Nonetheless, with regards to the sensitivity of its presence in the South China Sea (at least before tensions with Vietnam and the Philippines increased over the last few years over the Spratly Islands), China appeared to be happy to leave the heavy lifting of fighting the pirates to Malaysia, Indonesia and Singapore. The ASEAN states were able to come together to take active measures on a unilateral or multilateral basis to contain the situation. Owing to the War on Terror, there were a slew of successful initiatives such as the Department of Homeland Security's Container Security Initiative (CSI),[2] the Regional Co-operation Agreement on Combating Piracy and Armed Robbery against Ships in Asia (ReCAAP), and the Proliferation Security Initiative (PSI), but by and large these initiatives did not receive much attention from China.

Japan's dispatching of MSDF personnel to partake in the safeguarding of vessels passing through the Gulf of Aden is a remarkable departure from previous Japanese policy in a variety of ways. First, this was the first time

---

[2] Singapore, Malaysia, Hong Kong, South Korea and China are some of the countries participating in this US initiative.

that Japan had dispatched its maritime forces to the Middle East for an actual operation. Second, this was an independent deployment for anti-piracy missions in the Gulf of Aden, to safeguard Japan's own interests. Third, even though Japan was seizing the opportunity to deploy its navy on a far-flung mission and work in a multilateral setting, it also marked a first as Tokyo was also trying to match the Chinese in terms of such a deployment. Even though this began as some sort of "competition," as the following chapter will explain, the Japanese and the Chinese taskforces eventually came together to collaborate on the mission at hand. Their efforts to cooperate began under a multilateral setting, underscoring that it is entirely possible for the two Asian giants to come together to cooperate strategically.

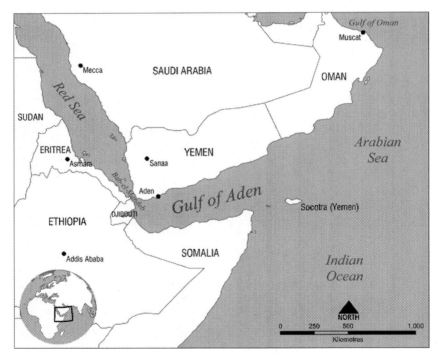

The Gulf of Aden. (Map showing the Gulf of Aden, located between Yemen and Somalia. Nearby bodies of water include the Indian Ocean, Red Sea, Arabian Sea and the Bab-el-Mandeb Strait. By Norman Einstein (Own work) [CC BY-SA 3.0 (http://creativecommons.org/licenses/by-sa/3.0) or GFDL (http://www.gnu.org/copyleft/fdl.html)], via Wikimedia Commons)

Piracy in the Gulf of Aden: An Overview

The Gulf of Aden is strategically located between Yemen on the southern coast of the Arabian Peninsula and Somalia, in the northern part of the Horn of Africa. The Gulf's importance is derived from the fact that the waterway is part of the Suez Canal shipping route between the Mediterranean and the Arabian Seas in the Indian Ocean with 21,000 ships crossing annually. The Gulf of Aden is also closely located to another critical chokepoint in the world: the Straits of Hormuz, which lie between Oman and Iran. The US government estimated that there was a flow of about 17 million barrels per day, up from 15.7 to 15.9 million barrels per day in 2001 (Komiss and Huntzinger 2011: 1). In 2011, 20% of the world's traded oil, with more than 85% of the crude oil exports, went to Asian markets, with Japan, India, South Korea and China as the largest destinations (United States Energy Information Administration 2012). The Gulf of Aden and the Straits of Hormuz are therefore extremely important areas of interest for China and Japan. Beyond the question of trade flows, a significant amount of petroleum-based imports destined for Northeast Asia transit through the Gulf. As the demand for transnational shipments between East Asia and the Middle East grows, the security of the sea-lanes and lines of communication in the Gulf of Aden become increasingly important.

The growth of piracy as an "industry" in the area can be traced back to the failure of the Somali state in the early 1990s. Ravaged by a civil war that was fought following the collapse of the ruling government in 1991, Somalia lapsed into anarchy characterized by clan-based rivalry and militia groups competing to control the national infrastructure (World Bank Report on Conflict in Somalia 2005). With the demise of the central government and the disbanding of state institutions such as the navy and the merchant fleet, foreign vessels allegedly engaged in toxic dumping activities and illegal fishing in Somali waters. (Ironically, there were reports that among those vessels engaged in illegal fishing, some belonged to Taiwanese fishermen who were fishing for tuna in Somali waters, and in turn their catches were being sold to the fish markets in Japan.) Captured Somalis engaged in piracy not only out of survival and desperation, but also to defend Somalia against these illegal activities, estimated to cost Somalia USD 100 million a year (Fox & AP, 25 July, 2013). In fact, among the Somalis, the pirates call themselves "saviors of the seas." The illegal fishing boats reportedly came from Yemen, Iran, Taiwan and Korea, among others.

The pirates' *modus operandi* is often to use single or multiple small but extremely agile speedboats to approach by stealth and board the larger merchant ships, using a combination of ropes with hooks and climbing up via the anchor chain, then hijacking the crew at gunpoint and steering the ship to one of their hideouts. There have also been instances where the pirates have used guile to commit their crimes, often pretending to be stranded fishermen asking for water, only to board and hijack the merchant ships (Westcott 2008). The pirates were also known to have launched rocket missiles to fire warning shots across the bows of fleeing ships to stop them (Walker 2009).

The economic costs to merchant fleets worldwide are tremendous. If ships were to avoid the pirate-infested waters off Somalia, there would be exponential costs to the shipping. For example, routing a cargo ship from Europe to the Far East via the Cape of Good Hope, rather than through the Suez Canal, would incur an estimated additional USD 89 million annually, which includes USD 74.4 million in fuel and USD 14.6 million in charter expenses. In addition, the rerouting would increase transit times by about 5.7 days per ship. This would result in the need for an additional vessel to maintain the service frequency. Additionally, these costs do not consider the disruption in logistics chains (United States Department of Transport 2010). For every USD 120 million seized by pirates in Somalia, the cost to the shipping industry and end-users is between USD 0.9 and USD 3.3 billion (Besley et al. 2012). The piracy industry grew partly because it was much cheaper and easier for ship owners to pay off the ransom to get back their ships than it was for them to try and pressure their respective governments to "retrieve" the ships. The two-year old Greek tanker, MV Smyrni, loaded with crude oil worth millions of dollars, was released after 11-month negotiations and a payment of around USD 15 million. (*The Guardian*, May 3, 2013).

Between 2005 and 2012, the number of hijackings increased exponentially, with 179 ships hijacked off the coast of Somalia and the Horn of Africa. Figures from the IMB indicate a similar pattern of increase, particularly from 2009 onwards. In 2009 alone, there were 46 ships hijacked, in 2010 there were 47, and by 2011, there were 25 successful hijackings out of 237 attempts. In 2012, there were only 14 successful hijackings out of 75 reported attacks (*The Guardian*, May 3, 2013). Statistics from the International Chamber of Commerce showed similar results. As of September 2012, there were 13 hijackings reported with 212 hostages taken, with 11 ships and 188 hostages still being held in Somalia at the time of reporting (International Chamber of Commerce n.d.).

According to the International Criminal Police Organization, the United Nations Office on Drugs and Crime and the World Bank, ransom payments to Somali pirates are estimated to have been between USD 339 million and USD 413 million for the same period. The average ransom paid was USD 2.7 million, with ordinary pirates receiving USD 30,000 to USD 75,000 each and bonuses paid to those who brought their own weapons or were first to board the ship (Harress 2013). This constitutes an "industry" because the pirates who carry out the actually hijacking get a relatively small portion of the ransom, with the "investors" (the warlords or the businessmen who invested in the equipment and the upkeep of the hostages) getting the lion's share of the ransom.

The case for concerted international intervention appears to therefore have been confined to a period of roughly eight years, from approximately 2005 to 2012. The sudden and sharp increase in piracy cases was prompted by both a lag in the international legal infrastructure and the inability of international governments to combat the piracy problem. As the efforts of the international community to combat the scourge came to bear, the number of cases reduced abruptly from 2013 onwards. In particular, the multilateral task forces with their lethal firepower and successful prosecutions with lengthy prison terms for the pirates meant that the costs were escalating for those involved in piracy. The section below will discuss in detail the evolution of the changes in international law, and contextualize Japan's efforts in this change.

INTERNATIONAL LAW AND THE PIRACY PROBLEM

The UNCLOS of 1982 (LOS Convention), stipulates that the extent of a state's territorial waters is confined to the region within 12 nautical miles of its coastline. The convention also recognizes the Exclusive Economic Zone (EEZ) of 200 nautical miles, whereby the state has special rights in terms of exploration and mineral rights. In particular, Article 58(3) of the convention stipulates that states shall have "due regard to the rights and duties of the coastal State and shall comply with the laws and regulations adopted by the coastal State in accordance with the provisions of this Convention and other rules of international law in so far as they are not incompatible with this Part."

This confers both a privilege and a burden on coastal states. Piracy in the traditional sense of the word could be construed as "armed robbery" in the territorial waters of the states, and for most part, it is the duty of the coastal state to ensure that such crimes are not committed in their territorial waters. Many states, in particular those without the capacity to enforce laws, have a hard time meeting these obligations insofar as piracy is concerned.

Thus, prior to 2008, the inapplicability of international law of piracy in territorial seas posed a problem in combating piracy in the Gulf of Aden. The international law accorded the Somali pirates a measure of safety, as the customary and conventional law of piracy provided that piracy could only occur on the high seas and not in areas subject to state sovereignty (Convention on the High Seas 1958; Convention on the Territorial Sea and Contiguous Zone 1958). Additionally, on the high seas, it is generally accepted that the flag state has jurisdiction over the vessels flying its flag, and may not be boarded, searched or molested by foreign flag vessels without the consent of the flag state, with the only possible exception being when the vessel(s) involved are linked to piracy. Thus, under modern international law, ships or vessels originating from Somalia related to piracy and pirates can be seized, arrested and prosecuted by other states or authorities (United Nations Convention of the Law of the Sea 1982).

The situation with piracy thus increased exponentially in the Gulf of Aden because of a mixture of circumstances—the failure of the Somali state, the inability of international law to deal with the situation, and most importantly the lack of protection accorded to the commercial fleet plying these treacherous waters. What started as a string of isolated incidents in the early 2000s had by 2008 developed into a mature business model, posing a significant threat to the busy shipping lanes near Somalia to the extent that the UN secretary-general and the Security Council requested international assistance to escort vulnerable World Food Programme (WFP) vessels (Hopkins and Swarttouw 2014).

The Security Council adopted Resolution 1816 in 2008 to overcome this difficulty and subsequently the mandate was renewed through resolutions 1846, 1897, 1950 and 2020 (Security Council 2010). Resolution 1816 authorized countries concerned to enter the territorial waters of Somalia and use "all necessary means" to repress acts of piracy and armed robbery at sea (UN 2008a). Additionally, the UN Security Council has also established various mechanisms to deal with the piracy problem in Somalia; Resolution 1846 endorses the seizing of vessels in Somalia territorial waters associated with piracy (UN 2008b); Resolution 1851 (Text of Resolution 1851) called for the cooperation of states with the transitional federal government in Somalia to include potential operations in Somali territorial land and airspace, to suppress acts of piracy and armed robbery at sea. The resolution also urged "countries to establish an international cooperation mechanism as a common point of contact for counter-piracy activities near Somalia, and to efforts to enhance the judicial capacity of regional states to combat piracy, including the judicial capacity to prosecute pirates." In 2009, the Contact Group on Piracy off the Coast of Somalia (CGPCS) was therefore established with 24 countries, including Japan, the US, China and nine other international organizations in Japan at the United Nations headquarters (Contact Group on Piracy 2009, 2015). At the meeting, the Contact Group delineated six areas of discussion and focus: (i) improve operational and informational support to counter-piracy operations; (ii) establish a counter-piracy coordination mechanism; (iii) strengthen judicial frameworks for arrest, prosecution and detention of pirates; (iv) strengthen commercial shipping self-awareness and other capabilities; (v) pursue improved diplomatic and public information efforts; and (vi) track financial flows related to piracy (Contact Group on Piracy 2015).

Resolution 1918 called on "all States, including States in the region to criminalize piracy under their domestic law and favourably consider the prosecution of suspected and imprisonment of convicted pirates apprehended off the coast of Somalia, consistent with applicable international human rights law." UN Resolution 1976 called for the creation of specialized courts to prosecute and house Somali pirates, as well as for laws to be created in their own national jurisdictions so that pirates could be prosecuted. UN Resolution 1897 encourages states to "conclude special agreements or arrangements with countries willing to take custody of pirates. Those arrangements should allow for the embarkation of law enforcement officials—or 'shipriders'—from these willing countries to facilitate the investigation and prosecution of persons detained as a result of anti-piracy operations, provided that the advance consent of the TFG was obtained for third State jurisdiction in Somali territorial waters and that such arrangements did not prejudice the effective implementation of the 1988 Convention for the Suppression of Unlawful Acts against the Safety of Maritime Navigation" (UNSC 2010). One of the most significant outcomes was that since 2009, any pirates captured by international naval forces are handed over to Kenya for trial. Effectively, from 2008 right through to 2011, no less than ten resolutions were passed to encourage third state intervention in Somali territorial waters (United Nations Security Council Resolutions 2012).

Japan had little experience operating in the Gulf, but the exigencies of the piracy challenge gave each power the reasons to consider deploying to the Gulf. This problem provided these Asian giants with an opportunity to join the multilateral movement, proving that cooperation as opposed to competition in strategic realms between China and Japan is entirely possible under the right conditions.

Japan's Response to the Piracy Problems in the Gulf

Even though Japan's anti-piracy efforts stemmed from a genuine need to protect its commercial shipping, its efforts cannot be divorced from its larger diplomatic and security strategy. Japan's operations in the Gulf of Aden could be construed as a larger part of Japan's interest in expanding its influence and prestige in Africa and the Middle East. Conducting naval operations in the name of providing a public good in an area outside their traditional area of influence would provide excellent opportunities for Japan,[3] and also other countries such as China (Kaufman 2009), to gain a foothold in the affairs of the region and familiarize themselves with the regional actors. To be sure, such gestures in so quickly dispatching naval deployments might also have been prompted by what another country was doing—such as Japan and China competing to be a global power prompted by nationalistic impulses—but this was something to be expected. Furthermore, their involvement in the provision of public goods (anti-piracy) is also an extremely important indicator of their great power aspirations, as it indicates a readiness to perform international public services. The willingness to participate, serve and lead on these global platforms also enables Japan to socialize other powers (such as China) to their presence, and if anything, allows them to garner capital for their global leadership credentials. Japan's deployment also cannot be divorced from Japanese observations of what China is doing in the region, as the government's response is meant to ensure that Japanese efforts and capabilities are "matched up" to her close neighbor's.

Even though the Chinese economy grows from strength to strength, China's foreign policy is still relatively reactive and conservative. China still largely does not attempt to exercise leadership in international affairs, particularly in situations where the use of force is required, as Beijing

[3] For a detailed survey of the activities undertaken by Japan, please see the Japan Ministry of Defense website on "Measures Against Piracy", http://www.mod.go.jp/e/d_act/somalia/index.html; see also the pamphlet "Counter Piracy Initiatives," Japan Ministry of Defense, http://www.mod.go.jp/e/publ/w_paper/pdf/2013/39_Part3_Chapter2_Sec3.pdf

adheres to the doctrine of non-intervention in the affairs of others and has always held the sanctity of sovereignty in high regard. In this instance, the situation with Somalia and the UN resolutions that were passed paved the political context for China's deployment to the Gulf (Lin-Greenberg 2010).

In 2008, China initiated the first escort mission for its merchant ships to Somalia. The first escort mission was prompted by two incidents that had occurred just prior to the Chinese deployment (*People's Daily*, December 29, 2009a). The most widely advertised incident involved a Chinese cargo merchant ship, the Zhenhua 4, which was almost captured by the Somali pirates on December 17, 2008. The incident was widely and graphically covered by the Chinese state and social media when the Shanghai head office of the shipping company provided photographs transmitted by the Zhenhua 4's crew to them (QQ News, January 22, 2009).[4] The Chinese foreign ministry subsequently announced that it would extend the escort missions to Hong Kong, Macanese and Taiwanese ships, with 15 merchant ships applying for escort within four days of the scheme being announced on January 6, 2009 (*People's Daily*, January 6, 2009b). The independent nature of China's deployment was made adequately clear: the deployment was not to accept any assignments or instructions from any other countries or regional organizations. This also registers one of the first times that the modern People's Liberal Army's navy (PLAN) sent an expeditionary force abroad (Weitz 2009).

The initial escort mission consisted of three ships. The flagship was a DDG-169 Wuhan (Guangzhou-class) multi-purpose missile destroyer built in Shanghai in 2002, with a displacement of 7000 tons, equipped with 16 anti-ship missiles, 48 surface-to-air missiles, close-in weapons systems and a helicopter. It was accompanied by a DDG-171 Haikou, the

---

[4] Photographs of the abovementioned encounter with the pirates were taken by a crew member named Wu Mingxiang on the Chinese vessel Zhenhua 4, while it was in the process of being hijacked. One of the photos showed the crew defending themselves against the pirates with Molotov cocktails, drawing intense public attention to the piracy issue. The pictures and videos were transmitted to the shipping company's headquarters and the images were transmitted widely to the media. See "The Story Behind the Merchant Ship's Successful Defence against the Somalian Pirates", *QQ News*, January 22, 2009, http://news.qq.com/a/20090122/000727.htm; more pictures can be found in the Xinhua News Agency article, "Yading Wan Tou Tufei Ji" ["Fighting the Pirates in Aden"] 2015, http://www.china.com.cn/news/txt/2008-12/19/content_16974634.htm. The CCTV clip of this episode can be viewed here: "Zhonguo chuanyuan yong zijiranshaodan jitui suomali haidao," YouTube, https://www.youtube.com/watch?v=Mnq4NrR4-V8

PLAN's latest Lanzhou-class destroyer completed in 2003. The Haikou destroyer is equipped with China's first generation of phased-array radar and vertically launched long-range air defense missile systems, providing air defense to the fleet. Both ships were supplied by the Weishanhu, a PLAN Qiandaohu-class supply ship. The Weishanhu is an indigenous multi-product replenishment ship and can take part in offensive operations using its eight 37 mm guns (*People's Daily*, December 27, 2008). In addition, the destroyers are equipped with Russian-built Kamov Ka-28 helicopters, greatly expanding the surveillance and response coverage of the destroyers (editorial – Naval Technology n.d.). In the initial deployments, China's naval tasks were principally "escort" missions, as opposed to a more permanent presence in the region (America's Navy 2009).

Japan's presence was to work with the UN and the US deployment. The combined Task Force 150 (TF150) is a task force formed out of the 25-nation Maritime Task Force operating out of Manama, Bahrain. Commissioned in 2002, the initial aim of the Maritime Task Force is to participate in and support the Global War on Terror, with the primary task of mounting maritime security operations around the Horn of Africa region and the Indian Ocean. For example, between 2006 and 2008, the TF150 conducted operations to interdict vessels and personnel associated with piracy off the coast of Somalia. In 2009, a new combined task force, TF151, was established to focus on combating piracy in the region. Its mission was to disrupt piracy and armed robbery at sea and to engage with regional and other partners to build the capacity and improve relevant capabilities to protect and enhance the freedom of navigation. TF150, and subsequently TF151, were naval coalitions of the US and its allies, established to respond to "distress calls" or mission orders from the coalition (China was not involved initially in the maritime security operations mounted by the US-led Combined Maritime Forces), NATO's Operation Enduring Freedom or the EU's Operation Atalanta—all three acted as the main forces operating in the region.

By 2010, China had lobbied for an increased role in the international fight against piracy and had agreed to participate and co-chair Shared Awareness and Deconfliction (SHADE) meetings, to share in planning joint operations for TF151, as well as sharing intelligence with the other task forces (BBC, January 29, 2010). It must be emphasized that even though China sought to work more closely with the international task force, its participation was still on a voluntary basis, as Beijing had been careful to ensure that Chinese forces did not get incorporated into a command structure outside the Chinese chain of command—in particular TF151, Operation Atalanta and Operation Enduring Freedom.

By the end of 2013, 16 Chinese task forces (comprising three ships each) had been sent consecutively to the Gulf of Aden since China had first started the deployments on December 26, 2008. These ships account for almost half of the latest Chinese destroyers, frigates and replenishment ships from the three PLAN fleets. The Chinese task forces had escorted 5460 ships, including 2765 foreign ships. Additionally, they also escorted seven ships of the WFP in cooperation with the EU CTF-465 (Zhou 2013).

Japan's journey toward their piracy efforts in the Gulf (Sakurai 2013) was undertaken on a radically different and difficult route (Japan MOD Fight Against Piracy website 2009). Prior to 2009, Japan's ability to protect merchant naval assets on the high seas was constrained by its domestic laws. There was no special law to deter piracy on the high seas, and any action undertaken by the Japanese authorities was only legal if the ships involved were Japanese (defined as Japanese flagged ships and foreign ships with Japanese crews). Operating under Article 82 of the Self Defense Force Law, this meant that JSDF ships were also hampered in their operational tactics in their engagement with the pirates, as well as the handling of captured pirates as part of "maritime security operations." From March 2009 onwards, the Japanese MSDF deployed two destroyers and two P-3C aircraft for surveillance activities. The Japanese deployment was initially headquartered in the US Army Camp Lemonnier, south of Djibouti airport. The destroyers were DD Sazanami and DD Samidare of the MSDF, both of which are among the MSDF's most capable naval assets. The two destroyers have a complement of about 400 officers with eight officers of the Japanese Coast Guard sailing along as judicial police officers. In dispatching the P-3C patrol and surveillance planes, alongside the helicopters on the destroyers, the MSDF proved to be extremely effective in counter-piracy operations (Japan Ministry of Defense 2009a, b). The operational efficiency of the Japanese deployment was remarkably enhanced after the passage of the "Anti-Piracy Law," which allowed the Japanese forces to escort foreign commercial ships and also engage (i.e. fire at) pirate vessels if they ignored warning signals.

From June 2011, Japan was able to conduct anti-piracy efforts from a new base, built north of the airport, which also served as the local coordination facility. This facility was built at a cost of JPY 4.7 billion, and would house the headquarters building, dormitories, a P-3C patrol plane maintenance hangar, and a gymnasium for MSDF members. The MSDF had previously moved from the US military base located to the south of the airport (*The Somaliland Times*, June 4, 2011). By 2014, Japan had conducted 567 escort measures under its anti-piracy laws, and had escorted 3469 merchant vessels in total (Japan Ministry of Defense 2013, 2014; US Department of Homeland Security 2014).

Japan's involvement in the anti-piracy campaign fitted remarkably well with the prevailing political ambitions of the neo-conservative government's plans, the exigencies of Japan's attempt at the normalization of Japan's presence, as well as the conditions required of and for the strengthening of the US-Japan alliance. Even though it was largely the Aso administration that started the initiatives associated with the dispatch of the naval assets, it was the DPJ governments (from September 2009 onwards) that pushed for these deployments. This is despite the fact that Prime Minister Yukio Hatoyama had very different ideas about what Japan's relations with its neighbors should be like vis-à-vis the US.

Working with the Chinese PLAN and the Multilateral Provision of International Public Goods

Even though Japan had therefore come to the Gulf of Aden under very different circumstances, this coincidence of events resulted in some happy circumstances. Japan had initially entered the region under the auspices of supporting the US in the Global War on Terror, but subsequently moved to the anti-piracy missions. The UN Security Council resolutions and the anti-piracy law passed in 2009 in Japan provided the legitimacy and the flexibility needed for Japan to integrate their efforts more closely with other navies in the region. The Chinese naval forces were dispatched owing to the exigencies of circumstances and the call for the UN Security Council to combat the pirates. Yet, as the number of piracy attempts increased from 2008 onwards, it was evident that many other countries had become concerned enough with the situation to dispatch naval assets to that area to help in this effort. India, Singapore, South Korea, Pakistan, the Philippines and even Iran had dispatched naval assets to the Gulf for anti-piracy missions. As most of the naval task forces in the region were led by either the US or EU, many countries, including China and India, established independent mandated missions from these "presence" groups, for political as well as operational reasons.

The instrument that facilitated the Japanese forces to come into contact and work with the Chinese ironically was a multilateral forum initiated by the coalition task force. The SHADE forum was reportedly established in December 2008 as a means of sharing "best practice," conducting informal discussions and deconflicting the activities of those nations and organizations involved in military counter-piracy operations in the region. This forum is organized at the officer level, and initially only involved those forces based in Bahrain, but it grew to include the forces operating with independent mandates, such as Japan, China, Russia and India. It is important to note that this was a "bottom-up" process, rather than one willed from the top.

One of the most under-rated and undiscussed implications of SHADE is the coming together of Japan's deployment forces with the Chinese in this multilateral setting. Facilitated by SHADE, Chinese and Japanese forces worked together with other navies to enhance the mission objectives. This formal cooperation between China and Japan (and South Korea joining subsequently) in the anti-piracy efforts began in 2012, when together with India they formed the Joint Escort Convey Coordination group (CNN 2011). Also, under the auspices of SHADE, the Japanese MSDF agreed to share information on their warship movements and relevant intelligence on piracy (Gokhale 2012). This arrangement occurred from January 1 2012 onwards (*The Economic Times*, February 1, 2012). Likewise, the Chinese deployment forces made reciprocal arrangements.

This was the first time that the Japanese military forces had worked closely with the Chinese. As stipulated in China's white paper in 2013, the Chinese navy was the reference navy for the first round of coordination in 2012. Together with India and Japan, they harmonized their maritime assets' patrol schedules on a quarterly basis, and were able to optimize the available ships on duty, enhancing escort efficiency (State Council of China 2013). South Korea joined this coordination in the last quarter of 2012, just a year after mounting an impressive and daring rescue operation code-named "Dawn of Gulf of Aden" (Roehrig 2015). Compared with the preceding years, when all the navies with independent mandates worked separately, this was a significant improvement. The most important aspect of this cooperation was the fact that China and Japan (and by extension, India and South Korea) were able to work jointly together, and were able to change the leadership of this loosely formed group on a rotational basis. They were even able to organize mutual exchanges and other social events.

Sailors visiting the Chinese navy frigate Yang Yi in Gulf of Aden in 2012. (Sailors from the guided-missile destroyer USS Winston S. Churchill (DDG 81) board the PLAN frigate Yi Yang (FF 548) to meet on Monday, September 17, 2012, prior to conducting a bilateral counter-piracy exercise in the Gulf of Aden. (Copyright held by: US Navy. Photo by mass communication specialist 2nd Class Aaron Chase/ Released on Flickr) 120,917-N-YF306–107; made available by a Creative Commons License Attribution 2.0 Generic license)

This cooperation between the navies was not promoted widely in Japan's or China's domestic media and public narratives. The domestic media in both countries only focused on the achievements of their respective maritime forces in undertaking anti-piracy missions as part of an international effort. Little attention was given to details of Japan's cooperation with China, largely because this would not be a popular or a politically correct thing to report. This collaboration is something that is "not" to be hyped up or promoted—but there is much potential in such cooperation.

One of the most important aspects that is lacking in Japan's rejuvenation is whether or not Japan can work independently or outside of the auspices of the US-Japan alliance. Being in an alliance does not necessary mean that Japan cannot act alone or in concert with others. Granted, Japan does get an "A" grade for being an all-weather ally (at least under Prime Minister Abe) to the US—but the incremental willingness to deploy Japan's forces and to act in a multilateral setting certainly suggests that Prime Minister Abe's vision of the US-Japan alliance as being a "global" alliance is being operationalized. Bearing in mind that this deployment was undertaken during President Obama's era, Japan certainly has had years to prepare for this deployment and eventuality.

The value of this cooperation, however, is not in Japan's deployment to provide a much needed international public good. It is not entirely clear whether Japan did engage in combat or policing actions while undertaking this. What is truly important is also what is not said—that it is possible for Japan to cooperate with China (and not just the US) in (a) security matters, (b) humanitarian affairs, and (c) in the provision of international public goods. This type of cooperation sends a powerful message that security cooperation is indeed possible between China and Japan (and by extension South Korea), and that their interactions could transcend the economic and commercial cooperation which the two giants are so used to. This message would also undermine the assumption that China is Japan's biggest foreign policy challenge, and open up new avenues for thinking about Japan's normalization and rejuvenation. It would enable the Chinese audience to see that Japan is open to cooperation with China. Additionally, the prospects of cooperation also immediately shed light on the fact that good relations with China need not necessarily come about at the expense of the US-Japan alliance and vice-versa. Japan need not give up the US-Japan alliance to work with China, in particular when it involves the provision of international public goods. It is entirely possible that more cooperation could alleviate challenges which China and Japan face in striving for a greater global role, as long as this is not framed as a "leadership" struggle. In this instance, the revolving leadership role that China and Japan undertake in the task force is important to socializing and cementing this role.

Plate: Prime Minister Abe visiting the anti-piracy base Japan established in Djibouti (East Africa). (Photo from Prime Minister's Office, Japan, https://japan.kantei.go.jp/96_abe/actions/201308/27djibouti_e.html)

Conclusion

Japan's willingness to deploy a naval group to participate in a multilateral anti-piracy mission is a major step forward in its rejuvenation as a global power. If a nation like Japan cannot assist in the provision of international public goods, then there are very few candidates left that can do this. Japan has the requisite economic strength, wealth and motivation to do this.

Due to the exigencies of circumstances, Japan's foreign policy should evolve with its changing aspirations. Indeed, Japan and China might find that their diplomacy had more room to grow if both countries could take stock of what they could achieve together. Japan's relations with China should develop in tandem with its relations with the US, perhaps on an even keel. Japan's work with China in the Gulf of Aden is a good starting point, and when properly promoted would provide the kind of confidence building that can reconcile their aspirations to an extent. At the very least, it might kick-start the relationship that by most indicators is shown to be a faltering one, at least at the time of writing. Tokyo and Beijing need to ensure that the traditional realpolitik maneuvers do not derail the potential cooperation both countries could undertake, particularly when the United States is pressuring third countries not to harbor any Chinese military presence, particularly in the Gulf of Aden (Lo 2017). This is the very sort of "medicine" that would help boost confidence and trust—ingredients sorely needed in Sino-Japanese relations. Japan and China should bear in mind that Asia can only become more harmonious if, and only if, both countries are able to work together. This small step in the Gulf of Aden demonstrated that China and Japan can work together (even though it had its genesis in nationalistic impulses, it ended in a joint effort). If anything, this is a case that should be promoted precisely because it could counter and erode the sensationalization and securitization of Sino-Japanese relations, both at home and abroad. Japan and China might find that such a move would actually reduce the political and diplomatic frictions they have and alleviate the diplomatic burden that now plagues their foreign policies.

REFERENCES

BBC. China's anti piracy role off Somalia expands. *BBC News*. 29 Jan 2010, http://news.bbc.co.uk/1/hi/world/asia-pacific/8486502.stm

Beckman, R.C., Forbes, V.L., & Grundy-Warr, C. *Acts of Piracy in the Malacca and Singapore Straits*. Durham: International Boundaries Research Unit, 1994.

Besley, T., Fetzer, T., & Mueller, H. The economic costs of piracy. International Growth Centre Paper. London School of Economics and Oxford University, 2012, http://www.theigc.org/project/the-economic-costs-of-piracy/

Black, L. Debating Japan's intervention to tackle piracy in the Gulf of Aden: beyond mainstream paradigms. *International Relations of Asia-Pacific* 2012, 12(2), 259–85.

Bradford, J.F. Japanese anti-piracy initiatives in Southeast Asia: policy formulation and the coastal state responses. *Contemporary Southeast Asia: A Journal of International and Strategic Affairs*. 2004, 26(3), 480–505.

Burnett, J. *Dangerous Waters*. New York: Random House Penguin Plume Books, 2003 Reprint edition.

Chan, G., Chan, L., & Lee, P.K. *China Engages Global Governance: A New World Order in the Making?* London: Routledge, 2012, p 170.

CNN, South Koreans pull off daring rescue of pirated ship. January 21, 2011. *CNN News*. http://edition.cnn.com/2011/WORLD/asiapcf/01/21/south.korea.pirate.rescue/

Contact group on Piracy, Piracy off the Coast of Somalia. 2015. CGPCS Newsletter. http://www.lessonsfrompiracy.net/files/2015/03/CGPCS-Newsletter-March-20152.pdf

Contact Group on Piracy off the Coast of Somalia. *First Communique*, 14 Jan 2009, http://www.lessonsfrompiracy.net/files/2015/03/Communique_1st_Plenary.pdf

Convention on the Territorial Sea and Contiguous Zone, Apr. 29, 1958, 15 UST 1606, 516 UNTS 205. Centre for International Law. http://cil.nus.edu.sg/1958/1958-convention-on-the-territorial-sea-and-the-contiguous-zone/

Ece, N.J. The Maritime Dimension of International Security: Piracy Attacks. (2012). *Maritime Security and Defense against Terrorism*, ed. F. Bora Uzer. Amsterdam: IOS Press, 12.

Editorial – Naval Technology, Ka-27/28 and Ka-29 Helix, *Naval Technology*, https://www.naval-technology.com/projects/ka272829-helix/

Fort, B. Transnational Threats and the Maritime Domain. In *Piracy, Maritime Terrorism and Securing the Malacca Straits*, ed. Graham Gerard Ong-Webb. 2006, Singapore: Institute of Southeast Asian Studies, 34–36.

Fox News, Somali pirates now protecting illegal fishing ships, says UN report, citing AP. 25 July 2013, http://www.foxnews.com/world/2013/07/25/somali-pirates-now-protecting-illegal-fishing-ships-says-un-report.html

Gokhale, N. India, China and the pirates. *The Diplomat*. 6 March 2012, http://thediplomat.com/2012/03/india-china-and-the-pirates/

Halloran, R. Japan at crossroads. April 2011 *Air Force Magazine* 62.

Harress, C. (2013, November 4). Secret flow of Somali piracy ransoms: 179 hijacked ships generated some $400M in payments since 2005. So where has it all gone? *International Business Times*. http://www.ibtimes.com/secret-flow-somali-piracy-ransoms-179-hijacked-ships-generated-some-400m-payments-2005-so-where-has

Hopkins, D.L., & Swarttouw, H. The Contact Group on Piracy off the Coast of Somalia: genesis, rationale and objectives. In *Fighting Piracy off the Coast of Somalia: Lessons Learned from the Contact Group*, ed. Thierry Tardy (Institute for Security Studies, European Union), 2014 http://www.iss.europa.eu/uploads/media/Report_20_Piracy_off_the_coast_of_Somalia.pdf

International Chamber of Commerce, Piracy news and figures. http://www.icc-wbo.org/products-and-services/fighting-commercial-crime/imb-piracy-reporting-centre/piracy-news-and-figures/

Japan Ministry of Defense Anti-piracy operations off Somalia and the Gulf of Aden., 30 March 2009a. http://www.mod.go.jp/e/jdf/no14/policy.html

Japan Ministry of Defense, A start of escorting ships by MSDF vessels in the Gulf of Aden. March 30 2009b. Press release.

Japan Ministry of Defense, Counter piracy initiatives. 2013. http://www.mod.go.jp/e/publ/w_paper/pdf/2013/39_Part3_Chapter2_Sec3.pdf

Japan Ministry of Defense, Record of mission, Escort operations conducted by MSDF units off Somalia and Gulf of Aden. 2014 November 14. Press Release http://www.mod.go.jp/e/d_act/somalia/pdf/20141114b.pdf

Japan MOD Fight Against Piracy website 2009, Measures against Piracy off the Coast of Somalia and in the Gulf of Aden Website, http://www.mod.go.jp/e/d_act/somalia/

Kaufman, A. *China's participation in anti-piracy operations in off the Horn of Africa: Drivers and Implications* CAN China Studies Conference report. Virginia, USA: Centre for Naval Analyses, July 2009. http://www.cna.org/sites/default/files/research/Piracy%20conference%20report.pdf

Komiss, W. and Huntzinger, L. 2011. The Economic Implications of Disruptions To Maritime Oil Choke points. CAN Analysis and Solutions, March 2011.

Lin-Greenberg, E. Dragon boats: assessing China's anti-piracy operations in the Gulf of Aden," *Defense and Security Analysis*, 2010, 26 (2), 213–30.

Lo, K. Japanese frogmen approached Chinese warship at Djibouti, State Media say, *South China Morning Post*, 2nd August 2017 https://www.scmp.com/news/china/diplomacy-defence/article/2105024/japanese-frogmen-approached-chinese-warship-djibouti

McCormack, G., & Norimatsu, S.O. *Resistant Islands: Okinawa Confronts Japan and the United States.* 2012, Washington DC: Rowman & Littlefield Publishers.

People's Daily, China navy to send its most sophisticated ships on escort mission off to Somalia. 2008, December 27 *People's Daily Online.* http://en.people.cn/90001/90776/90883/6562939.html

People's Daily, Chinese naval fleets sails into the Straits of Malacca. 2009a, December 29. *People's Daily Online.* http://en.people.cn/90001/90776/90883/6564180.html

People's Daily, Hong Kong, Macao, Taiwan ships can request escort of Chinese mainland navy. 2009b, January 6. *People's Daily Online.* http://en.people.cn/90001/90776/90785/6568223.html

PRC State Council, Defense White Paper April 2013. State Council of China, see in particular, Section V, Safeguarding World Peace and Regional Security. Available at: http://eng.mod.gov.cn/Database/WhitePapers/index.htm

QQ News, *Qiemi: zhongguo shangchuan jitui suomali haidao de muhou gushi* [The story behind the merchant ship's successful defence against the Somalian pirates]. 2009, January 22. QQ News. http://news.qq.com/a/20090122/000727.htm

Roehrig, T. South Korea's anti-piracy operations in the Gulf of Aden. Global Korea Report. Harvard Kennedy School, 2015. http://belfercenter.ksg.harvard.edu/files/globalkorea_report_roehrig.pdf

Sakurai, T. The fact sheet of anti-piracy activities off the coast of Somalia and the Gulf of Aden. Japan Peacekeeping Training and Research Center, Joint Staff College, Tokyo, Japan Ministry of Defense 2013. http://www.mod.go.jp/js/jsc/jpc/research/image/eng01.pdf

Security Council, Unanimously Adopting Resolution 1918 (2010), Calls on All States to Criminalize Piracy under National Laws, (Press Release), https://www.un.org/press/en/2010/sc9913.doc.html

Strait of Hormuz is chokepoint for 20% of world's oil. United States Energy Information Administration. 2012, http://www.eia.gov/todayinenergy/detail.cfm?id=7830

Takeda, I. Taking the lead in regional maritime security. *Japan Echo*, 2004, 31(6), 47–50. This article was translated from "Nihon ga shudo suru 'kaiyo anzen hosho' no shin chitsujo," *Chuo Koron*, Oct 2004, 70–77.

Text of Resolution 1851. United Nations. Available at http://cil.nus.edu.sg/2008/2008-united-nations-security-council-resolution-1851-on-the-situation-in-somalia-unscr-1851/

The Economic Times, India, China and Japan coordinating in anti-piracy operations. 2012, February 1. *The Economic Times*. https://economictimes.indiatimes.com/news/politics-and-nation/india-china-japan-coordinating-in-anti-piracy-operations/articleshow/11716849.cms

The Guardian, No Somali hijacking in nearly a year. 2013, May 3. http://www.theguardian.com/world/2013/may/03/somali-pirate-hijacking

The Somaliland Times. Japan sets up first overseas base in Djibouti to fight piracy. 2011, June 4. http://www.somalilandtimes.net/sl/2011/488/20.shtml

UN, Security Council Resolution 1816. (2008a). United Nations. http://www.refworld.org/docid/48464c622.html

UN, Security Council Resolution 1846. (2008b). United Nations. Available at http://cil.nus.edu.sg/2008/2008-united-nations-security-council-resolution-1846-on-the-situation-in-somalia-unscr-1846/

UNCHS, Convention on the High Seas, Art. 15, Apr. 29, 1958, 13 UST 2312, 450 UNTS 11. Centre for International Law. http://cil.nus.edu.sg/rp/il/pdf/1958%20Convention%20on%20High%20Seas-pdf.pdf

United Nations, Art 105, United Nations Convention of Law of the Sea, Dec. 10, 1982, 1833 UNTS 397. United Nations. http://www.un.org/depts/los/convention_agreements/texts/unclos/unclos_e.pdf

United Nations Convention of Law of the Sea (UNCLOS), Dec. 10, 1982, 1833 UNTS 397. United Nations. In particular see Art 58(3). http://www.un.org/depts/los/convention_agreements/texts/unclos/unclos_e.pdf

United Nations Security Council Resolutions on Piracy. 2012. United Nations. http://www.un.org/depts/los/piracy/piracy_documents.htm

US Department of Homeland Security, Container security initiative ports. (2014). United States Department of Homeland Security. http://www.dhs.gov/container-security-initiative-ports

US Navy News, New counter piracy task force established. (2009, August 1). *America's Navy*. http://www.navy.mil/submit/display.asp?story_id=41687

US Transportation Dept, Economic impact of piracy in the Gulf of Aden. 2010, http://www.marad.dot.gov/wp-content/uploads/pdf/Economic_Impact_of_Piracy_2010.pdf

Wagner, D., & Cafiero, D. Japan's Influence in the Middle East, 24 Jan 2014, *Huffington Post*, https://www.huffingtonpost.com/daniel-wagner/japans-influence-in-the-m_b_4159850.html

Walker, R. Inside Story of a Somali Pirate Attack. *BBC News*. 4th June 2009 http://news.bbc.co.uk/1/hi/world/africa/8080098.stm

Watanabe, H. A Global Perspective on National Security. *Japan Echo*, 34 (4), 40–44. This article originally was translated from "NATO to no taiwa ga Nihon ni tsukitsuketa mono" *Chuo Koron*, May 2007, 160–67.

Weitz, R. Operation Somalia: China's first expeditionary force? *China Security*, 2009, 5(1), 27–42. http://www.washingtonobserver.org/pdfs/Weitz.pdf

Westcott, K. Somali pirates face battles at sea. *BBC News.*, 2008 http://news.bbc.co.uk/1/hi/world/africa/7358764.stm

Woolley, P. Japan's 1991 Minesweeping Decision: An Organizational Response. *Asian Survey*, 1996, 36(8), 804–817. doi:https://doi.org/10.2307/2645440

World Bank Report, Conflict in Somalia: drivers and dynamics. (January 2005). http://siteresources.worldbank.org/INTSOMALIA/Resources/conflictin-somalia.pdf

Yading wan tou tufei ji [Fighting the pirates in Aden]. 2008. http://www.china.com.cn/news/txt/2008-12/19/content_16974634.htm

Zhonguo chuanyuan yong zijiranshaodan jitui suomali haidao. Youtube, https://www.youtube.com/watch?v=Mnq4NrR4-V8

Zhou, B. Counter-piracy operations in the Gulf of Aden: implications of PLA Navy. *US-China Focus*, 30 December 2013. http://www.chinausfocus.com/peace-security/counter-piracy-in-the-gulf-of-aden-implications-for-pla-navy/

Open Access This chapter is licensed under the terms of the Creative Commons Attribution 4.0 International License (http://creativecommons.org/licenses/by/4.0/), which permits use, sharing, adaptation, distribution and reproduction in any medium or format, as long as you give appropriate credit to the original author(s) and the source, provide a link to the Creative Commons licence and indicate if changes were made.

The images or other third party material in this chapter are included in the chapter's Creative Commons licence, unless indicated otherwise in a credit line to the material. If material is not included in the chapter's Creative Commons licence and your intended use is not permitted by statutory regulation or exceeds the permitted use, you will need to obtain permission directly from the copyright holder.

CHAPTER 6

Recalibrating Japan's Foreign Policy

Japan's rejuvenation as a "normal" nation has been an arduous and difficult journey to say the very least. Contrary to conventional wisdom, Japan's normalization and rejuvenation is not just the purview of the LDP conservatives, but remains at the heart of the nation's debate on constitutional revisionism, on the future of Japan's alliance with the US and the status of Japan's commitment to global intervention through the deployment of the JSDF. There is a consensus across the broad political spectrum in Japan concerning the importance of the US to Japan's global strategy, security posture and foreign affairs, just as there is broad-based support for Japan's shouldering of more responsibilities globally, particularly in terms of humanitarian and disaster relief. This is significantly positive as even though Japan underwent a two-decade economic stagnation, its impulses to act for UN mandated aspirations and goals remained strong. In the post-Cold War period, Japan evolved from a passive bystander to a nation that is more able and capable than ever before in its recent history to meet with key foreign and security policy challenges. This journey has been exceedingly difficult, primarily because no one, even at the policy elite levels, has known exactly where Japan was heading strategically, particularly in the early 1990s. The Japanese people as a society have always had the tradition of consultation and consensual decision-making. Together with a vicarious press, increasingly assertive politicians and Diet members

© The Author(s) 2019
V. Teo, *Japan's Arduous Rejuvenation as a Global Power*,
https://doi.org/10.1007/978-981-13-6190-6_6

who tend to get rowdy when things don't go their way,[1] the debate on the way forward has of late become very difficult.

The rejuvenation of Japan today rests on three important pillars—the management of the US-Japan alliance, the erosion of pacifism and changing mindsets in Japan on the deployment of the JSDF globally lastly, the revision of the postwar constitution. All these items have always been extremely important to the conservative agenda in the immediate postwar era, even though they have never had the opportunity to be brought to the forefront of Japan's political agenda. Across the decades, postwar Japanese prime ministers have slowly but surely worked out how to manage Japan's security and interests by combining traditional influences, realpolitik considerations and lessons drawn from past experiences.

Without question, the most important element by far for Cold War prime ministers was the management of the US-Japan security alliance. During the early postwar decades in the 1950s and 1960s, Japan as a nation had always debated upon the extent to which it could and should cooperate with the US in military and strategic terms. Right up to the 1960s, after the revised US-Japan security treaty was put in place, the rationale and logic of the US-Japan alliance was neither always clear nor uncontested. Initially, cooperation with the US came as a natural result of the Occupation—but for many Japanese, particularly those with ties to the pre-war government, this turn of affairs was far from natural. Yoshida Shigeru, Hatoyama Ichiro, Ishibashi Tanzan, Kishi Nobusuke, Ikeda Hayato, Sato Eisaku, Tanaka Kakuei, Fukuda Takeo, Miki Takeo, Ohira Masayoshi, Suzuki Zenko, Nakasone Yashuhiro, Takeshita Noboru, Miyazawa Kiichi, Kaifu Toshiki, Hosakawa Morihiro, Murayama Tomiichi, Ryutaro Hashimoto, Keizo Obuchi, Mori Yoshiro and others all had to contend with evolving demands and tensions in Japan's relations with the US, even though on the surface things appeared to be rosy. For many of the other prime ministers born during or after the war, this might have mattered less. Koizumi Junichiro, Abe Shinzo, Taro Aso, Yukio Hatoyama, Kan Naoto, Noda Yoshihiko are of this era.

---

[1] As the LDP attempted to push the contentious security bills through the legislative committee, catching the opposition party by surprise, the Upper House committee chairman Yoshitada Konoike was surrounded by the opposition, who attempted to prevent bills to increase military influence from being heard and passed. The bills allowed Japan's military to conduct operations abroad for the first time in 70 years. See video of the scuffle in Japan's Upper House after the panel approves the military bills, and where an estimated 13,000 people rallied outside Parliament: https://on.rt.com/6rl1

The retrospective evaluation of the foreign policy records of these are varied, but one dominant theme that stands out is the vexing difficulty most prime ministers faced in managing the demands of the US and reconciling public mood and the capabilities of Japan with these demands at any particular point. Many of those who grew up in the 1950s and 1960s understood that what the US wanted did not always coincide with what Japan desired. There was widespread resistance to the US during the 1960s, because many believed that the Cold War goals were antithetical to the pacifist and democratic spirit that the Japanese nation embodied.

Contrary to the popular idea that Japan had slavishly followed the strategic lead of the US, an important but subtle question for Tokyo has always been how to incorporate resistance through cooperation with the US, and in doing so maintain a more equidistant relationship with the US. Generations of prime ministers worked hand in hand to ensure that the relationship was never an easy one-way relationship. Japan's alliance with the US evolved from one where Japan had relatively little say or choice in the immediate period after the Occupation, to one that saw a confident Japan emerge as a challenger to the US, to what looks like a true partnership today. Thus, the US-Japan security alliance was managed as a Cold War institution initially and viewed as a suspect and anti-democratic institution by the Japanese during the initial postwar years. As we have already seen, the idea of this US-Japan relationship being an "alliance" was only first mooted in the early 1980s. What everyone takes for granted today as the "bedrock of peace and stability" was therefore only conceived as an intellectual construct about four decades ago. Since then, Japan has come to increasingly rely on the US for strategic direction, even though its national strength grows.

By the end of the Cold War, the US had become a truly global power that had significant sway over regional affairs across the globe, from Latin America to Southeast Asia. Often integrated deeply into regional affairs, the US has more times than not found itself at odds with one (or more) of the regional hegemons. In the Middle East, the US is constantly challenged by Iran and the radical groups, in Europe by Russia and in East Asia, China. Insofar as Tokyo is concerned, the US-Japan alliance has served Japan in a largely positive way in the Asia-Pacific region. Outside the Asia-Pacific region, Japan's close association with the US brought about knock-on difficulties. As exemplified by the discussion on the Middle East, the difficulties are brought about in two dimensions.

First, even though Tokyo has had varying differences with Washington in their approaches over certain issues (for example on the Iran nuclear challenge and their handling of the Arab-Israeli conflict), Japan has chosen to harmonize its policies with the US, as alliance unity is paramount and prioritized. Second, close political association with the US often imposes an opportunity cost almost immediately. In its bid to cultivate strong relations with important Middle East countries such as Saudi Arabia, Tokyo found that the latter was more interested in Beijing than in Tokyo for the simple reason that China can act as a counterweight and leverage to the US in a way that Japan cannot. For that reason, Japan often finds itself frustrated because it is unable to pursue its interests in an adulterated manner. Japan's own preference to play a supporting role and privileging US policy goals is a major stumbling block to Japan's rejuvenation. The question going forward for Japan is therefore whether it would be able to move beyond this political culture and the attendant constraints it has imposed upon itself to adopt a more independent foreign policy in instances when it serves its interests to do so.

With the inception of the Trump administration, the nature of US domestic politics changed drastically. Trump's unconventional political strategy and the vicious overdrive by his political enemies to topple his administration have impacted upon US foreign policy. To that end, it has had several fundamental spill-over effects on Japan's foreign policy. First, Trump's America First policy has provided a change in the way the US worldview and priorities are framed, and this has severely impacted on the mainstream politics and agenda of both parties, particularly in the way costs of alliance and foreign intervention are discussed. This goes far beyond the bipartisan political bickering that observers of US politics are used to. At the heart of this debate is whether the US should continue to bear the costs for its global presence, as this is now framed as a "burden" for US taxpayers, and undermines the support built up over the decades domestically for global US presence. When it comes to cost calculations, the US has neither enemies nor allies, and "issues" to do with burden sharing are taken care of—the US will not be "ripped off" by its allies. Needless to say, such rhetoric affects the leadership credentials of the US, thereby alienating and increasing tensions with its traditional allies. From Germany to France to Australia, every incumbent leader appears to have taken political potshots at President Trump and the values that the US now appears to stand for. Tokyo is concerned about the impact this has had for US leadership and the cohesiveness of the liberal democratic order that Japan's security has come to rely on so much. Second, the Trump administration has undertaken policy adjustments that impacted directly on the US-Japan alliance, such as the unilateral withdrawal from TPP, pressuring Tokyo on trade concessions and undertaking negotiations with North Korea without prior consultation with Tokyo. This has both shocked and dismayed many within the Abe administration, but at the same time provided the impetus for Japan to reconsider its own policy adjustments. Third, at the risk of great political cost, Prime Minister Abe has built a close personal relationship with President Trump in service of the bilateral alliance. Through his deft personal diplomacy, Abe has quietly and stealthily taken the senior statesman role in steering the US-Japan alliance, despite the policy setbacks originating from Trump's decisions. The inclusion of India and Australia as part of the Quadrilateral Security Dialogue, Japan's constant urging of an improvement in India-US relations, and Tokyo's active measures to support the Philippines and Vietnam in the South China Sea are some of Japan's initiatives to help enhance its security in the region vis-à-vis China. Prime Minister Abe has become the person most instrumental in pushing for initiatives to shore up the alliance, as the Trump ascension has provided an unprecedented opportunity for Tokyo to try and strengthen its position in the alliance and steer it in the direction Tokyo desires.

The second pillar of Japan's rejuvenation—that of restoration of Japan's military prowess and the restoration of the JSDF's status—is probably one of the more successful elements of the neo-conservatives' strategy so far. Even though this aspect has been critically stifled by the Japanese nation's preference for pacifism in the immediate aftermath of the Second World War, the neo-conservatives have successfully changed the way the military is being conceived in Japan today. For much of the postwar period, pacifism acted as both the moral compass of the people and the ideological shield that the Japanese government used to fend off US demands for Japan to do more. In realpolitik language, Tokyo used pacifism to protect Japan from the possible dangers of alliance chain-ganging, of being dragged into an unwanted war that Japan had no wished to be involved in. The provisions of the treaty were such that there is no obligation for Japan to come to the aid of the US should it be attacked, but this did not prevent unwanted criticisms of free riding and evading rightful international obligations. A turning point came in the aftermath of the Gulf War, where a frustrated and bewildered Japan struggled to understand why, despite contributing more than USD 7 billion to the war effort, "boots on the ground" mattered more politically and symbolically to the international community. In the early post-Cold War period, Japan's normalization took shape with increasing UN missions within Asia, as evidenced by Japan's UN peacekeeping missions in Cambodia and East Timor, as well as the deployment of elements of the JSDF to assist in operations in Iraq, Afghanistan, the Indian Ocean, Somalia and Sudan. With generation change, strategic shifts in Japan's external environment, and increased nationalistic sentiments within Japan, the neo-conservative's normalization agenda and rejuvenation aspirations were propelled to the forefront.

Even though Japanese elites and the Japanese people agree that Japan should support UN mandated operations and contribute to worthy global missions, the debate often centers on the extent and the manner by which Japan should do so, as Japan is constitutionally prohibited from waging war or maintaining "war potential." Japan has certainly made adjustments to its defense posture vis-à-vis the US-Japan security alliance. These adjustments are incremental, and often take on mundane administrative measures or Dietary legislations—but nonetheless, they do help the government skirt constitutional constraints incrementally. This started in earnest after the Hashimoto–Clinton agreement in the mid-1990s, when a series of guidelines were put in place to help support Japan participating more actively (and legally) in US-Japan alliance operations. Since then, Japan and the US have worked closely to ensure that Japan continues to improve the JSDF operational capabilities through better legislation, joint training and closer coordination. The Japanese government began to interpret "threats to Japan" in a "situational" manner to protect Japan and its people, shifting the doctrine of strict self-defense to one that allowed Japan to exercise the right to collective defense. This is a much bigger step from the Japanese government's official decision in February 1956 that deemed that it is constitutional to possess capability to attack enemies when there is no other measure to defend itself from external aggression (Tatsumi, 2018).

This right to collective defense was deliberated in the Diet in 2015, and the security bills were pushed through by the Abe government. This would include situations such as a contingency involving North Korea and US forces off the Korean Peninsula to a China-Taiwan conflict involving US forces in the Taiwan Straits. Japan could also in theory engage in military action in the Gulf if its ships laden with petroleum were endangered. Through the security bills passed in 2015, the JSDF is now able to participate in collective defense and fight a foreign conflict as long as the government deems it appropriate. In 2017, Defense Minister Itsunori Onodera went further, saying that a North Korean ballistic missile attack on Guam would also constitute a survival-threatening situation, as this would degrade the capabilities of the US military that are important for Japan's national security. Today, the Japanese military is one of the best armed and best equipped in the Asia-Pacific region, if not the world. Be that as it may, the neo-conservatives are now waging a public relations and political battle, as well as a court battle, to have their policy upheld (Aibara 2018).

In January 2018, Prime Minister Abe stipulated that rather than following the traditional linear project used in previous National Defense Program Guidelines (NDPG), there would be an honest assessment of the challenges facing Japan and that 2018 would see the operationalization of his plans (Tatsumi, 2018). By December 2018, the Abe cabinet had finalized a new set of National Defense Policy Guidelines that endorsed the Japan defense ministry's plans to retrofit two helicopter carriers to become aircraft carriers. Additionally, Japan also committed to purchasing around 100 F-35s fighters to replace aging F-15s, and additional 42 F-35b variant aircrafts to be used on the two Izumo-class carriers. Japan also began to cultivate abilities for cyber and space warfare. Naturally, critics of the Abe government and opponents of the neo-conservatives inside and outside of Japan were outraged by these developments. To have bureaucrats interpret whether something is "constitutional" or not is clearly problematic, as is the slippery slope logic presented by the Abe cabinet. If indeed the aircraft carriers are "escorts," then clearly there is nothing stopping Japan from manufacturing more of these "escorts" in the future, should the need arise. Furthermore, it does not take many of these advance fighters to cause widespread destruction, given the advancement of military technology. There is a belief among scholars that the pacifism, moral compass and ideological restraint infused into Japan since the end of the Pacific War has all but eroded. The popularity of this view might be due to governments attempting to disseminate the view through its official narratives and the media, but it is also popularized by Japan watchers in the West, who are often keen to advocate for the containment of China, and lastly, but also ironically, by narratives coming out of China itself. Certainly the conversion of Izumo from helicopter carriers to aircraft carriers, or the purchase of 142 (estimated) F-35s and the institution of cyber defense and space warfare capabilities, does not make the "pacifism" look real anymore. The neo-conservatives' rhetoric that Japan has to change with the times, live up to its alliance responsibilities, fulfill its obligations as a responsible global power and look after its own interests and security has certainly been operationalized.

The third and most important pillar in the rejuvenation effort—that of constitutional revisionism—is arguably the most difficult pillar for the neo-Conservatives to achieve. In retrospect, as the prime minister with the greatest stock of political capital and strategic instincts, and what looks like a divine opportunity coming to power again in 2012 in the aftermath of DPJ's mishandling of the Senkaku issue with China, Shinzo Abe struggles with uphill support for constitutional revisionism despite the LDP's relentless attempt to chip away at the obstacles. During his first term (September 2006–September 2007), the prime minister made a political mistake of privileging this goal above all others, and this contributed to his early resignation as prime minister. Prime Minister Abe was reelected in 2012, becoming the first Prime Minister to return to office since Shigeru Yoshida in 1948. He was reelected in 2014, and then again in 2017. At the time of writing, the Prime Minister is the fourth longest serving Prime Minister in history. This resilient Prime Minister has miraculously just survived two political scandals and, at the time of writing, is now enjoying improved approval ratings. The August 2018 victory for Prime Minister Abe for the leadership of the LDP thus presents one of the best opportunities for the neo-conservatives to renew their push for, and to effect, such a change. Prime Minister Abe himself has indicated that this is to be achieved by 2020.

The attempt to revise the constitution must be viewed as a 70-year old exercise, stemming from attempts by Japanese conservatives from the Yoshida era, even before the existing constitution was put in place. The roots of the complaints are common-place enough, even though they have been repeatedly articulated by various factions attempting to justify constitutional revisionism over the past few decades. Today, the neo-conservatives parrot the same reasons: The constitution is: a foreign imposed document; an infringement of Japanese sovereignty; a manifestation of victor's justice; a blatant violation of the Japanese people's right to self-defense; an obstacle to the rightful status of the Japanese military. Thus, allowing the Japanese people a right to choose (through a referendum) as times and circumstances change is important and a valid point that needs to be considered.

However, the key lies in understanding what ordinary Japanese people want for themselves. The popularity and longevity of Prime Minister Shinzo Abe do not lie in his normalization or rejuvenation of Japan i.e. his foreign policy agenda alone. Most of the Japanese electorate just believe that Prime Minister Abe will be able to help maintain stability needed for economic growth. While many Japanese are convinced by some of the neo-conservative arguments, there is no indication that they do agree with Abe's proposed solution entirely. There is dissent toward a military rearmament agenda, however, and certainly there is a sizable opposition to constitutional amendment. There are many questioning whether Abe's agenda is indeed the best way forward for Japan, and no amount of official narratives and media messages would change that easily. A certain segment of the Japanese public remains relatively suspicious of the Japanese government's attempt to remilitarize Japan unconditionally and without restraint. Thus, even though the Abe administration has so valiantly tried, they have had limited support. The postwar generation, infused with the spirit of pacifism, is thoroughly conflict adverse. This pacifism is not only manifested in Japanese institutions such as the liberal democratic structures that have been put in place, but also lives on among the people as both a culture and a tradition. Many of those at the forefront of the protests against the security bills, in Okinawa and even in Tokyo, are of the younger student generation. Even though they might not like China, there is every reasonable expectation that they also might not like what the neo-conservatives are proposing. One should not automatically assume that just because there are popular negative perceptions of China in Japan, one would necessary agree with Constitutional revisionism.

Japan's Rejuvenation from the Perspective of the US and China

The US: The Preservation of Pre-Eminent Status

From the perspective of the US, constitutional revision has been something that successive US administrations have asked for as soon as the Japanese constitution was imposed on Japan by Truman and MacArthur during the Occupation period. The main motivation behind this was that the US needed an ally in Asia to fight its Cold War and to prevent the spread of communism. Particularly with the onset of the Korean War, this emerged as an issue of critical strategic importance, not only of political expediency. The best anti-communist leaders, the US learned, were ironically the right-leaning politicians of the pre-war and wartime cabinet. Rehabilitating such personnel and putting them in place in the new system that had been set up ensured both loyalty (to the anti-communist cause at least) and competence in leading the nation. McArthur's aims of both containing and punishing wartime criminals had all but dissipated by the

1950s. Many of the rehabilitated wartime elites who adopted pacifism as their political philosophy and outlook became founders of reputable firms and institutions in Japan. However, there are others with revisionist views of the war who have also risen to positions of powers and influence—and the views of these politicians sit uncomfortably with those who fought in the Pacific War. It is in the interest of the US to cultivate a Japan that is entirely devoted to its strategic goals—a Japan that tries to align its goals to the US, but when this is not possible, subordinates Japan's national interests while maintaining the narrative of alliance unity.

During the tenure of Prime Minister Koizumi, US-Japan relations blossomed, driven largely by Japan's unwavering support for the US War on Terror, and Prime Minister Koizumi's friendship with President George W. Bush. The deterioration of Sino-Japanese relations during this period was often blamed on the US War on Terror, and for its neglect in maintaining its relations with Japan and China to keep a balance. Yet, in retrospect, this could alternatively be seen as the period that was most successful for US policy in the region. The neglect caused the Japanese to struggle and come to terms with the prospect of dealing with China on their own, and the anti-Japanese riots have reaffirmed the Japanese conviction that their alliance must be tightened, even though they seek normalization in their foreign and security affairs. At the same time, China learned through the Koizumi era (and the subsequent DPJ era, especially from the Senkaku Islands dispute), that the Japan that China is dealing with is a radically different Japan from yesteryear. Even though the Chinese believed for years that it was the security alliance with the US that prevented Japan from reaching out and building closer relations with China, this assumption began to look questionable, particularly from the Koizumi year onwards. Without the assistance of the US, China does not quite know what it could do to handle its relations with Japan. In a nutshell, even though the US neglected to pay more attention to Asia during the War on Terror years, its policy had inadvertently driven both China and Japan to seek closer relations with the US in their bid to hedge against each other.

The US, however, did not find Japan unproblematic. Washington D. C. became truly vexed, with relations with Japan under the tenure of the first DPJ prime minister stalled. Keen to "rebalance" Japan's foreign relations, Prime Minister Yukio Hatoyama's alarming (perceived or real) tilt toward China and Korea did not go down well with neo-conservatives in Japan or Washington. The reaction in Hatoyama's Japan was telling. The speed by which public opinion turned against Hatoyama was an indication that his election was premised upon what the LDP was not doing right rather than upon his professed agenda of recalibrating Japan's foreign relations with the US and its neighbors. Even China found the DPJ's tenure frustrating, as it became apparent that the DPJ did not have a handle on the domestic politics situation in Japan, and even Beijing found it difficult to decide locate someone who can speak for Japan at the height of the Senkaku crisis. From Beijing's perspective, it was easier to deal with a nationalistic LDP than a friendly DPJ who was not able to rein in the factions, bureaucracy, the military, the political opposition and press. Beyond that, the United States' ability to handle Japan suddenly found a new appreciation in Beijing.

This new-found confidence in the LDP certainly did wonders for the incoming Abe administration. For Beijing, it was a relief that the period of anti-Chinese sentiments seemed to be handled nicely by this administration, whose hawkish position on these issues appeared to rein in excessive nationalistic calls. The US was relieved that this sense of Hatoyaman adventurism had subsided by the time Prime Minister Noda came to power. The last DPJ prime minister went further than his predecessors in his "nationalization" of the Senkaku Islands, and in the reaffirmation of the US-Japan Security alliance. Noda even reversed Hatoyama's positions on the Okinawa Islands, and went ahead to put in place several policies that were more traditionally LDP (or Japanese) in nature. Both the US and China heaved a sigh of relief when Japanese politics returned to "normality" with the election of Abe.

The election of Prime Minister Abe for the second time was well received in Washington. What could be better for the US than for the scion of Prime Minister Kishi, (who single handedly pushed through the revised US-Japan security treaty bill through the Diet in the 1960s) be appointed Prime Minister after the tempestuous DPJ era. The Japan of the Abe 2.0 era was certainly more decisive and forward looking than under his predecessors. Even though various US scholars and commentators question the effectiveness of Japan as an alliance partner under Koizumi, their wishes for a Japan to be led by a leader with staying power came through. As far as the US was concerned, an end to the revolving door prime ministers that had so come to characterize the post Cold War era were certainly a dream come true. The Abe administration exhibited a kind of attitude that is reminiscent of China's "leaning one side" (with no question of ambivalence) at all toward the US, but this is not surprising at all. Prime Minister Abe campaigned vigorously for a revival of the US-Japan Alliance, publishing his manifesto through his book, (*A Beautiful Japan*) which was never translated into English for wider circulation as planned.

The question is whether the US could count on the neo-conservatives to support this strategy, after the Cold War. There is no question that this is entirely possible—but it begs the question whether there is merit to the neo-conservative's often-articulated strategy to tighten the alliance in order to obtain more latitude and independence from the US. Such articulation, however, opens up the debate as to the real intent of the neo-conservative politicians: is closer collaboration with the US an instrumental strategy by which more latitude for Japan is sought, and if so, would a strategically more independent make Japan remain beholden to US policy goals in the future?

Between Revisionism and Realpolitik: China's Japan Problem

From China's perspective, Japan's constitution serves as a political and legal latch on Japan. How "useful" this latch is in time to come remains to be seen. Given the incremental legal and administrative approaches the post-Cold War Japanese governments have taken to bypass constitutional constraints in terms of advancing the military deployments or revamping the JSDF to support US operations, the constitution remains more effective in spirit than perhaps in practice. Today, the Chinese know that the Japanese military possess the most formidable military hardware in Asia, and have the technological might to dominate the most important fields with military applications. The problem, however, is not so much with the fact that Japan wants to revise its constitution, so that its appeal and operations are commensurate with the new strategic realities surrounding Japan. China's concern is the perceived historical whitewashing and the general historical narratives that have been constructed by the conservatives with regards to history and how this narrative stokes wholesale anti-Chinese nationalism at home and abroad. This certainly begets enmity among the young people in Japan toward the Chinese government and the Chinese nation. Ironically, this is exactly what the neo-conservatives in Japan are accusing the Chinese government of—the instrumental usage of history and nationalism to stoke anti-Japanese sentiment.

More worryingly, China has always viewed the handling of Japanese issues in its foreign policy as a subset of its relations with the US. This is a logical extension of the Cold War practices, a by-product if you will of the Yoshida Doctrine. Yet, the end of the Cold War did not bring about the improvement in Sino-Japanese relations that many Chinese commentators had hoped for. Japan-China relations deteriorated over a series of issues—

some involving the US and some not. It became increasingly clear that Japan needs to be dealt with in its own right, particularly with the LDP (whom many Chinese consider as China's old friends). From 2000 onwards, from the election of Junichiro Koizumi to the present, Chinese leaders have been shocked to discover a new breed of LDP conservatives in power—unlike their older colleagues in the LDP such as Yoshida, Tanaka or Nakasone—whose ideology seems to be centered on all things anti-Chinese. The key here is that Koizumi had detached Japan's treatment of history from being a factor in the state of Sino-Japanese relations—and this is a fact that has not sunk in with the Chinese.

The assessment of Japan's strategic proclivities had also started to change in Chinese discourse. From Beijing's perspective, the qualitative change in the way China was presented in Japanese narratives was alarming. In 1998, when North Korea fired the first missile that overflew Japan, North Korea was constituted as the primary threat in Japanese strategic narratives. While the defense community in Japan continued to fixate on North Korea, the place of China moved from expressions of "concern" to outright security "threat" by the early 2000s. The difficulty China had with Japan was in understanding Japan's psyche, as their understanding of being able to "handle" Japan through managing relations with the US were completely negated by the time Koizumi stepped down as prime minister.

To that extent, elites debating in Beijing had a hard time understanding what it was about China and its rise that Japan feared so much. Even though common Chinese people are gleeful at the prospect of "catching" up with the US and Japan, most Chinese elites are sanguine about the real situation, as China is still decades away from truly catching up with Japanese or American hard and soft power (Van Ness 2001; Farley 2018). This view optimistically assumes Chinese growth rates remain constantly high or that Japan and the US continue growing at their current rates. Thus, China perceives with some anxiety the "normalization" of Japan, and assesses that Chinese elites have taken a decisive position not to in anyway show signs of friendliness and good neighborliness to Japan.

Senior Chinese scholars and policy elites have interpreted Japan's attempt at constitutional revisionism with a suspicious and a somewhat ambivalent manner. They are not sure whether China prefers a Japan that is more independent strategically to a Japan that is assertive under the general US-Japan alliance (as it is now). They would certainly prefer a "friendly" Japan, but there is no agreement what this actually means to the

Chinese elites. One fundamental standard is the way perhaps is to see how history, particularly the war with China, is being explained to the younger generation. Chinese commentators have indicated that while Japanese leaders certainly have the right to cultivate patriotism among the young, inculcating historical revisionism over issues such as the Nanjing Massacre or comfort women certainly does not help matters. It cultivates anti-Chinese sentiments and inculcates an entire generation of young Japanese with a misguided sense of history.

There are of course counter-allegations from Japan on the similar state practices over history (over events such as the Great Leap Forward, the Cultural Revolution or the Tiananmen Square Massacre) or the Chinese propensity to use "victimhood" (in the words of so many scholars) to gain the diplomatic upper hand. However, these narratives miss the point: China, Korea and many other parts of Asia did suffer from Japanese imperialism—and raising these allegations about the post-1949 communist government in China does not negate the unfortunate period of history in pre-1949 China.

Memories are a lot more tangible and consequential than people assume them to be. These generational memories are not derived from thin air. They come from the memories inherited and passed down by the previous generations. These memories are mediated and transformed through various media—museums, performing arts, stories, literature and oral history. Some memories are actively manipulated, while others are pristinely preserved. What is true is that as society changes, these memories morph and transform with generations—perhaps through new ways of interpretation. Generational memories interact in a strange way with national identity. The latter guides what memories are to be retained and given a prominent place, and what memories to discard or delegate to the deep recess of social remembrance, and in turn, social memories help heed and evolve national identities. National governments might have short memories because of the exigencies of the moment, but nations have long ones.

The debate over the content of certain events such as the Nanjing Massacre or the atomic bombing of Hiroshima and Nagasaki in social memories in China and Japan are well known and need not be rehashed here. What needs to be highlighted is this: while attempting to cultivate the "correct" political orientation toward history, societies often choose to repress certain memories. These memories while being repressed might still figure prominently in a people's identity—memories repressed by state or nation might not be discussed in public but the likelihood is that they will not be forgotten because of their poignancy to social history and conscience, but also, because they are essential for nation-building and identity forging. The problem as it happens is that the memories of the unpleasant interactions over the last 30 years have morphed into layers and layers of social memories that have prevented the Chinese and Japanese nations, particularly the younger generation, from having a shared sense of history and a common narrative.

China therefore views Japan's attempt to revise the constitution and eradicate pacifism as parts of an attempt to eradicate an understanding of the Pacific War and the aftermath reached by the interpretation of the previous generation. This revision means that younger Japanese people do not get told clearly why the Second World War was fought, and why Japan should bear the majority of the responsibility. If the revisionist interpretation offered by Prime Minister Abe has become the bedrock of modern Japan, and informs the subsequent state policy, it is only natural that China, as much as the Koreans, takes issue with Japanese policies. Abe's efforts to revise the constitution, to have closer relations with the US and reform the status of the JSDF, have encouraged Japan to play a global role that has become suspect and inappropriate in Chinese eyes. Simply put, China complains that the revival of Japanese militarism does not come out of nowhere—it is linked to Abe's and the general right wing's revisionist projects that are going on in Japan.

Therefore, to say that the Chinese are using the "history card" might not actually be quite on the mark, as the effectiveness of the "history card" is not entirely clear either, and in reality it might backfire on the Chinese government more than it affects the Japanese government. Most importantly, since the Koizumi administration, the Japanese government has made it abundantly clear that their China policy is not one that will be affected by what the Chinese (or the Koreans) say about history.

Resistance from Below: Democratic Resilience and Rejuvenation

The resistance against Abe is ironically echoed by some segments in Japanese society who have reacted to the Abe administration policies positively over the past few years. Abe's normalization and rejuvenation agenda is increasingly facing resistance from various segments of society, even though the prime minister has skillfully capitalized on the recent geopolitical developments—particularly the rise of China and the belligerence of North Korea—to make the case for Japan to remilitarize, undertake collective security responsibility and increase its global and military role, particularly through the deployment of the JSDF. If anything, the Prime Minister has also skillfully manipulated and propelled Japan onto the path of becoming a global power—continuing the good work done by successive generations of Japanese leaders since pre-modern times. However, there is resistance to the prime minister's plans, making his mobilization efforts difficult to sustain. This is particularly so because the strategies that Japan has undertaken over the decades to address its security challenges seem to have worked (such as incremental secondary legislations and administrative workarounds), and also because tensions in Sino-Japanese relations often ebb and flow over time, even if the narratives over the China threat are sustained.

The younger students that show up to protest against Abe, however, do not necessarily share the concerns of the Koreans and the Chinese over historical revisionism and revived militarism. The constituent makeup of these groups of protestors is diverse—ranging from elderly Japanese from the wartime generation who have participated in the Second World War, to pacifist housewives and civic activists who are suspicious of the LDP and young people.

The younger generation has often expressed the idea of apologies fatigue, but often is receptive of the security challenges that China and North Korea pose. The problem, however, is that many of the younger protestors do not see these as important enough reasons for Abe's erosion of Japan's unique postwar cultural traditions and practices. These protests argue that the LDP under Abe is acting above the law and subverting the democratic process. Others object to the militarization by arguing that the JSDF are nothing but tax thieves. Some are concerned by the possibility of being drafted to fight for Abe's wars.

Viewed from China's and Korea's perspective, the fact that not too many are standing up to the historical revisionism that underpins the militarism advocated by the prime minister and his supporters is worrying. Many of the younger Japanese who do protest (against the Japanese government) might ironically agree with the right wing's view that the Nanjing Massacre never happened, or that comfort women were "prostitutes" or that the judgment by the International Tribune for the Far East is a "victor's justice." They protest against Abe and the neo-Conservatives because they feel principally that they have not been consulted or that the policies were undertaken in an undemocratic manner. This does not necessarily mean they are sympathetic to the Chinese or Korean concerns. It is not just about the rearming, but really also about the intent behind this, and the misguided notion of "blaming" the victim, that concerns the Chinese and Koreans—something that is seemingly ignored or overlooked, even by those who are resisting the prime minister's efforts.

CHALLENGES FOR THE FUTURE

The rejuvenation of Japan, and the three important pillars of reforms are, in the view of the Abe administration, necessary to securing Japan's future. Taking a step back—the question is, securing Japan against what? There are domestic and foreign criticisms against current Japanese strategy beyond those of the pacifists. Japan's foreign policy has been criticized for being overtly reliant on the US; premised on an erroneous historical revisionist narrative that undermines Japan's pacifist image and democratic values; and self-fulfilling in its China threat sentiments. Where does that leave Japan?

PUTTING JAPAN'S SELF-INTEREST FIRST: ASIA AND BEYOND

The rejuvenation of Japan is an important exercise, and sufficient time has passed since the end of the Cold War for Tokyo to have understood the challenges and difficulties for its normalization as a nation-state and its rejuvenation as a global power to achieve a status commensurate with its strategic aspiration and ambition. Even though there have been clear and articulate voices, such as that of Yoshihide Soeya, who has argued since the mid-2000s that Japan should adopt a "middle power" strategy. This "middle power" strategy is born out of a neo-realist appreciation that Japan would likely eschew any ambition to contend with the US and China in terms of power capabilities. Soeya perceives such strategic competition to be self-defeating. It is therefore unlikely that Japan would change its position on the constitution and the US-Japan security alliance, and should strive to close the gap between its economic prowess and military capabilities. Japan's natural partners lie with South Korea, Australia and ASEAN, since they situate themselves with the US on one hand and China on the other, and allying with these powers would give Japan more flexibility in the region's diplomacy. This approach is typically Japanese: virtuous, strong and displays the utmost humility, and this is the kind of thinking that generates the most respect for Japan when viewed from the outside.

Yet, on the face of it, the neo-conservatives of the LDP have not taken this recommendation wholly on board. Under the Abe administration, Japan has embarked on embracing the US in a whole-hearted manner— with an increasingly strident anti-China tone, that has grown louder and shriller since the mid-1990s. China has given many reasons for the LDP to capitalize on the "China threat" theory, from increasingly assertive postures (in reality insecure and defensive reactions in most cases), to non-compromising rhetoric, to opaque military budgets. However, the question before Japan is this: in enacting this policy of leaning one side toward the US unquestioningly, and backing the US unconditionally, would such an allegiance benefit Japan in its quest to achieve the security and the global power status that is commensurate with its economic status around the world?

A cursory survey of Japanese foreign relations in East Asia would provide a clue to this. In Northeast Asia, Japan can count on Taiwan to be usually positively predisposed to it, particularly after Ma Ying-jeou stepped down as president of the Republic of China. Japan's relations with South Korea, a US ally, can hardly be described as good, even though they have both appeared to stand side by side with the US on many matters, such as Terminal High Altitude Area Defense (THAAD) deployment and North Korea in particular. However, Japan's relations with South Korea are still dogged by the territorial dispute over Dokdo/Takeshima; historical burdens concerning the Second World War, particularly over the comfort women issue; and Japanese colonization of Korea. Japan-China relations have been at a low point, with the Chinese and Japanese leaders having little high-level contact for the past seven years, until the 2018 official visit by Abe to Beijing to celebrate the fortieth anniversary of the Treaty of Peace and Friendship. Japan's relations with North Korea are probably the worst among all its East Asian neighbors. North Korea has kidnapped Japanese nationals, fired missiles over Japanese territories and most likely would target Tokyo for military strikes in the event that US relations with North Korea deteriorate substantially. In other words, in the two decades following the end of the Cold War, Japan's security environment has deteriorated to a large extent despite the LDP's policies of "handling" these challenges through the tightening of the US-Japan security alliance. How could Japan possibly enhance its security in East Asia?

A possible way would be for Japan to recalibrate its role in the US-Japan alliance. Rather than leaning unconditionally toward the US, Japan might consider that a critical aspect of normalizing/rejuvenating would be to posit a certain measure of independence from the US if it is in Japan's interests. Unconditionally subordinating Japanese interests in the name of alliance unity erodes Japanese sovereign dignity politically, undercuts Japanese diplomatic initiatives and undermines Japanese democracy at home. Putting Japanese interests first is critically important as a hallmark of Japanese normalization and rejuvenation. It would be fallacious to assume what is in the national interests of the US would always be in the national interests of Japan. Likewise, it would be foolish to assume that what has worked in the past will always work in the future.

First, the logic is simple, becoming more independent strategically might increase the value and attractiveness of Japan's cooperation in the alliance rather than decrease it. Unthinking subordination in the name of "holding the alliance partner closer to achieve more independence" defeats the point of the "alliance" in the first place—of advancing Japanese national interests and security in the long run. As the hegemonic struggle between China and the US is projected to increase over the years, the dangers of entrapment by the alliance into a conflict with China is every bit a possibility. There is no guarantee in terms of continuity of policies with the US—as Prime Minister Abe learned when the Trump administration scrapped the TPP and agreed to a summit with the North Korean leader Kim Jong-un. Japan could and should learn how to say no (again) to the US when it is not in its interests to say yes, and should not be worried about diverging from the US position if needs be. It may be far from obvious to the LDP elites, but Tokyo's fear of "abandonment" is misguided. The alliance is just as important to the US as it is to Japan, and it is difficult to see how the US would "abandon" Japan, just because Japan speaks its mind. Tokyo brings concrete benefits to the table in the alliance, and should not be afraid to assert its rights. After all, the US is clearly no longer the hegemon in the Asia-Pacific (Ikenberry 2014; Chellaney 2018).

Second, it demonstrates a Japan that is actually capable of exhibiting a normality in its foreign relations instead of being voluntarily entrapped in an alliance in service of another nation's goal, even when it is against its interest to do so. This is **not** the equivalent of calling off the alliance or behaving difficultly with Japan's long-time alliance partner. This is also certainly not suggested with "Chinese interests" in mind. The basis of normalization and rejuvenation presupposes Japan acquires greater autonomy, not less as a result. Years of subordination to the US position has conditioned Japanese diplomats and politicians to respond with a defensive and knee-jerk reaction to any suggestions that Japan should adopt a more independent stance (from the US politically and militarily) by dismissing such suggestions as "Chinese propaganda". There is a difference here: becoming more independent from the US does not mean that Japan should naturally become more pro-Chinese. This kind of thinking constricts the Japanese diplomatic position in a "black or white" binary way. It just means that Japan should privilege its interests above affinity with, or alliance against, any other nation. At the same time, Japan should be mindful that the abandonment might come even if Tokyo adopts a "leaning to one side" posture if cooperation with China results in significantly greater benefits for the US, if the US assumes they have the Japanese position locked down under any circumstances.

Third, the "invisible" price of membership of this alliance might be significant, particularly in terms of opportunity costs, both in Asia and beyond. Japan's choices are not binary in nature but could be more varied and nuanced than imagined. Japanese foreign policy elites might think they are piggy-backing on a US global presence to globalize Japanese foreign policy, but the fact remains that such a strategy might hinder rather than help Japanese ambitions. Beyond tangible material benefits, these costs also manifest themselves in potential relations with foreign states where Japan might have an interest in cultivating security and diplomatic breakthroughs. Historical evidence has shown that Japan's interests have always been subordinated to the US position, either by design (Japan voluntarily subsuming its interests and aligning its position with the US) or by compulsion through negotiations (as in the case of Iran, for example). In certain areas where Japan has interests that diverge from US interests, it is likely that Japan would have to give up its interests, particularly where the US interests are considerable. Once that happens, then it does not matter what the Japanese have done or are doing, US interests will no doubt come first. The recent developments (2017–2018) in US relations with North Korea certainly showed that Japan would be forced to accept a US position rather than reject it. Prime Minister Abe's multiple visits certainly did not help mitigate the situation with North Korea, and in the end, the way the US agreed to the summit was eerily reminiscent of the 1972 rapprochement between the US and China. From US statements, Japan has reportedly shouldered the bulk of the burden sharing. It has borne the cost of every generation of new US weapons and supported most of the US deployments in Asia.

Fourth, the persistent over-riding of Okinawa resident's interests by Tokyo in favor of arrangements for the US military on Okinawa is undemocratic in nature. Given how Prime Minister Abe has articulated again and again Japan's democratic credentials as a fundamental basis for Japan's values-based diplomacy, and in reaching out to allies such as India and Australia, this comes across as being a little hypocritical. Why should the democratic rights of the Okinawa people or the young students protesting outside the Diet over the various legislations be ignored, while the neo-conservatives harp on about the fact that Japan is a democracy? Externally, such strain on democracy does not help either if it is only coached in anti-China terms. If Japan were really democratic (since Prime Minister Abe has been fixated on the idea of a values-based diplomacy), then Japan's relations with Vietnam or Laos should not be as good as they are now, since these countries are still communist. Consequently, the neo-conservatives actually give Japanese democracy a shade of doubt. The democratic narrative becomes every bit as hypocritical whether from the perspective of Okinawa or from the perspective of Southeast Asia.

Pre-Requisites for Global Leadership: Gaining Respect of Asian Neighbors

The privileging of the US in Japan's foreign relations, particularly vis-à-vis China or Korea suggests that Tokyo is not at all worried about the opinions of its neighbors. Yet Japan has always made a case that it would like to speak for Asia, particularly when in its narrative it asserts the rule of law in the region (against China in the South China Sea, for example). The problem is this—if Japan wants to lead (in Asia), then it needs to have not only the support of its neighbors in Southeast Asia, but also in East Asia. Japan's relations with China and South Korea face a fair amount of difficulties, and currently relations with North Korea are as good as non-existent. Only relations with Taiwan are good, but Taiwan is not a sovereign nation-state.

Japan's diplomacy has more traction in Southeast Asia. Of the 11 states in Southeast Asia, Japan maintains good relations with most if not all of them, cultivated through long decades of meticulous diplomacy, particularly through the implementation of the ODA mandated by the Fukuda Doctrine in the 1970s. Tokyo has undisputedly assumed leadership of the region as its economy recovers from the ashes of the postwar era, leading the growth of

East Asia's and Southeast Asia's newly industrializing economies (NIEs) of Singapore, Taiwan, South Korea and Hong Kong, and closely behind the ASEAN NIEs. This episode of steady and reinforcing growth was interrupted in the 1990s when Japan's growth stagnated, and was subsequently sidelined by the rise of China. Despite this, Japan did not retreat strategically from Southeast Asia after the end of the Cold War. Japan stepped in to provide humanitarian assistance, and participated in UN operations in Cambodia and East Timor. Since 2012, Japan has been at the forefront of a multilateral effort to confront China in the South China Sea, backing the Philippines and Vietnam in their claims against the Chinese. Needless to say, this act of supporting the US, Vietnam and the Philippines could be construed as confronting the "bully" in the region, but it also reinforces the realpolitik hegemonic tensions caused by the US in trying to curb a rising China strategically. This might have the unfortunate consequence of forcing the Southeast Asian countries to choose sides. Southeast Asian countries do not wish for the region to become an arena for great power competition, and Japanese (as well as American or Chinese) pressure is not welcome.

Unlike most Asian countries, Japan identifies itself as closely associated with the industrialized West. This identification goes back to the Meiji era, and certainly has helped build Japan's sense of national mission and industrial efforts. The vestiges of Japan's ambition to join the valued Western colonial club of the last century can still be felt in Japan's membership of the OECD and G7, where Japan is ostensibly the only Asian country in the developed nations club. Alongside its preference for the US, there is an impression that Japan is first and foremost a Western power as opposed to an Asian one. The operative word here is first and foremost. Japan's interests are seen to be more tied to US interests. At the same time, most Asians, including a significant percentage of Chinese and Koreans, have an admiration for aspects of Japanese society and culture. The humility, intelligence and diligence of the Japanese people are well known and highly respected throughout Asia, and Japan's industrial prowess and technical advancement have meant that Asian countries look to Tokyo for leadership in many aspects of economic and industrial development. Japanese cultural developments and consumerism provide the requisite leadership that further fuel Japan's prestige and soft power. For other Asians, for the most part, daily interactions with Japan and the Japanese people have been largely positive, and the misdeeds of Japan's imperial past do not automatically cast a shadow on these daily interactions. The election of nationalist politicians—the likes of Shintaro Ishihara, Toru Hashimoto, Junichiro

Koizumi and Shinzo Abe—have given the impression that right-wing views are prevalent and popular in Japan. Historical revisionism gets advertised, and it damages Japan's image in its immediate neighborhood in a big way.

Japanese nationalism, particularly when based on misogynistic and radical interpretations of history, does a disservice to Japan's foreign relations, particularly with China and Korea. Diplomats in China and Japan have often dismissed questions whether history has affected their bilateral relations, citing the paramount importance of national interests in making foreign policy, not wishy-washy influences of the "burden of history." Sadly, these diplomats and policymakers schooled in thinking about national interests conceived of them in mainly material terms but in reality history issues are identity issues. Revisionist accounts affect the effectiveness of Japan's diplomacy. They also detract from an inclusive sense of Asian identity that Japan might want to inculcate in the region if it is indeed building some sort of pan-Asian identity. Revisionists suggest that contemporary Japan and modern Asia are prosperous because of the "rightful" acts of those who wage war. Calling events such as the Nanjing Massacre a fabrication, or protesting that comfort women were all prostitutes, or suggesting that the judgments imposed by the International Tribunal for the Far East represent a form of victor's justice, seems to put the blame on Japan's neighbors, and undoes decades of goodwill inculcated by Japan's pacifism and atonement. If Japan is unable to gain the respect and support of its closest neighbors in its backyard, it is bound to have tremendous difficulties achieving the kind of normalization that contemporary leaders in Japan have spoken about—from the likes of Nakasone to Hosakawa to Koizumi to Abe. Historical revisionism unfortunately can only be confronted domestically within Japan by the kind of democratic resilience we have seen, not by the Chinese or Korean commentators.

In the short term, it might seem like a good strategy that right-wing politicians such as Abe utilize revisionism in their domestic campaigns and capitalize on the confrontations with China (such as over the Senkaku Islands) to boost the neo-conservative rejuvenation agenda. This could even be construed as a continuation of Japan's statecraft since pre-modern times to bandwagon with the prevailing hegemon and balance against the rising power. The problem, however, is that this strategy only gets one so far. Underpinning the rejuvenation agenda with revisionist rhetoric only serves to erode Japanese security and undermine Japan's credentials as a democracy and pacifist credentials in the long run and hurts Japanese security. These are the very sources of Japan's soft power that it should seek to grow, rather than replace. These two critical aspects have helped Japan become the role model it is already in so many ways to the rest of the world, particularly at a time when the US is undergoing so much change domestically and globally.

Unfortunately, this consensual and non-confrontational nature of Japanese culture means that most of the progressives within Japan, particularly well-respected intellectuals and critics who are best poised to challenge and confront revisionist interpretations of history, are uncomfortable doing so loudly and assertively in public. This goes against the grain of Japaneseness, and the interest of preserving civility and maintaining professional opportunities. The opposite is also true—revisionism encourages more bigotry across the political spectrum and truly offends the victims of the Second World War. This actually degrades Japanese security in the long run, because popular opinion in both Japan as well as in the neighboring countries might not support cooperative gestures. For a period of eight years, between 2011 and 2018, there was virtually no high-level contact between China and Japan (notwithstanding the couple of times where President Xi and Japanese leaders attended regional conferences together). Even though there are signs in 2019 that Sino-Japanese ties are warming, the situation is far from ideal.

The existing institutions such as the US-Japan alliance can be made stronger without the revisionist narratives and rhetoric. Certainly, the elder generation of American soldiers who fought in the Second World War will disagree with such revisionist rhetoric, as would any right-minded individuals in Japan. Even the neo-conservatives in the US are ambivalent, but most prefer to privilege the alliance over the difficulties in history, given the urgency of containing China or confronting North Korea. However, this does not mitigate the situation, as some are wary that this nationalism could be aimed at the US some day in the future. They are not far wrong—anti-US sentiments have always been present, but the fact remains these sentiments are exceeded in a large way by anti-Chinese and anti-Korean sentiments.

Genuine normalization and rejuvenation for Japan should therefore entail a certain recalibration of Japan's relations with both the US and China. This recalibration would shift the basis of cooperation toward a truer partnership where there is room for Japan to disagree with the US, and for Japan to develop a more rounded and comprehensive partnership with its Asian neighbors independent of the US. Given the trade war and changing economic circumstances in 2018, Japan might do well to rally with China and try to starve off the effects of a US going into deep recession (Rowley 2018).

Closer relations between China and Japan would present Japan with the opportunity to live up to its promises of upholding democracy, values and principles as it stakes out a position to be pro-peace as opposed to being just pro-alliance. The author believes that the majority of the Japanese people remain deeply invested in both the spirit and the operationalization of the peace constitution, and perceives this as one of the most important apology statements that Japan as a nation has made and continues to choose to make. Chalmers Johnson, one of the most respected political scientists in recent times, too has stated publicly that it is his belief that the peace constitution is the best apology that Japan could make to her neighbors because it is a conscious choice Japan has made to give up her sovereign war-making right.

Working with US in the Asia-Pacific and with China Beyond

The chapters within this book have shown that Japan could do well to contribute to important global causes and issues beyond just check-book diplomacy. It has already done so in Southeast Asia (and continues to do so in Southeast Asia and elsewhere). Japan's choice during the post-Cold War era has been to increase its cooperation with the US, and this choice has been implemented at an accelerated pace, in reaction to the rise of China but ostensibly sold as China's threat to the Japanese domestic audience. This strategy might well have suited Japan over the course of the last two decades or so, but it actually will not help in the long run for two reasons. The first and the most important is that this kind of rhetoric is self-fulfilling. China-Japan relations were relatively amicable in the early 1990s, and even though there were difficulties in bilateral issues that emerged in the mid-1990s, the relationship only reached a new low during the tenure of Junichiro Koizumi and Abe. Prime Minister Koizumi actually visited the Museum of the War of Chinese People's Resistance Against Japanese Aggression at Marco Polo Bridge in Beijing when he visited China in October 2001. During this visit, he expressed 'deep remorse and a heartfelt apology' (Fukuda 2015), but his repeated visits to the Yasukuni Shrine managed to drive relations to one of the lowest point in history, resulting in the massive anti-Japanese protests in 2005. Prime Minister Abe is even more hawkish and at the same time more systematic in advocating for his normalization agenda. Like Prime Minister Koizumi, Prime Minister Abe has largely similar policies, but unlike Prime Minister Koizumi, Prime Minister Abe's family background provided him with the nationalist credentials he needed without needing advisors such as Isao Iijima to mold his media image (Strom 2001).

The chapters on Japan's cooperation with China in combating piracy in the Middle East demonstrate that China and Japan can work together on security issues. It also demonstrates that there is actually no barrier to cooperation in wanting to deliver an international public good together, and if both sides have the will to do so. In this case, the initiative to cooperate came at the working level of the task force in a multilateral setting, working alongside other navies. If China and Japan found it difficult to cooperate within East and Southeast Asia in the past, either because of Japan's normalization agenda or particularly because of its alliance with the US, Japan could now undertake an alternative strategy to help its normalization without taking on an anti-China bias. In seeking a global role, Japan could seek a partnership with China in places where there is resistance to the US. There are numerous places around the globe where China arguably faces less resistance than the US, and an ad hoc partnership not only would enable Japan to show that it can work well with the US in its traditional security agenda, but also forge new partnerships with China worldwide to contribute to causes never previously imagined possible.

China has traditional links to the blocs and countries not in the "traditional" alliance bloc of the US—in Latin America, in Africa and Middle East—more so than Japan, for both historical and political reasons. Japan's cooperation with China in the Gulf of Aden did not come about as a result of an intentional political desire on the part of both Beijing and Tokyo to cooperate. This happy turn of events started out perhaps as a parallel and somewhat competitive effort, but as a result of a multilateral cooperative effort at sea, both Chinese and Japanese task forces did work together. This episode, however, proves that there is no real reason why this cooperation cannot be built on, and that China and Japan can work together on security issues outside of the Asia-Pacific if the time is not ripe to do so within the Asia-Pacific, and also possibly collaborate independently of the US. This is a choice, and is something that Japan has a sovereign right to decide, and it should therefore not be construed as betrayal of the US as such.

Japan's credentials as a pacifist power are unparalleled and Tokyo enjoys soft power which many other nations can only envy. Unfortunately, Tokyo's humility and fidelity to the US-Japan alliance has prevented it from capitalizing on becoming the global political power it is capable of becoming. In this instance, Japan is suited to be the peacemaker—more so than the US. The recent move by the Trump administration to support

Israel unconditionally means that it is more important than ever that an even-handed treatment of Arab and Palestinian causes be advocated. For a substantial time, the view in the Middle East of Japan is that it is firmly entrenched in the US-Japan alliance, and would follow the US assiduously without questions. Now more than ever, Japan would be able to make a difference, and Japan should be able to use its expertise and clout in the Middle East to mediate in the conflicts between Israel and the Arab world, particularly with the Palestinians. Japan has always been active in peacekeeping operations, joining UN blue helmets in the Southeast Asian countries of Cambodia (1992) and East Timor (2002), Rwanda (1994), Golan Heights (2002), Iraq (2004), Congo (2004), Haiti (2012) Sudan and Southern Sudan (2011). Even though these UN missions (as well as those in support of the US, such as the anti-piracy missions) do raise the role of the JSDF, Japan's focus cannot be on peacekeeping alone. Granted, such activities help provide more opportunities for a Japanese peacekeeping presence. There is no reason why Japan cannot expand beyond these peacekeeping operations to assume a greater political role in peacebuilding and conflict prevention. Consequently, it might be in Japan's interest to take a more independent posture vis-à-vis the US.

Japan has a sovereign right to decide what kind of great power that it wants to become. This should be the decision of the Japanese nation alone. The wisdom of the postwar generation in choosing pacifism and democracy has helped Japan extend its soft power further than possibly imagined, and endeared it with its neighbors. Unfortunately, Asian countries have not appreciated enough that Japan's renunciation of its war-making power through Article 9 is a sovereign choice that represents the deepest embodiment of an apology a nation can make. Today's neo-conservatives are advocating the revision of the constitution, and at a symbolic level, Japanese leaders are revoking the apology that Japan made decades ago in the name of national security. The changing conceptualization of "peace" can be worrying—as wars were almost always justified in the name of defense and peace rather than ambition, greed or pride. Be that as it may, the struggle within Japan today reflects the democratic resilience of Japanese society—an indication of how far the Japanese nation has traveled since 1945 and how contemporary Japanese foreign policy cannot be separated from influences of traditional Japanese thinking, philosophy and politics. As Satoh notes, democratic participation is truly replacing quiescent citizen obedience, and the desire to be a responsible member of the international community is [resisting] an assertive nationalism so that perhaps since the first time since Meiji Restoration, a new national path beckons (Satoh 2010: 586). As Japan continues down its path of rejuvenation and normalization, it will come under increasing pressure externally from countries such as the US and China, and internally from the often divisive forces at home. Japan's democratic resilience in all likelihood will win through in the end. As Tadokoro (2011: 38–71) notes, [Japan's] quest for traditional great power status compared to that of the US or China is an untenable goal, even if it were possible, as postwar Japan's value orientation would suggest an inclination toward multilateralism and international rule of law, not the attainment of economic or strategic supremacy. Japan in short is now at a political crossroads, and the extent of the political support that the neo-conservatives receive will determine the future of Japanese diplomacy. If Japan is able to further work on intra-regional integration with Southeast Asia, increase cooperation with China to provide for international public goods and work for joint development in third countries, and moderate the excesses of the US by becoming a true and equal partner in the US-Japan alliance, one can be assured that Japan's rejuvenation as a global power is not too far away.

References

Aibara, R., Abe government called two-faced over threats to Japan's survival, Asahi Shimbun, 26 Feb 2018, http://www.asahi.com/ajw/articles/AJ201802260029.html

Chellaney, B., US Struggles to Counter Chinese Maritime Hegemony, *Asia Times* 14 June 2018.

Farley, R., The One Important Ingredient for Regional Hegemony that China's Still Missing, *The Diplomat*, 4 March 2018.

Fukuda, M., (2015), Japan's Koizumi years, a time of lost opportunities, *East Asian Forum* 14 Oct 2015, available at: http://www.eastasiaforum.org/2015/10/14/japans-koizumi-years-a-time-of-lost-opportunities/

Ikenberry, G. J., From Hegemony to the Balance of Power: The Rise of China and American Grand Strategy in East Asia, *International Journal of Korean Reunification Studies*, Vol. 23, No. 2, 2014, 41–63.

Rowley, A., "Japan and China could be about to forge an alliance that will shield them from the coming recession", *South China Morning Post*, 30 Dec 2018.

Satoh, H., Legitimacy Deficit in Japan: The Road to True Popular Sovereignty, *Politics and Policy*, Vol. 38, No. 3 (2010), pp 571–588.

Strom, S., Man in the News; Plain-Spoken Leader; Junichiro Koizumi, April 21, 2001, *The New York Times*, https://www.nytimes.com/2001/04/25/world/man-in-the-news-plain-spoken-leader-junichiro-koizumi.html

Tadokoro, M., "Change and Continuity in Japan's 'Abnormalcy': An Emerging External Attitude of the Japanese Public in Soeya, Y., Tadokoro, M. & Welch, D.A., *Japan as "Normal Country"? A Nation in Search of its Place in the world*. Toronto: University of Toronto Press, 2011.

Van Ness, P., Hegemony, not anarchy: Why China and Japan are not balancing US Unipolar Power, Working Paper 2001/4, Department of International Relations RSPAS, Australia National University.

Open Access This chapter is licensed under the terms of the Creative Commons Attribution 4.0 International License (http://creativecommons.org/licenses/by/4.0/), which permits use, sharing, adaptation, distribution and reproduction in any medium or format, as long as you give appropriate credit to the original author(s) and the source, provide a link to the Creative Commons licence and indicate if changes were made.

The images or other third party material in this chapter are included in the chapter's Creative Commons licence, unless indicated otherwise in a credit line to the material. If material is not included in the chapter's Creative Commons licence and your intended use is not permitted by statutory regulation or exceeds the permitted use, you will need to obtain permission directly from the copyright holder.

Index[1]

A
"Abandonment"
  circumstances under which it may occur, 214
  dilemma of alliance theory, 119
  fear of, 120–121, 213
  strategic, by, US 18, 88
  US–Korea case, 4
Abe, Shinzo
  advocating normalization agenda, 219
  areas of success, 29, 60, 135, 187
  as author, 1, 6, 17, 92
  China–Japan relations, 219
  China's views on, 209
  comparison with Koizumi, 62, 85, 92, 219
  concerns of young protesters, 11, 26–27, 210
  core vision for Japan, 1, 92
  effects of Senkaku dispute, 68–69, 202
  efforts to amend constitution, 12
  elements in garnering public support for rejuvenation, 88–89, 117–118
  on foreign policy and China, 23, 169
  on grandfather's goal, 71
  handling of nationalization of Senkaku Islands, 118–119
  historical revisionism, 92–93, 216–217
  imperialism and democracy, 97
  involvement in industrial park, 148
  as leader of LDP, 83, 202
  lessons learned, 156–157
  lifting ban on weapons exports, 113–114
  measures to effect changes across pillars of rejuvenation, 117–118
  meeting with Trump, 2–3
  as neo-conservative, 95, 112
  new Conservatism, 93
  new national defense policy guidelines, 201
  North Korea relations, 2
  one of first to highlight Korean threat, 28–29

---

[1] Note: Page numbers in italics refer to photographs.

© The Author(s) 2019
V. Teo, *Japan's Arduous Rejuvenation as a Global Power*,
https://doi.org/10.1007/978-981-13-6190-6

Abe, Shinzo (*cont.*)
  opinions of election to Prime Minister, 93
  opposition from Japanese people, 98, 111, 153, 201, 203, 209–210
  pacifism and democracy, 96
  popularity and longevity, 202–203
  possible hypocrisy, 215
  "proactive pacifism" doctrine, 112, 159
  projecting strong and appealing image, 96–97
  in pro-military quadrant, 64
  pushing for help to contain China, 127–128
  pushing through security bills, 200
  re-election in 2012, 112
  relations with China, 158–159
  relations with Trump, 199
  remilitarization of Japan, 113
  repressive stance, 98
  as right of center, 12, 65, 173
  rising above US–China hegemony, 128
  stance with Middle East, 160
  struggling with support for constitutional revisionism, 202
  succeeding Koizumi, 111
  US–Japan relations, 196, 205, 212–214
  visit to anti-piracy base, 188
  visit to China, 121, 124, 212
  wishing to build freedom and prosperity, 22
Adventurism, 108, 121, 161, 205
Americanization of Japan, 51–52
Anti-piracy operations, *see* Piracy
Arab–Israeli conflict
  candidates for mediation role, 149
  Japan's involvement in, 140–144, 147, 150–151, 154, 198
  overview, 136–140

Article 9 "No War Clause"
  and Conservatives, 67–68
  Japan's narrow interpretation of, 170
  and LDP, 22, 52, 66–67
  as legal and political, 13
  neo-liberal and neo-realist approaches to, 19
  pacifism enshrined and materialized in, 56, 76–77
  presence of US–Japan forces negating, 82
  question of whether to amend, 6
  serving as formal apology, 27, 77, 221
  Yoshida's perspective, 67, 70, 112–113
ASEAN states
  apprehension over US efforts with piracy, 173
  China, Japan and US, 125, 127–128, 130
  China's growing trade with, 124
  Japan helping in disaster relief efforts, 16
  Japan sharing weapons technology with, 114
  Japan's natural partners, 211
  newly industrializing economies, 216
  preference for multilateral negotiations, 124
  reservation about Japan acting as major military power in, 129–130
  US–China divide causing concern, 30
Asia
  and beyond; gaining respect of, 215–219; putting Japan's self-interest first, 211–215; working with China, 219–222
  Japan's strategy for, 108–114
  winning hearts and minds in Southeast, 124–130
  working with United States in, 219–222

Aso, Taro
   appointment on revolving door basis, 111
   associate of Abe, 93
   as author, 6, 17
   holding relatively conservative views, 173
   perspective on cooperation with US, 196
   starting dispatch of naval assets, 184

B

Balance of power
   during First and Second World Wars, 15
   historical overview, 54–55
   Japan–China, 217–218
   Japan–Korea, 4
   Japan–Middle East relations, 142, 154, 160–161
   US–China divide, 130
   US–Japan alliance and China, 30, 55, 65, 128, 204
   US–Japan relations, 115, 117
"Balfour Declaration," 137
Berger, T., 9–10, 15, 82
Binary choices, 12, 23–27, 214
"Burden of history," 9, 61, 95, 217
Bush, George W., 2, 26, 88, 97, 111, 140, 204

C

Cha, V., 10–11, 25
Checkbook diplomacy, 85, 109, 172
China
   belief in erosion of Japan's pacifism, 201–202
   China dilemma, 42–50
   crude oil exports to, 175
   foreign policy, 180–181
   historic overview, 54–55
   involvement in Middle East, 158–159, 161, 198
   Japanese people; believing necessary to confront, 170; recognizing challenges of, 98, 210
   Japan's strategic attention fixed on, 153, 169
   military, 65, 114, 119, 123, 127, 189
   perspective on Japan's rejuvenation, 206–209
   and piracy, 173, 179, 181–183
   PLAN, 182, 184–189, 186
   reactive and conservative foreign policy, 180–181
   See also Sino–Japanese relations; US–China divide
"China threat," 5, 24, 65, 85, 109–110, 210, 212
Clinton, Bill
   agreement with Hashimoto, 85, 88, 112, 200
   anger with Japan, 154
   Israeli–Palestinian peace process, 146, 154
   signing Oslo Accords, 140, 142
Clinton, Hillary, 119, 127
Cold War
   China and Middle East during, 158
   China–US capability gap, 169
   conservatism in Japan during, 53, 56–58
   Japan and Middle East during, 154
   Japanese electorate during, 84
   Japan's pacifist position during, 134
   nuclear weapons, 71
   "pragmatic wing" of LDP during, 65
   Sino–US relations, 122
   US–Japan relations, 108
   US–Japan security alliance, 196–197
   US seeking alliance systems, 51, 203
   US wanting to rearm Japan for, 52, 77, 81, 116, 122
Collective security, 18, 89, 210

Collective self-defense, 18, 78, 112–113, 200
Conceptual survey, 7–12
Confucian philosophy, 15, 42–43, 45, 47–48, 54
Conservatism
  during Cold War, 53, 56–58
  compared with neo-conservatism, 90–95
  historical narratives constructed by, 206
  of LDP, 59–61, 195, 207
  opportunity for resurgence, 110
  in postwar Japan, 76, 79–81, 196
  "reactionary," 62
  reaction to Constitution, 67–69, 202
  rewarded with political longevity, 11–12
  steering right-of-center political agenda, 173
  tension with democracy, 82, 84
  See also Neo-conservatism
Constitution
  amendment as detrimental to Japan's values, 98
  as conscious decision of people, 76–77
  consensus towards amendment, 64
  guiding politics, social development and foreign policy, 56
  major progress made by, 66
  neo-conservatives against, 90
  Nippon Kaigi's goal to amend, 93–94
  and pacifism, 76–77
  as pillar of Japan's rejuvenation, 56–57
  political and legal challenges, 63
  as political and legal instrument, 89
  reaction of Japanese society to, 67
  in relation to US–Japan alliance, 74
  year of adoption, 56
  See also Article 9 "No War Clause"

Constitutional revisionism, 27, 53, 66–69, 74, 92, 195, 202–203, 207
Constructivists, 20–21, 172
"Corridor for Peace and Prosperity," 147–148, 159
Cultural factors, 7–8
Culture of deference, 155–156

D
Democracy
  during 1950s, 51–52
  during 1980s, 57
  Cold War goals as antithetical to, 197
  current movement, 26–27
  debates about quality, 22
  deep effect of, 22–23
  existence with historical revisionism, 85–90, 211
  fusion with pacifism, 76–77, 153, 203, 221
  institutionalization of, 78
  and Japan–China relations, 219
  LDP position, 22, 56, 210
  and Okinawa people, 11, 22, 97, 169, 203, 215
  paradoxes of, 90, 95–98, 215
  replacing quiescent citizen obedience, 221–222
  right wing nationalism belying, 79
  "social," 53
  spectator, 81–85
Democratic Party (DPJ)
  economic problems of, 93
  former presidents, 65, 89
  protest against, 91
  pushing naval deployments, 184
  Senkaku Islands crisis, 117–119, 202, 205
  US and China's frustration with, 204–205
  years of tenure, 22, 111

Democratic People's Republic of Korea (DPRK), *see* North Korea
Democratic resilience, 12–16, 23, 209–211, 221–222
Demonization, 109, 153
Diaoyu Islands, 71, 85, 118
Diet
  Abe increasing neo-conservative presence in, 89
  deliberations on right to collective defense, 200
  inviting Yasser Arafat to Tokyo, 141
  Kishi pushing security treaty bill through, 205
  Koizumi forcing legislation through, 168
  LDP bureaucrats serving in, 53
  Nippon Kaigi members, 93
  opposition to Constitutional revision, 67
  rowdiness of some members, 195–196
  streamroller-voting in, 98
  young students protesting outside, 215
Dower, J., 7, 10, 52, 77

E
Economic realism, 52
Egalitarianism, 14, 28, 47–49, 52, 81–82, 95
Emperorhood, 43–45, 50–51, 66
Emperor, institution of, 46–47, 81, 93
"Entrapment," 18–19, 121, 213
Equality, 14, 42, 46–47, 50, 66, 70, 72, 75, 88
Exceptionalism, 28, 44–50, 58

F
Foreign policy, *see* Japanese foreign policy
Fukuda, Takeo, 73–74, 78, 196

Fukuda, Yasuo, 111, 167
Fukuda Doctrine, 20–21, 57, 74, 84, 134, 215
Fukuzawa, Y., 41–42, 47–48
Funabashi, Y., 10, 53, 60

G
Global leadership
  aspiring to, 26
  pre-requisites, 30, 180, 215–219
"Golden Age," 53, 58, 75
Great Britain, 15, 46, 48, 54, 137–138
Green, M., 10–11, 57, 121
Gulf of Aden, 174
  constructivist approach, 172
  departure from previous Japanese policy, 173–174
  deployment marketed as US assistance, 168
  international law and piracy, 177–180
  Japan and China working together, 170, 180, 184–189, 220
  Japan's response to piracy in, 180–184
  as most high profile Japanese military deployment, 31
  as "peace" activity, 134
  piracy overview, 175–177
Gulf War, 85, 109, 117, 142, 156, 168, 172, 199–200

H
Hashimoto, Ryutaro
  agreement with Clinton, 85, 88, 112, 200
  legislation on troops abroad, 20
  right-of-center political agenda, 173
  US–Japan relations, 196
Hashimoto, Toru, 11, 95, 97, 117–118, 216

Hatoyama, Ichiro, 67, 70–71, 80, 83, 196
Hatoyama, Yukio
  from brand-name political family, 85
  perspective on cooperation with US, 196
  as president of Democratic Party, 65, 89
  pushing naval deployments, 184
  tenure, 111, 117
  tilt towards China and Korea, 204–205
Historical revisionism, 27, 85–90, 92–95, 208–211, 217–218
History
  central pillars of rejuvenation, 66–85
  China dilemma, 42–50
  Cold War, 53, 56–58
  debate on rejuvenation, 63–66
  erosion of pacifism, 85–90
  evolving strategic posture, 54–55
  neo-conservatism; and paradoxes of democracy, 90–98; rise of, 59–63
"History card," 209
Hong Kong protestors, 118
Hosokawa, Morihiro, 196
Hughes, C.W., 6, 16, 18, 98

I
Ideational influences, 9–10, 20, 52, 56, 89, 169
Inoguchi, T., 11, 20–21
International law
  definition of piracy, 171
  and piracy problem, 177–180
International Maritime Bureau (IMB), 171, 176
International public goods, multilateral provision of, 33, 170, 184–189, 222

International relations
  pacifism as dominant worldview for, 56
  principles governing, 48
  quest for exceptionalism in, 47
Ishihara, Shintaro
  accounting for success of, 95
  advocate of abrogation of US–Japan alliance, 19
  as author, 8, 15, 107–108
  involvement in Senkaku Islands dispute, 117–118
  as prizing sovereignty above all else, 65
  projecting strong and appealing image, 96–97
  as pro-military, 64
  as right wing nationalist, 11, 216–217

J
Japan
  abnormal status, 5, 9, 13, 21, 28, 58
  as "adaptive" state, 15, 28
  Asia strategy, 108–114
  "beautiful," 1, 33, 93, 161
  cautioning America's unilateralism, 115–121
  contradictory tendencies, 12–16
  credentials as peacemaker, 149–153
  defense strategy pillars, 18
  as developmental state, 8, 14–15
  genesis of anti-piracy efforts, 171–174
  as "Global Ordinary Power," 21
  impact of US "anti-China" position, 122–124
  importance of status, 14
  Middle East; building better socio-economic conditions, 145–148; foray into, 134–136;

INDEX   231

involvement in Arab–Israeli
    conflict, 140–144, 147,
    150–151, 154, 198;
    peacebuilding in, 144, 149–161
political and economic model,
    7–8, 57
political and philosophical traditions,
    42–50
politics during Cold War, 53, 56–58
putting self-interest first, 211–215
response to piracy in Gulf of Aden,
    180–184
shape-shifting ability, 15–16
soft power, 26, 30, 57, 96, 128,
    134, 216–218, 220–221
uniqueness, 7, 151–153, 210
See also Postwar Japan
Japan as Number One, 8, 13
Japan–China relations, *see* Sino–
    Japanese relations
Japanese foreign policy
    "autonomous" streak, 73–74
    categories and worldviews, 64–66
    challenge of managing US
        demands, 197
    and Constitution, 13, 56, 67, 170
    contradictory tendencies, 11
    criticized for over-reliance on US,
        211, 214
    and democracy, 97–98
    of DJP, 118–119
    evolving alongside its aspirations, 188
    historical, 49–50, 54–55, 64
    important questions, for 4–5
    as inseparable from traditional
        thinking, philosophy and
        politics, 221
    "irrationality" and paradoxes, 88
    and Koizumi, 26, 61, 86, 110, 158
    and LDP, 24, 62, 80, 82, 195
    need for greater independence,
        155, 198

    neighborly policy as priority, 21, 23
    and neo-conservatives, 62, 95,
        157, 200
    neo-realism, 11, 20
    and normalization, 16, 18, 20, 28,
        187, 202
    as not all about China, 23, 169
    "Omni-directional," 74
    and rejuvenation, 21, 28–29, 202
    resistance to exporting liberal
        democracy, 22
    three pillars of, 63
    understanding, 7–12
    US–Japan security alliance,
        57, 112–113
    US spill-over effects, 198
    values-based, 95
Japan Institute for International Affairs
    (JIIA), 157
Japan International Cooperation
    Agency (JICA), 134, 136, 147
Japan–Korea relations, *see* North Korea
Japan Ministry of Defense, 180, 183–184
Japan Self-Defense Forces (JSDF)
    amending Article 9 to
        acknowledge, 68
    amphibious aircraft, 115
    anti-piracy deployments,
        156, 183, 221
    categories of activities undertaken,
        134, 168
    China's concerns, 206, 209
    circumscribed activities abroad, 134
    example of aversion to, 78
    greater acceptance of, 89–90
    harmonizing with US missions, 112
    impact of 2015 security bills,
        200–201
    normalization and rejuvenation,
        195–196
    vs. pacifist traditions and democratic
        culture, 29

232 INDEX

Japan Self-Defense Forces (JSDF) (*cont.*)
  reactions to deployment to Iraq, 158
  in relation to normalization and rejuvenation, 199–200
  resistance to, 210
  training opportunities for, 153
Japan–South Korea relations, *see* South Korea
Japan's rejuvenation
  Abe's strategy for, 88–89, 117–118, 202, 209–210, 217
  ability to play role in global affairs as indicator of, 134
  anti-piracy deployments, 168, 188
  as arduous journey, 195
  central pillars of, 66–85, 196–203
  contours of debate on, 63–66
  contradictory elements of strategy, 22
  as difficult, 12–16
  future challenges, 211
  as hopefully imminent, 222
  idea of, 16–23
  impetuses for, 117
  as increasingly major challenge, 23, 29
  and involvement in Middle East, 30–31, 151, 155–157, 161
  and Japanese foreign policy, 21, 28–29, 202
  latitude of freedom for true, 33
  and neo-conservatives, 28, 200, 217
  from normalization to, 59–63
  from perspective of China, 206–209
  from perspective of United States, 203–206
  problem of understanding, 1–7
  processes, 6–7, 21
  putting Japanese interests first, 213
  requirements; greater independence, 213–214; greater role in international affairs, 30; increased westernization, 64;
  re-evaluation of priorities re US and China, 26; recalibration of relations with US and China, 218
  resistance to, 209–211
  transcending "with us or with them" divide, 30
  US–Japan security alliance; acting alone or with others, 187; becoming true and equal partner, 222; as central pillar of, 56–57, 196; confines of, 155; facilitating and hindering, 32; globalization of, as assisting, 135; importance of strengthening, 29; as major stumbling block, 198; piggybacking on, 22; US containment as part of reason for failure, 116
  working with China as possible strategy, 25
"Japan threat," 8
Japan–West relations, *see* West–Japan relations
Johnson, C., 7–8, 30, 68, 219

K
Kaifu, Toshiki, 141, 196
Kan, Naoto, 89, 111, 117, 196
Kantei, 60, 62, 110, 116
Katzenstein, P., 7, 9–10, 20, 82
Kim Jong-il, 86
Kim Jong-un, 1–3, 213
Kishi, Nobusuke, 23, 52, 65, 67–68, 70–71, 73–74, 80, 196, 205
Koizumi, Junichiro
  Abe as chief cabinet secretary, 2, 28, 89
  achievements, 59–60, 85–88
  comparison with Abe, 62, 85, 92, 219

as Conservative leader, 95
on cooperation with US, 196
deployment in Iraq, 168
effectiveness of Japan as alliance partner under, 205
historical revisionism, 216–217
industrial park conceived during era of, 147–148
and Japanese foreign policy, 26, 61, 86, 110, 158
as left of center leader, 11–12
as more nationalist than right of center, 65
parallels with Ozawa, 64
populism, 61
primary concerns of, 110, 158
pro-military quadrant, 64
relations with Bush, 2, 88
right-of-center political agenda, 173
Sino–Japanese relations during period of, 25–26, 61–62, 86–88, 111, 125, 204, 207, 209, 219
strong and appealing image, 96–97
unconventional methodologies, 60–61
on US–Japan Treaty, 107
"Kono Principles," 159

L

Lam, P.E., 11, 16, 21, 143
LDP, *see* Liberal Democratic Party
Left wing ideology, 20
Liberal democracy, 15, 22, 48
Liberal Democratic Party (LDP)
 1955 system, 70
 Abe as leader of, 202
 Abe as Secretary General of, 93
 Article 9 "No War Clause," 22, 52, 66–67
 attempts to push security bills through, 196
 Beijing's preference for, 118, 205
 change in mainstream conservatism, 59–60
 China's shock at new breed of conservatives in, 207
 during Cold War, 53, 56, 84
 and Constitution, 67–69, 94
 democratic credentials, 22
 foreign policy, 24, 62, 80, 82, 195
 Japanese youth on, 26–27, 210
 Koizumi's dislike of, 60–61, 110
 Koizumi's unconventional methodology, 86
 left wing politics against grain of, 91
 longevity, 83
 misguided fear of "abandonment," 213
 Ozawa credited with ending rule of, 18, 64
 reasons voters elected, 12, 82–83, 97, 111
 research interest in dominance of, 8
 US preference for, 80
 views on relations with China and US, 65, 212

M

Magosaki, U., 5, 71, 122–123
Maritime Self-Defense Force (MSDF), 87, 152, 168–169, 172–174, 183–185
McCormack, G., 10, 22, 71–72, 94–97, 112, 122, 169
Meiji
 Constitution, 66
 elites, 42, 47–48, 50, 78, 110
 era, 15, 44, 50, 54, 76, 107, 216
 Restoration, 42, 50, 222
Middle East
 Arab–Israeli conflict, 136–144
 China's involvement in, 158–159, 161, 198

Middle East (*cont.*)
  Japan; building better socio-economic conditions, 145–148; credentials as peacemaker, 149–153; dispatching troops to, 173–174; foray into, 134–136; impediments to peacemaking, 153–157; neo-Conservative's peacebuilding efforts in Trump era, 157–161; rejuvenation, 30–31, 151, 155–157, 161
  shipping lanes, 167–168, 175
  view of Japan, 221
  See also Piracy
Middle Kingdom, 46
"Middle power diplomacy," 64
"Middle power" strategy, 21, 211
Militarism
  Japan eschewing, 77–78, 96
  revival of, 26, 209–210
  "slippery slope" of, 68
  stances on, 64–65
Military
  during 1990s, 84–85
  ASEAN reservations, 129
  Chinese, 65, 114, 119, 123, 127, 189
  constraints of law, 13
  counter-piracy operations, 185
  dispatch to Middle East, 135, 153, 168
  dissent towards rearmament, 203
  foreign adventurism, 108
  historical, 43, 48, 52, 76
  increasing role of, 210
  influences, 82, 96, 98, 113–114, 196
  Japan lifting ban on exports, 115
  Japan owning formidable hardware, 116, 206
  Japan working with China, 185
  lopsided focus on, 136
  and normalization, 18–20, 30, 89, 120, 156, 168

  North Korean threat, 212
  personnel, 122
  restoration of Japan's, 199–202
  subjugation of, 78–79
  United States, 69, 70, 120, 184, 215
Ministry of International Trade and Industry (MITI), 7–8
Miyazawa, Kiichi, 196
Mochizuki, M.M., 10, 15, 18
Mori, Yoshiro, 196
Murayama, Tomiichi, 83, 196

N

Nakasone, Yasuhiro
  as author, 17
  balancing China militarily, 65
  "*Kantei*" style foreign policy, 62
  Nakasone–Reagan, 2
  normalization, 217
  obsessed with international status, 23
  older-style LDP, 207
  projecting strong and appealing image, 96–97
  in pro-military quadrant, 64
  shrine visits, 58
  success as Prime Minister, 74–75
  technology transfer protocol with US, 75
  US–Japan relations, 196
National Defense Program Guidelines (NDPG), 201
Nationalism
  Chinese, 72, 118, 206
  East Asian, 89
  grassroots, 22, 26
  igniting, 118
  Koizumi's, 61
  in postwar Japan, 79–81
  preventing work with neighbors, 27, 217
  resisting, 221–222
  revisionism, 95

right wing, 78–79
techno, 10
ultra, 15, 50, 76
young people's sense of, 91
Nation-states, 13–14, 42, 158
Neo-conservatism
   Abe boosting agenda of, 217
   Abe laying groundwork for, 88–89, 112
   agenda to transform Japan into substantial power, 136
   ambivalence over revisionist rhetoric, 218
   and closer collaboration with US, 206, 212
   commanding most attention for way forward, 12
   compared with conservatism, 90–95
   and constitutional revisionism, 28, 202–203, 221
   emergence of, 85
   eroding Japan's liberal credentials, 22
   extent of support determining future of Japanese diplomacy, 222
   and Japanese foreign policy, 62, 95, 157, 200
   Japan's anti-piracy campaign fitting well with, 184
   and Japan's rejuvenation, 28, 200, 217
   Koizumi associated with, 65, 87
   main ideas behind, 5
   measured support for, 109
   more successful element of, 199
   operationalized rhetoric, 201–202
   and pacifism, 5–6, 22, 28, 87, 90, 94–95
   and paradoxes of democracy, 90, 95–98, 215
   peacebuilding efforts, 157–161
   and reliance on United States, 32
   resistance to, 153, 201, 210
   rise of, 59–63
   sidestepping constitutional constraints, 168
   support for focus on security, 87–88
   three major tenets of, 28
   US–Japan security alliance, 28
   using traditional culture and values, 118
   views on United States and China, 116
   See also Conservatism
Neo-liberalism, 19–20
Neo-realism, 9–11, 18–20, 67, 77, 115–116, 211
Newly industrializing economies (NIEs), 216
Nihonjinron, 7
Nippon Kaigi, 93–94
Noda, Yoshihiko, 89, 111, 117, 196, 205
Norimatsu, S.O., 22, 71–72, 96–97, 169
Norinaga, Motoori, 45
Normality
   efforts to rejuvenate Japan to, 21
   idea of, 13
   in Japanese politics, 81
   Japan keen to demonstrate, 173
   Japan's capability of exhibiting, 213
   Japan's return to, 205
Normalization
   Abe as systematic in advocating, 219
   Abe's idea of fundamental barrier to, 89
   China's concerns, 207
   deployment of naval vessels to deter piracy, 168, 173, 184
   examples of efforts, 31
   under external and internal pressure, 222
   factor driving efforts, 169
   idea of, 16–23

Normalization (*cont.*)
   and Japanese foreign policy, 16, 18, 20, 28, 187, 202
   in Middle East, 134–135, 151, 155–156
   and military, 18–20, 30, 89, 120, 156, 168
   move to rejuvenation, 59–63
   neo-conservatism driving, 28
   origins of discourse on, 52–53
   processes, 6–7, 21
   putting Japanese interests first, 213
   requirements; alternative strategy, 220; greater autonomy, 213–214; recalibration of relations with US and China, 218; respect and support of neighbors, 217
   resistance to, 209–210
   UN missions within Asia, 200
   and US–Japan alliance, 32, 120–121, 204
North Korea
   Abe emphasizing threat from, 28
   and China; need to increase interaction with, 23; *vs.* US–Japan alliance, 28, 109–110, 169–170, 199, 207, 213, 218
   as dictatorship, 95
   DPRK, 83, 85–86, 89, 98
   escalating threat from, 1–4
   Japan's interests subordinate to US, 214
   Japan's relations with, 212, 215
   nuclear weapons, 19
   security bills relevant to, 200–201
   Trump's unconventional diplomacy, 24
   younger generation's perspective on, 210

Nuclear protection
   Japan relying on US for, 57
   US extending umbrella of, 72
Nuclear threat
   China, 85, 109
   Iran, 154, 198
   North Korea, 2–4, 125
Nuclear weapons
   advocacy for Japan acquiring, 19
   hosted on US warships, 83, 122
   Japan's need to defend itself, 108
   in Japan's strategic thinking, 18
   Japan's Three Nuclear Principles, 71, 82–83, 122
   peace movement objecting to, 77
   US obstructing Japan's repossession of, 74

O
Obuchi, Keizo, 53, 196
Occupation period, 50–52, 69–70, 73–74, 77, 79–81, 96, 196–197, 203
Ohira, Masayoshi, 58, 73–74, 141, 196
Okinawa
   in history, 46
   LDP repressing views in, 22
   location of US bases, 11, 82, 122
   Noda reversing Hatoyama's position on, 203
   opposition in, 169, 203
   reversion of, 71–72
   rights of residents sacrificed, 97, 122, 215
One Belt One Road (OBOR), 158
Onishi, N., 83–84, 86
Oros, A.L., 11, 16, 98
Oslo Accords, 140, 142–143, 150
Overseas developmental assistance (ODA), 20, 57, 114–115, 147, 215
Ozawa, Ichiro, 18, 20, 52–53, 63–65, 78

P

Pacifism
  becoming "normal" at expense of, 53
  China's view of Japan's attempt to eradicate, 209
  deployment to Middle East testing notion of, 135
  engrained in Japanese identity, 13, 22
  erosion of, 59, 85–90, 96, 196, 201
  fusion with democracy, 76–77, 153, 203, 221
  as ideational influence, 52
  Japanese people's preference for, 96, 199, 203
  as key institution of postwar Japan, 5–6, 221
  nationalists and conservatives in postwar Japan, 79–81
  and neo-conservatism, 5–6, 22, 28, 87, 90, 94–95
  as pillar of Japan's rejuvenation, 56–57
  "proactive pacifism" strategy, 112–113, 159
  of rehabilitated wartime elites, 204
  vs remilitarization, 12
  scholarship on impact of, 9
  and spectator democracy, 81–85
  subjugation of military, 78–79
Palestine, *see* Arab–Israeli conflict
"Paternalism," 82
Peacebuilding
  assuming greater role in, 221
  diplomacy, 16
  Japan's credentials, 149–153
  Japan's long history of, 136
  need to revamp strategy, 144
  neo-conservatives' efforts, 157–161
  or peacekeeping, 136, 149, 156
  reasons for not taking larger role in, 153–157
  resistance to, 31
  understated aspect of, 134–135
Peacekeeping
  in Cambodia, 59, 84, 200, 221
  dominant narratives on, 17
  focus of activities, 134, 168, 221
  Japan's focus on traditional dimensions of, 30
  or peacebuilding?, 136, 149, 156
  Yoshida on, 133
"Peace senility or idiocy," 5, 12
People's Republic of China (PRC)
  as dictatorship, 95
  Japanese governments highlighting dangers posed by, 89
  nuclear test, 85
  possibility of US partnership, 88
  as rising power, 55
  Senkaku/Diaoyu islands, 71–72
  See also China
Philippines, 58, 97, 114–115, 119, 127–128, 173, 199, 216
Pillars of Japan's rejuvenation, *see* Constitution; Pacifism; US–Japan security alliance
Piracy
  collaboration with China, 31–32, 161, 184–189, 220
  definition, 171
  genesis of Japan's anti-piracy efforts, 171–174
  in Gulf of Aden; international law impact, 177–180; Japan's response to, 180–184; nature of mission, 31; overview, 134, 175–177
  multilateral provision of international public goods, 184–189
  as security challenge, 167–170
Populism
  Abe, 62
  Koizumi, 61
Pork-barrel politics phenomenon, 53, 83, 110

"Postwar conservatism," 28, 53
Postwar Japan
  Abe seeking departure from regime of, 92
  Abe's erosion of cultural traditions, 210
  achievements and rehabilitations efforts, 68, 98
  central tenets of conservatism, 28
  clear role for military, 78
  democracy at work in, 81, 83
  at "emotional" stalemate, 26
  extension of soft powers, 221
  first generation of literature, 7
  foreign policy and strategic direction not dominant in, 82
  funds and aid contributions, 26, 59
  "golden age" of, 53
  ideational matters, role of, 10
  interests in Middle East, 30–31, 140–141
  internationalist outlook, 74
  Japan–China relations, 87
  nationalism and conservatism in, 79–81, 91–92, 94–95
  neo-conservatism revisiting ideas of, 62
  new ideological framework, 52
  one-party state, 22
  pillar of politics and foreign policy, 63
  piracy construed as threat to security, 172
  prime ministers characterizing, 205
  revision of constitution, 196
  state protests modern feature of, 76
  strength of pacifism, 76–77, 81, 84, 96, 199, 203
  successful Prime Minister, 74–75
  US–Japan alliance, 196–197
  value orientation, 222
  viability of institutions, 90
Pyle, K., 52, 67, 70–71, 96

Q
Quest for excellence, 14, 16, 23, 28, 47, 95

R
Realpolitik
  considerations, 196
  in foreign relations, 97
  hegemonic tensions, 216
  indicators, 14, 48
  Japan–China relations, 75, 188–189, 206–209
  Japan–Great Britain alliance, 15
  limiting remilitarization, 52
  and pacifism, 199
  US–Japan alliance, 115–116
Regional Maritime Security Initiative (RMSI), 172
Rejuvenation, *see* Japan's rejuvenation
Revisionism
  constitutional, 27, 53, 66–69, 74, 92, 195, 202–203, 207
  historical, 27, 85–90, 92–95, 208–211, 217–218
Revolving door prime ministers, 111, 205

S
Samuels, R.J., 10–11, 15, 19, 48, 64–65, 121
Samurai class, 15, 42–43, 78
San Francisco system, 50–53, 58, 69, 108, 116, 157
Sato, Eisaku, 71, 73, 196
Satoh, H., 53, 87, 97–98, 130, 221–222
Schaller, M., 7, 68, 88
Security Council, *see* UN Security Council

INDEX

Senkaku Islands dispute, 59, 68–69, 71–72, 112–114, 117–119, 204–205
Shared Awareness and Deconfliction (SHADE), 182, 185
Singapore, 8, 51, 84, 86, 127, 173, 216
Sino–Japanese relations
  during 1970s, 73–74, 84
  during 1980s, 57–58, 75
  during 1990s, 59, 75–76, 85, 109, 216
  Abe's strategy, 88–89, 97, 212, 217
  competing to be global powers, 180
  danger of entrapment into conflict, 213
  deteriorating at end of Cold War, 206–207
  ebbing and flowing tensions, 210
  global awareness of tensions, 161
  as historically rooted and geographically fixed, 130
  during Koizumi period, 25–6, 61–62, 86–88, 111, 125, 204, 207, 209, 219
  leaning to one side, 29, 214
  "middle power" strategy, 211
  need for closer relations between, 218–219
  neo-conservatives view on, 90–92, 95
  signs of warming, 218
  US blocking reconciliation, 122
  working together, 161, 170, 180, 184–189, 219–222
  worldviews of, 65
  See also China; US–China divide
Soeya, Y., 11, 16, 21, 64, 112, 211
Somalia, 174, 175–182
South China Sea
  China's militarization of, 24, 129
  history of China's involvement in, 124
  Japan selling arms to countries in, 114
  Japan's initiatives to help in, 199
  multilateral dispute, 123, 216
  Philippines and Vietnam confronting China in, 119
  piracy hijackings in, 171–173
  sensitivity to China's presence in, 173
  territorial claims in, 126, 127–128
  US–China contestation, 30, 124–130
Southeast Asia
  humanitarian concerns, 123
  and Japan; anti-piracy efforts, 172; continued efforts in, 219; diplomacy in, 215–216; intra-regional integration efforts, 222; need for support from, 30, 215; no longer "abnormal" power in, 21; overseas development assistance, 16, 84; peacebuilding efforts, 149; peacekeeping efforts, 221; postwar focus on, 74; striving for cooperation, 173, 220
  neutral stance as norm, 114
  territorial disputes, 124–130
  views on US–Japan alliance, 30
South Korea
  anti-piracy collaboration, 185–186
  anti-piracy deployments, 184
  claims to South China Sea, 127
  in Cold War period, 51
  concerns about US–Japan alliance, 113
  as Japan's natural partner, 211
  as nationalistic, 169
  newly industrializing economies, 216
  participation in US initiative, 173
  in postwar period, 75
  relations with Japan, 9, 25–26, 91–92, 212, 215
  as "Tiger" economy, 8
  traded oil, 175
Spectator democracy, 81–85
Spratly Islands, 125–128, 173
Structural realism, 10

T

Taiwan Straits crisis, 59, 73, 109, 200
Takahashi, T., 58, 69, 92–93
Tanaka, A., 11, 16, 53, 89
Tanaka, Kakuei, 21, 73–74, 196, 207
Task Force 150 (TF150), 182
Tawara, Y., 93–94, 118
Teo, V., 9, 11
Terminal High Altitude Area Defense (THAAD), 212
Threat perception, 5, 8, 15, 24, 32, 59, 61, 90–91, 109–110, 123, 159, 172, 178, 200, 207, 212
Thucydides' Trap, 109
"Tiger" economies, 8
Trans-Pacific Partnership (TPP), 24, 199, 213
Truman, Harry S., 51, 77, 139, 203
Trump, Donald, 1–3, 23, 24, 31, 115, 120, 130, 161, 198–199, 213, 220–221

U

"Uganda Scheme," 137
Unilateralism, 13, 32, 115–121, 130, 199
United Nations Convention on the Law of the Sea (UNCLOS), 178
United States
  "anti-China" position, 122–124
  bases in Japan, 11, 82, 122, 184
  efforts in Middle East, 134–144, 146–147, 149–150, 159–161
  foreign policy, 111, 136, 155–156, 170, 198
  global presence, 135, 198, 214
  military, 69, 70, 120, 184, 215
  opposition to Japan's involvement in Arab–Israeli conflict, 154, 198
  perspective on Japan's rejuvenation, 203–206
  pivot to Asia, 119, 127
  preservation of pre-eminent status, 203–206
  unilateralism, 13, 32, 115–121, 130, 199
UN Security Council, 64, 84, 151, 178–179, 184
US–China divide
  "anti-China" position and Japanese interests, 122–124
  cautioning against unilateralism, 115–121
  as challenge, 108–114
  Southeast Asia territorial disputes, 124–130
  transcending, 23–27
US Department of Homeland Security, 173, 184
US–Japan cooperation
  firm basis for, 51
  as goal in itself, 155
  greater independence increasing, 213
  guidelines document, 113
  incorporating resistance through, 197
  Japan's choice to increase, 219
  Ozawa for, 63–64
  problematic aspects, 122
  as result of Occupation, 196
  technological, 120
  towards truer partnership, 218
US–Japan security alliance
  1980s strain in relations, 116
  1990s concerns over, 108–109
  Abe's achievements, 89, 199, 205
  activities undertaken under auspices of, 134
  adjustments to defense posture through, 200
  American responsibility for Japanese security, 77
  America privileging, 4
  argument of overreliance on, 119–120

balancing China through, 65, 128
China's view on, 207–208
during Cold War, 196–197
collapse of USSR as raison d'être,
    59, 108
elements of tension in, 121
ending of political career over, 117
as fundamental bedrock of Japanese
    foreign policy, 10–11
globalization of, 135, 156, 187
"globalizing" strategic reach, 68
Hashimoto–Clinton reaffirming,
    85, 88
impact of North Korea episode, 4, 29
India as alliance partner, 114
interim review report, 113
Japan; culture of deference,
    155–156; fidelity to, 220;
    impact in different regions,
    197; interests never taking
    precedence, 170; possible
    recalibration of role in,
    212–213, 218; privileging,
    154; unlikely to change
    position on, 211
Japanese people's attitude towards,
    6, 22, 83, 98, 218
and Japan's rejuvenation (see Japan's
    rejuvenation)
Koizumi–Bush achievements on,
    88, 107, 204
management of, 69–76, 196
Middle East's view on, 221
nature and tone of, 69–76
negating Article 9, 82–83
neo-conservative focus on, 87–88, 90
and normalization, 18–19, 29,
    92, 112
portrayed as anchor of stability, 110
Senkaku Islands dispute, 118–119
Southeast Asia's attitude towards, 30
towards greater tightening of,
    23–24, 33, 62, 111, 120, 184

and Trump, 2, 199
year of establishment, 3, 55–56
US–Korea security cooperation,
    1–4, 24
USSR
    in Arab–Israeli conflict, 138–140
    Cold War period, 10, 55, 59
    collapse of, 59, 85, 108, 135, 142
    comparison with China, 119
    no longer strategic threat
        to Japan, 172
    postwar period, 15
    US détente with, 72–73
    US–Japan alliance, 75, 80

V
Values-based diplomacy, 97, 215
"Victor's justice," 93, 202,
    210, 217
Vietnam
    communist regime, 97, 215
    confronting China, 119, 126, 173
    Japan selling arms to, 114–115
    Japan supporting, 199, 216
    Spratly Islands dispute, 125–127, 173
    War, 71–73, 109
Vogel, E., 8, 13

W
War on Terror, 25, 86, 111, 134, 144,
    152, 173, 182, 184, 204
Watanabe, H., 42, 44–46, 114, 172
West–Japan relations
    close association, 216
    historical, 41–44, 47, 49–50
    popularity, 26
White, H., 24, 119, 122

X
Xi Jinping, 114, 121, 218

Y

Yamamoto, M., 76–77, 80, 82, 88
Yasukuni shrine, 58, 61, 86, 91, 92, 110, 219
Yom Kippur War, 138–140
Yoshida Doctrine, 10, 31, 56–57, 63, 77, 115–116, 154, 206
Yoshida, Shigeru
  1948 return to office, 202
  Article 9 "No War Clause," 67, 70, 112–113
  as author, 67, 70, 107, 133
  Doctrine enacted by, 10, 56
  involvement in US–Japan alliance, 69–71, 74, 77, 80, 196
  as leader of Liberal Party, 83
  neo-realist nature of, 77
  obsessed with international status, 23
  older-style LDP, 207
  regret over Japan's inability to play more global role, 78
  withstanding demands from US to rearm, 52

Z

Zero-sum games, 23–27

Printed in the United States
By Bookmasters